IRON HULLS
IRON HEARTS

MUSSOLINI'S ELITE ARMOURED DIVISIONS IN NORTH AFRICA

IAN W. WALKER

The Crowood Press

First published in 2003 by
The Crowood Press Ltd
Ramsbury, Marlborough
Wiltshire SN8 2HR

www.crowood.com

British Library Cataloguing-in-Publication Data
A catalogue record for this book is available from the British Library.

ISBN 1 86126 646 4

Typeset by Textype, Cambridge

Printed and bound in Great Britain by The Cromwell Press, Trowbridge

Contents

Introduction

In Britain and the wider English-speaking world almost everyone is familiar with the Desert War fought in North Africa between June 1940 and May 1943. They have all heard of the famous Field Marshal Bernard Montgomery and his 8th Army. They are equally familiar with his legendary opponent Field Marshal Erwin Rommel and his *Deutsches Afrika Korps* (*DAK*). The epic encounter between these rivals and their élite forces that took place at El Alamein is viewed as one of the key battles of World War II. There are countless books on the North African campaign, ranging in scope from academic studies of the grand strategy through to personal memoirs. In their entirety these works manage to touch on almost every conceivable aspect of the conflict.

In spite of all this, I hope to offer an entirely fresh perspective on this familiar campaign of World War II. This will come from a focus on the hitherto neglected story of the Italian involvement. In all previous accounts in English, the Italians have been either ignored completely or afforded little more than an acknowledgement of their presence – yet they made up the bulk of the Axis forces involved in this campaign, a fact not reflected in existing accounts. They are sometimes allowed a place during the first phase of the campaign as Britain's only opponents, but the arrival of Rommel's *Afrika Korps* in early 1941 quickly relegates them to obscurity thereafter. This book will seek to redress this imbalance by focusing directly on the activities of the Italians, particularly in the period following Rommel's intervention.

In the historiography of World War II generally the Italians are undoubtedly poor relations, especially in English works. In some ways this is natural, since Italy was undoubtedly the weakest of the Axis powers. Its military were able to claim few significant successes during the war, while suffering a number of disastrous defeats, especially in their opening year of war. Thereafter Italy was effectively overshadowed by its German ally. In a real sense, however, the fighting that raged around the Mediterranean Sea and along the coast of North Africa was Italy's war, and more precisely Benito Mussolini's war, since it was the Italian dictator's decision to declare war on Britain in June 1940 alongside Germany that plunged the Italians into a war for which they were unprepared. And it was his decision to invade British-occupied Egypt in September 1940 that first ignited the North

African campaign – a campaign that would only end in May 1943 with the surrender of the Italian 1st Army to the Allies. If Italy had not entered the war it is unlikely that there would ever have been a North African campaign at all: the German war effort was almost entirely focused on the European continent, and from June 1941 onwards increasingly on their immense Russian campaign. This concentration of German resources was only occasionally distracted and to a minor extent by the need to rectify Italian failures in the Balkans and North Africa.

The central role of Italy in initiating the North African campaign makes it all the more surprising, therefore, that so little has been written about Italy's role therein. In spite of the fact that the fighting raged across Italian colonial territory, and that Italians made up the bulk of the Axis forces engaged, they are seldom allotted more than a passing mention. This is the case with almost all works in English, and especially those dealing with the period following German intervention, with a few notable exceptions. Moreover, this remains the case regardless of whether these works examine the campaign from an Allied or an Axis viewpoint. There are no works that concentrate specifically on the Italian forces involved in this campaign. What is the reason for this continued omission sixty years later?

There are, quite naturally, many works in English that deal with almost every aspect of the British and Commonwealth contributions to this campaign. Perhaps more surprisingly, there are almost as many that concentrate on the German forces involved. But in all these works the Italian forces remain a shadowy presence, although almost always acknowledged: the records of overall troop strengths and orders of battle make them all too obvious. In terms of their influence on the fighting, however, they are usually dismissed in a few paragraphs that primarily concentrate on describing their many deficiencies. Thereafter they are usually ignored, except to record their defeat or surrender, or to comment on their failure in a particular action. Was this really the full extent of their influence on the North African campaign?

In Britain, many people are familiar with wartime propaganda images of endless lines of dejected Italian prisoners of war being escorted by a single plucky British soldier. This strong visual image was reinforced by contemporary newsreel and newspaper accounts of Italian military incompetence and cowardice, often involving the use of racial stereotypes. This picture was often deliberately contrasted with German military efficiency and ferocity. This produced a strong British prejudice against the Italians very early in the war, which has been constantly reinforced in most histories produced since its end. It was a viewpoint supported by German accounts that were often openly contemptuous of their wartime allies. All of this has left a powerful legacy in English-speaking accounts, in which the Italians are widely seen as a nation of dilettantes, devoid of military skills and entirely lacking in courage. It is high time, however, that this view was re-examined to reveal what, if any, truth lies behind it. It is only by doing so that we will be able to assess what impact the Italians actually had on this campaign.

This process really requires a complete re-evaluation of the Italian economy and the political and military systems, because it was this that effectively restricted Italy's ability to wage war, whether in North Africa or elsewhere. This is far too ambitious a task for a single author or book, so it is fortunate that a number of authors have already made significant progress in exposing the complex economic, political and military factors that lay behind the poor performance of the Italian armed forces in World War II. They have demonstrated the fundamental weakness of Italian industry, the instability of political leadership under Mussolini, and the inefficiency of the Italian military system at many levels. These works are immensely important in understanding the reasons for Italian military weakness. It still remains, however, to consider what this overall weakness meant to those at the sharp end of war; it is only in this way that we can achieve a realistic assessment of the overall performance of Italian troops on the field of battle. I have chosen to focus my attention on a review of the performance of the Italian armoured divisions – *Ariete*, *Littorio* and *Centauro* – during the North African campaign. The armoured divisions have been selected because they represent an élite force within the Italian Army, and might therefore be expected to represent Italian military effectiveness at its best. This narrow focus will hopefully allow me to study in some detail the impact of wider Italian economic, political and military deficiencies on the actual battlefield performance of these units. In turn this should permit an assessment of their overall effectiveness, which takes account of these larger factors. In the end we should be able to provide a more accurate assessment of the contribution of at least part of the Italian forces to this campaign, and perhaps to offer a reassessment of the established 'myth' of Italian military failure.

In the following chapters I will briefly review the economic, political and military background of the Italian Army, drawing heavily on the work of those recorded in the bibliography. This will reveal an Italy completely unprepared for modern war in 1940, but a country that nevertheless became involved to achieve the expansionist aims of Mussolini. I will review the development of the Italian armoured units, guided by the work of the late John Sweet, and consider their composition and armament on the eve of war. I will then move on to my main purpose, to relate and review the performance of Italian armoured units during the long and complex battles of the North African campaign. The story will range from the Western Desert of Egypt in autumn 1940, to the hills of Tunisia in spring 1943. It will consider the role of Italian armoured units in many well-known engagements – Tobruk, Gazala and El Alamein – and in some possibly less well-known encounters at Bir el Gubi and Bir Hacheim. It will also consider their brief but important role in the Tunisian campaign against the Americans. Finally, I will review their overall battlefield performance in the light of their own military weaknesses and their opponents' strengths. This should reveal whether there really is an Italian predisposition to military incompetence and cowardice, or whether their performance can be traced to real economic, political and military weaknesses. In any event it will, I hope, offer, even to those already familiar with the Desert War, a new and fresh perspective on an otherwise familiar campaign.

This book has proved to be a tougher task than was originally anticipated; it was particularly difficult to obtain and translate some of the Italian source works. However, it has also been a rewarding one. I hope that others will follow and make the Italian operations as familiar a feature of this campaign as those of the Germans and British are already. It is certainly an interesting area, and one that is well worth study.

I would like to thank the following for their assistance: first, the staffs of the National Library of Scotland and Edinburgh University Library, for their help with my research and particularly Jill Evans at NLS for securing some Italian sources from abroad; and David Fletcher and his staff at the Tank Museum, Bovington, for their assistance with original British sources, Italian sources and photographs, and for preserving the only surviving Italian M14/41 medium tank in Britain, which provides a flavour of what the Italians put up with. Thanks are due to the Imperial War Museum and the various organizations and individuals who helped locate the photographs that feature in the book; in particular Ted Neville of TRH Pictures. Thanks are also due to Iain and Stefania Martin who managed to obtain another Italian source for me in Italy and to Robert Adamson for technical advice.

Thanks also to Graham Thompson and Bruce Stewart, who took part in many discussions about this book and to my parents, who have helped with the proof reading at several stages; and to The Crowood Press and all of those who have encouraged me during the writing process. I must, of course, accept the blame for any inadvertent errors or omissions in the finished work. If anyone notices any, particularly where the Italian armoured divisions are concerned, I would appreciate their comments or suggestions for improvement through my publishers.

Finally, I would like to dedicate this book to all of those on both sides who fought in the North African campaign between 1940 and 1943, but especially to those who did not come back.

1
Mussolini's War

Why were the Italians fighting with Nazi Germany against the British during World War II? Why did the deserts of North Africa become the main arena in which this struggle was played out? Why were the Italians almost entirely unprepared for this conflict? This chapter will attempt to answer these questions, and briefly outline how Italy became involved in a protracted war with Britain before it was ready.

It is probably no coincidence that the states that generated much of the international unrest in the period between 1860 and 1945 were Germany, Italy and Japan. They were new states of the 1860s; Germany and Italy had been formed by the unification of smaller states, and Japan had emerged from centuries of self-imposed isolation. This triad had to find their place in the hierarchy of the established powers: France, Britain, Russia, China and the United States. These had already secured their colonies, their spheres of influence and their economic zones; the new states had none of these things, but they wanted them. They were, naturally, opposed by the established powers, and the result was economic competition, international tension, colonial disputes and, ultimately, open conflict. Germany fought France in 1870, and France, Britain, Russia and the United States in 1914–18. Japan fought China in 1896, Russia in 1905 and Germany in 1914–18. Italy fought Ethiopia in 1896, Turkey in 1911 and Austria-Hungary and Germany in 1915–18. The outcome was a mixture of gains and losses, which left all the new states frustrated, unsatisfied, and still eager for change.

In 1918 Germany, defeated and forced to surrender territory and colonies, was clearly unsatisfied, and almost from the moment of defeat was planning revenge. In contrast, Italy and Japan had been on the winning side, and should have had few complaints. In fact, the Japanese remained frustrated despite securing additional territory. The Western Powers prevented them imposing colonial status on northern China, and treated them as racial inferiors – for example, by restricting Japanese immigration. This inflamed Japanese animosity towards the Western Powers, and fuelled their ambitions in Asia.

How did Italy fare in World War I? In 1914 the Italians had been allied with the Central Powers of Germany and Austria-Hungary. They had naturally gravitated towards Germany, another new state, with whom they shared a common interest in the revision of the status quo. They had been close allies during their respective unification struggles in the 1860s, when German assistance had proved instrumental in securing concessions from Austria-Hungary. This link was the primary reason for Italy's alliance with the Central Powers, since Italy and Austria-Hungary were natural enemies with little in common. The latter was a polyglot dynastic relic of the Middle Ages, facing decline in an era of nation states. Italy coveted its territory in South Tyrol, Istria and Dalmatia. It was not a situation that provided the basis for a solid alliance, and when World War I erupted in 1914, Italy chose to remain neutral, partly through weakness but also because of her animosity towards Austria-Hungary. However, the bloody deadlock on the Western Front encouraged the rival combatants to tempt Italy into the war to shift the balance in their favour, and in May 1915 the Allied Powers, Britain and France, succeeded by promising, in a secret treaty, to satisfy Italy's territorial ambitions against Austria-Hungary. As a result, the Italians endured more than three years of bloody fighting against the Central Powers, including a disastrous defeat at Caporetto, which almost forced them out of the war. They recovered with Allied assistance, and in November 1918 inflicted a crushing defeat on the Central Powers at Vittorio Veneto. In the end Italy suffered 460,000 casualties, though she now anticipated receiving the rewards promised in 1915.

In the event, while Italy did secure certain territorial gains from Austria-Hungary, these were significantly less than promised by the Allies in 1915. She secured South Tyrol, Istria and Zara on the Dalmatian coast, but was denied Fiume and the rest of Dalmatia. The Italian nationalist poet, Gabrielle D'Annunzio, described this as a 'mutilated victory', and it caused a great deal of resentment against the Allies, particularly amongst Italian nationalists. In September 1919, D'Annunzio staged a popular paramilitary occupation of Fiume, which the Italian government was unwilling to challenge, and Fiume was quietly absorbed into Italy. It was the first sign that Italian nationalists were not content with the post-war settlement, and were prepared to take direct action to change it.

Another source of Italian nationalist resentment, consequent on Italy's late appearance on the international scene, was the lack of African colonies. In the 1880s Italy had secured a couple of worthless stretches of desert in East Africa, Eritrea and Italian Somaliland, the scraps left by the other European powers. An Italian military expedition was sent to expand this foothold by conquering the independent kingdom of Ethiopia. In 1896 it met with disaster at Adowa, when 10,000 Italians were massacred by a much larger force of Ethiopians; as a result Italian designs on Ethiopia were effectively shelved. In 1911, Italy seized control of Libya in North Africa from Turkey, but this area, too, was largely desert. The lack of rich colonies and the humiliation of defeat by Ethiopia rankled with many Italians, who were denied the economic and political benefits that usually accrued from the ownership of colonies.

In 1919, therefore, Italy was a nation whose ambitions remained unsatisfied. This was the background to the rumbling discontent of the inter-war years, and to Italy's involvement in World War II. It did not, however, make an Italian alliance with the other discontented powers, Germany and Japan, inevitable; it merely showed that this triad shared a common dissatisfaction with the status quo that might draw them together. This had not been the case during World War I when they fought on different sides. The alliance of Italy with Nazi Germany and Japan was the result of events during the inter-war period.

In the immediate post-war period the European economy was bankrupt, and fear of imminent Communist revolution stalked Europe. On 28 October 1922, the Italian establishment therefore handed power to Benito Mussolini and his Fascist Party, and left them to deal with Italy's apparently insoluble economic and political problems. They were well organized and strongly anti-Communist, and could therefore be expected to oppose the threat of revolution. If they failed, they could easily be replaced. Unfortunately they had not placed Italy's future in safe hands. Mussolini had a strong will and natural belligerence, combined with a somewhat erratic temperament, and he introduced a considerable degree of instability to the heart of government. He was supported by a Fascist Party that was strongly nationalist and militarist. It included many of those who were most anxious for Italy to secure her rightful place in the world, and who would not shrink from using force to achieve their aims. They transformed Italy into a state that sought to increase its power and influence through military force.

The new regime made great play of its dominance of every aspect of Italian life – but it did not achieve as much influence as, for example, would later be secured by the Nazis in Germany. The Italian king, Vittorio Emmanuele III, remained head of state and commander-in-chief of the armed forces, which also remained largely independent; thus as prime minister, Mussolini could declare war and provide overall political direction for the armed forces, but he could not command the military in wartime. This restriction clearly rankled, and in the 1930s, Mussolini personally assumed control of all three individual service ministries with the intention of influencing detailed military planning. This actually caused more problems, since no single individual could possibly fill so many roles adequately, and especially not a dilettante like Mussolini. (In contrast, Hitler made himself head of state in Germany, and the armed forces swore allegiance to him personally.) This meant that Mussolini's power was not solidly based, and he was less able to impose his will on the military. As a result, in July 1943 the king was able to exploit his position as commander-in-chief of an independent military in order to depose Mussolini.

In the 1920s, Italy was a restless nation led by a belligerent demagogue supported by nationalists anxious to change the status quo. It was only the strength of the victorious allies, Britain and France, and Italy's own weakness, which prevented any overt aggression during that decade. In fact, Italian economic weakness would always restrict Fascist ambitions. In the 1930s, Italy was a nation of forty-four million, not far short of Britain's forty-eight million, but with a much smaller industrial base in comparison. An indication of this disparity can be gained by comparing production data for Italy, Britain and Germany: Table 1.1 below provides comparative figures for production of some key strategic materials, and Table 1.2 comparative figures for military production. The figures show that the Italians were short of many of the raw materials essential for military production, with no significant indigenous sources of iron ore, oil or rubber. The Italian colonies offered neither sources of raw materials nor significant markets for Italian agricultural produce or manufactures. They were a drain on resources, rather than a source of support for the economy. It is ironic that millions of tons of desperately needed oil lay undiscovered beneath the sands of Italy's otherwise worthless Libyan colony! At the time the Italians

Table 1.1

Production of Key Strategic Materials 1940

	Population (millions)	Coal (millions of tonnes)	Crude Oil	Iron Ore	Steel
Italy	43.8	4.4	0.01	1.2	2.1
UK	47.5	224.3	11.9	17.7	13.0
Germany	78.0	364.8	8.0	29.5	21.5

Table 1.2

Production of Military Aircraft and Armoured Vehicles 1940

	Population (millions)	Aircraft	AFVs
Italy	43.8	2142	250
UK	47.5	15049	1399
Germany	78.0	10826	1643

Table 2

Typical Annual Position on Key Strategic Materials – Italy

	Requirement (millions of tonnes)	Domestic Production	Shortfall	Imports	Deficit
Coal	16.5	2.2	14.3	11.6	2.7
Oil	8.5	0.1	8.3	1.1	7.2
Steel	4.8	2.4	2.4	0.8	1.6

had to meet most of their raw material needs through imports, and to expend a high proportion of their national income to purchase these; Table 2 above provides details of the levels required of some key materials, and the shortfall in securing these.

These stark economic facts of life meant that Italy had to restrict its ambitions to those that could be fulfilled in a short period of time and without coming into conflict with a great power. Alternatively, if they wanted to be more ambitious they needed to secure the support of one or more powerful allies. In this period, however, potential allies opposed to the post-war settlements, principally Germany and the Soviet Union, were themselves too weak to be of any help. This was the context within which Fascist Italy had to pursue its ambitions for territory and influence. A firm grasp of Italy's economic limitations should have resulted in a lowering of expectations, but it simply left the Italians more frustrated than ever. Thus in the unfavourable circumstances of the 1920s they were forced to shelve their more aggressive plans – but only until the situation improved.

In the 1930s the situation was completely transformed by the rise of Japan and Germany, who increasingly challenged the established order in pursuit of their own frustrated ambitions. In 1931 Japan occupied Manchuria in north-western China by military force. Britain and France responded with strong words of condemnation, but no retaliatory action. This demonstrated the potential of any power that was prepared to act ruthlessly and ignore diplomatic obstacles, to defy the status quo. However, it was not until 1933, when Adolf Hitler and his Fascist-inspired Nazi Party came to power in Germany and determined to overthrow the post-war settlement, that those Italians seeking to overturn the status quo finally had a potential ally. But in spite of superficial similarities, the fundamental nationalism of the two fascist regimes presented a serious obstacle to any prospective alliance. Thus, the Italians considered German nationalism to be a potential threat to the territories seized from Austria-Hungary, as these contained German-speaking minorities; and the Germans were concerned about Italian influence in Austria, which they themselves wanted to absorb. This tension made early relations difficult, and provided scope for mistrust and misunderstandings. In July 1934 Mussolini dispatched Italian troops to the Austrian frontier when it appeared that Hitler might exploit a Nazi coup in Vienna to occupy Austria. It was only gradually that the fascist regimes were drawn together by their shared interest in overturning the post-war settlement.

In March 1935, Hitler renounced the disarmament clauses of the Treaty of Versailles and revealed the reconstruction of German military power. The European powers, including Italy, met soon afterwards at Stresa to formally condemn Germany; but they took no practical action. This weak response was further undermined by the British, who were prepared to appease Germany to avoid another war: in June 1935 they signed the Anglo-German Naval Agreement, which declared British acceptance of German rearmament and effectively shattered the post-war consensus. They did so without consulting the French or Italians, and so broke the Stresa Agreement before the ink was dry. The instability created by these events presaged the effective abandonment of the post-war system; it also encouraged the Italians to resurrect their own expansionist ambitions, and their covetous gaze quickly fell on Ethiopia.

A great deal of Italian frustration centred on Ethiopia, an undeveloped area blighted by slave trading and other barbarous customs, which the Italians considered it their right and duty to colonize. They were willing to offer the Ethiopians the same benefits that European colonization had brought to the rest of Africa. The British and French declared they had no designs on this area, although – frustratingly for the Italians – they sought to prevent the Italians from occupying it. The Italians could not understand the British public enthusiasm for an independent Ethiopia, which appeared hypocritical in the face of their own colonization of most of the globe. In 1934 a minor dispute on the borders of Italian Somaliland and Ethiopia caused them to resurrect plans for military conquest. The existence of a powerful revisionist Germany meant that Britain and France could no longer simply block Italian plans: they had to be circumspect about opposing Italy for fear of driving her into alliance with Germany. On 30 October 1935, therefore, an Italian army 100,000 strong was launched against Ethiopia on the basis that intelligence that Britain and France would not intervene militarily.

In the campaign that followed the Italians exploited their technological superiority to crush the large but poorly equipped Ethiopian forces: they used aircraft, tanks, artillery, machine guns, flame-throwers, bombs and mustard gas against poorly armed, badly trained and often barefoot tribesmen. The unforeseen possibility of military intervention by Britain made the Italians anxious to complete their conquest quickly – maybe this

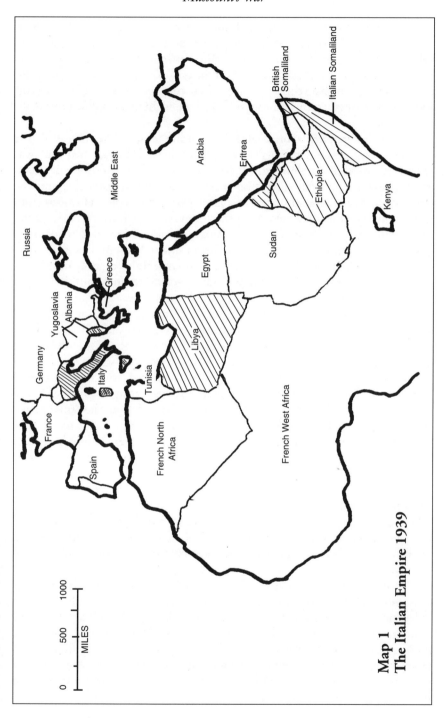

Map 1
The Italian Empire 1939

contributed to their ruthlessness, although it cannot excuse it. The Italians were condemned for this both at the time, and since, although they were behaving much like other European colonial powers before them. On 5 May 1936, the conquest was completed with the occupation of Addis Ababa, and the Italians finally had their empire. It had cost the lives of 2,766 Italians and 1,593 colonial troops on one side, and an estimated 50,000 Ethiopians on the other.

The Italian empire would also have other costs. The first was the economic cost of an Ethiopia that had not been fully pacified and was urgently in need of development. It consisted of a mosaic of different tribes, most of them hostile to each other and to any central authority, and the Italians had to install and maintain a large garrison of colonial troops from Eritrea. In addition they were obliged to improve the infrastructure of the country, initially by constructing the first network of metalled roads. As a result, Italian colonial expenditure rose from under 1 billion lire in 1934 to more than 6 billion in 1938. It was an expense that Italy could ill afford, and its new empire promised to be little more than a drain on resources, at least in the short term.

The wider political consequences of this Italian aggression were also important. In contrast to their appeasement of Germany, the British took a tough line towards Italy, introducing economic sanctions and mobilizing their Mediterranean fleet. This unexpected reaction briefly caused the Italians some anxiety, until they realized that the British could not risk open war in the face of the German threat. It is worth reflecting that if the British had allowed the Italians to occupy Ethiopia without demur, they might have secured a potential ally against Germany. And if, on the other hand, they had taken an even tougher line and imposed oil sanctions or closed the Suez Canal, they might have ended Italian ambitions there and then, and provided Hitler pause for thought. Instead, the British managed to antagonize Mussolini and unite the majority of Italians behind him without affecting military operations in Ethiopia. In addition, in March 1936 Hitler exploited the preoccupation with Ethiopia to reoccupy the demilitarized Rhineland: this was another blow to the post-war settlement. Furthermore, the British hostility towards the Italian occupation of Ethiopia pushed Italy towards Germany.

A common interest in overturning the status quo was beginning to draw Germany and Italy together. In July 1936 Mussolini and Hitler decided independently to exploit the outbreak of a right-wing military revolt in Spain to undermine the left-wing government. They provided increasing levels of assistance to the Nationalist rebels, including large amounts of military equipment and trained 'volunteers'. In response, Soviet Russia supported the left-wing Republican government with her own military advisers and supplies. The fascist dictators had a common interest in ensuring that the Nationalists under General Franco were not defeated, especially following Soviet intervention. The Italians invested more than the Germans in a Nationalist victory in the hope of securing a counter-weight to France in the western Mediterranean. This participation in a common venture almost inevitably drew the fascist powers closer together. The Italian and German forces sent to fight in Spain worked together and developed close, if not always amicable, relations.

In spite of – or perhaps because of – the scale of foreign intervention, the Spanish Civil War was protracted and only ended in April 1939. The Italians eventually succeeded in securing a friendly regime in the western Mediterranean, but at immense cost. They sent 78,500 men to Spain and suffered 3,819 dead and 12,000 wounded. They also lost a significant amount of military equipment, since everything sent to Spain was left behind: this included 3,400 machine guns, 1,400 mortars, 1,800 artillery pieces, 6,800 vehicles, 160 tanks and 760 aircraft, and it represented a loss to Italy's war inventory, although most of it was obsolescent. The financial cost of this war was probably more debilitating, amounting to between 6 and 8.5 billion lire, an immense drain at 14 to 20 per cent of annual expenditure. The heavy cost of this war severely handicapped Italy in the period leading up to the outbreak of World War II.

In the meantime, in November 1936 Italy and Germany signed the Anti-Comintern Pact to cement their common interest in opposing Soviet intervention in Spain. The fascist dictators had recognized the common features in their regimes and slowly developed a close, if mismatched, personal association. It was the first sign of the future Axis partnership that was intended to decide the fate of Europe, but instead brought war and ruin to both Italy and Germany. In Germany, Hitler acknowledged Mussolini as his fascist mentor, and respected him as a strong man despite his native Austrian contempt for Italians generally. In turn Mussolini, amidst jealousy of superior German economic and military power, admired Hitler's ability to exploit political opportunities to overthrow the post-war settlement, as he himself had hoped to do. Mussolini was fast coming to the conclusion that he would only achieve his own expansionist aims by drawing closer to Germany.

In this same period, Britain and France failed to draw Italy back from her increasing closeness to Germany, although they could probably have done so if they had really wanted to. It would have meant concessions on their part, since Italian ambitions were mostly directed at their areas of influence. In the end they were unwilling to make concessions, possibly out of fear that Germany would interpret this as weakness, or because they were doubtful as to whether making such concessions would actually secure Italy's alliance. The British Foreign Secretary, Anthony Eden, remarked that 'We are not in a mood to be blackmailed by Italy... If Mussolini thinks he has only to beckon and we will open our arms, he is vastly mistaken.' In addition the Western Powers did not fear Italy herself, and were perhaps not convinced that Italian assistance against Germany was worth having, although Italian weakness would only be fully exposed after the war began. Whatever the reasons, Britain and France failed to prevent Italy from drifting into an alliance with Germany.

In March 1938 Hitler increased the tempo of international events by annexing Austria. Mussolini, who had sent troops to the frontier back in 1934, was the only man who might conceivably have prevented this, but he was offered nothing by Britain and France that might have persuaded him to act. In contrast, Hitler offered him the prospect of support for Italian territorial ambitions; he therefore did nothing, and allowed Austria to fall into German hands by default. It was a crucial concession, and Hitler declared: 'Tell Mussolini that whatever happens, I shall never forget his gesture. Even if the entire world were to go up against him, or if he were in danger, he can always count on my support.' He would prove true to this pledge in September 1943 when he sent commandos to free the fallen Mussolini from imprisonment. In the short term, Hitler personally guaranteed that Germany would not pursue claims to Italian territory with German-speaking minorities. This seemed like a reasonable basis for future co-operation, though unfortunately for Italy, Mussolini, in common with many others, was completely unaware of just how radical Hitler's policies would prove in practice.

In September 1938 Hitler pressed forwards with his expansionist plans, demanding the surrender of German-speaking Sudetenland from Czechoslovakia. The Czechs were prepared to fight, and the French felt obliged to support them, and seemed to have British and, possibly, Russian backing. International tension reached fever pitch, and it seemed that war was imminent. At this time Italy was still heavily committed to the war in Spain, and was not prepared for a wider European war. Britain was also not prepared to fight, and broached a diplomatic solution. Mussolini leapt at this chance to avert war and achieve a peaceful solution that would satisfy Hitler. The Munich Agreement secured the Sudetenland for Germany with Mussolini's help and the blessing of Britain and France. There was no desire for war across Europe, and this peaceful outcome to the worst crisis since the end of World War I was almost universally welcomed. The only exceptions were Hitler, who had wanted war, and the Czechs, who had lost any chance of defending themselves against future German aggression. In Italy Mussolini was hailed as a hero, although ironically this adulation did not please him: he wanted to be hailed as a conqueror rather than as a statesman, though he was well aware that Italy was unprepared for full-scale war before 1943 at the earliest. Until then, he could only contemplate a short war that offered Italy significant gains at minimal cost. While Hitler's intense desire to overthrow the post-war settlement might offer the chance for Italian expansion, it looked increasingly as if it carried with it an escalating risk of war.

This appeared to be confirmed in March 1939 when Hitler tore up the Munich Agreement and occupied the rest of Czechoslovakia. In response, Britain and France could do nothing to save the Czechs, but they were finally sufficiently alarmed by this blatant German perfidy to offer Poland a guarantee against German aggression. This encouraged the Poles to resist Germany, and made the possibility of a peaceful settlement between them unlikely. It seemed that Hitler would have his war by invading Poland, although not quite as he intended. The occupation of Czechoslovakia also encouraged Mussolini into his own ill-considered response. On 7 April 1939, he was persuaded by Count Galeazzo Ciano, his son-in-law and foreign minister, to occupy Albania, virtually an Italian satellite already. This action, that was intended to register Italy's status as an expansionist power, impressed no one, and furthermore it had a number of unforeseen consequences. It caused Britain and France to issue further guarantees to Greece and Romania a few days later. In addition the Soviet Union made contact with the Western democracies about a potential alliance. It was firmly believed that Germany and Italy were already co-operating on plans for European domination. In fact Mussolini, although strongly drawn towards Germany, remained uneasy about the scope and timescale of Hitler's plans. It was the possibility that a European alliance was now being formed against them that finally brought Germany and Italy together.

This was the background to the signing of the Pact of Steel between Italy and Germany on 22 May 1939. It was customary for such pacts to be activated by aggression against a signatory. This extraordinary pact committed the signatories to assist each other should either of them engage in a war of aggression: it was designed so they would support each other's expansionist aims. It provided the Italians with reassurance of German support in pursuit of their own ambitions. More dangerously, it committed Italy to supporting Hitler's increasingly radical and belligerent agenda, a potentially disastrous arrangement. It appears that Mussolini's natural inclination to appear aggressive and militaristic persuaded him to accept these terms. The underlying assumption behind the pact, which was extensively discussed during the negotiations, was that neither signatory would be ready for war before 1943 at the earliest. There would be no prospect of the alliance coming into play before then. Unfortunately, although the Italian and German military commanders were working to this timetable, Hitler's own plans would bring war much sooner.

In the summer of 1939 it became increasingly apparent that Hitler's actions could lead to war with Poland at any time, and as a consequence of their guarantee, with Britain and France also. This time there would be no repeat of Munich. Hitler was intent on invading Poland, the Poles intended to resist, and Britain and France would almost certainly support them. It seemed that Hitler alone believed that the Western democracies would not fulfil their obligations. He considered that his last-minute non-aggression pact with the Soviets deprived them of any practical way of assisting Poland. In contrast, Mussolini was not convinced that Britain and France would stand aside again, and so it appeared that Italy, under the Pact of Steel, would find herself involved in a war for which she was not prepared. The condition of the Italian armed forces – the navy, the air force and especially the army – at this time made European war a terrible prospect for Italy.

The Italian armed forces suffered from significant weaknesses at the highest level. As noted above, Mussolini was ultimately responsible for military policy and planning. He had also held for a time the ministries responsible for the policy and planning of the three individual services: army, navy and air force. In May 1940, the king would grant his long-held wish by delegating the functions of commander-in-chief to him for the duration of the war, a post that also made him responsible for the wartime command of the armed forces. This was a formidable concentration of power in the hands of one man – although the reality was rather different. A corporal in World War I, Mussolini had no personal experience of command, and had to rely on military professionals in whom he had little confidence or trust. He held too many posts to be able to fulfil the duties of any of them adequately; he also had a natural aversion to administrative work, and he suffered frequent mood swings. The result was erratic changes in military policy, and a lack of consistency in the overall direction of the war.

This might have been of less consequence had the Italians possessed an adequate high command. Instead they had the grandly titled *Commando Supremo*, which consisted of a small staff that could do little more than inform the individual service commands of Mussolini's general intentions. It was left to the individual service commands to develop these into proper orders and commands, using their own staffs. As a result there was no central direction of plans, preparations or operations at the highest level. This duty was undertaken by the three individual service staffs, which tended to work independently and so focused narrowly on their own fields. There was little or no inter-service co-operation, and this was not a suitable structure either for preparations for war or for wartime command.

The *Regia Marina*, or navy, was arguably the best funded and best equipped of the three services, and its overall structure was basically sound. It had six battleships, although this was in a period when these were an indicator of national status. It has been condemned, unjustly, for its lack of aircraft carriers, at a time when the potential impact of air power on naval operations was little understood. In fact the central position of Italy in the

Mediterranean meant that land-based aircraft could support the fleet. The real failure was that air units had not been trained to operate with the fleet, and the navy suffered as a result. The fleet had originally been built to contest control of the Mediterranean with France, but was never asked to do so. It had been expanded after 1935 on the premise that it would have to fight against Britain, though its commanders remained reluctant to entertain this possibility. They had immense respect for the traditions and capabilities of the Royal Navy, and a distinct inferiority complex.

The apparent strength of the Italian navy concealed weaknesses that would undermine its actual performance. It suffered from fundamental flaws in the areas of ship design, training and gunnery. The majority of its surface ships were designed for speed and gun power, at the expense of protection, and this made them vulnerable to enemy fire. They had been built for fleet actions, but in practice these were few and far between, and they spent most of their time protecting supply convoys to North Africa. Most of its large force of 113 submarines had large conning towers and heavy guns for action on the surface. This made them slow to dive and easily visible underwater in the clear Mediterranean, and therefore extremely vulnerable to air attack. They were designed to sink independent merchant ships, but the British merchant ships in the Mediterranean always travelled as part of heavily escorted convoys. In common with the other services, the Italian navy suffered from a lack of practice, as training was often curtailed in order to save expense on fuel and ammunition. In consequence, opportunities for fleet manoeuvres and live firing were minimal, and there was no training for night actions. As a result, Italian naval commanders remained unaware of the poor concentration of their gunnery salvos and the unreliability of their shells, which often failed to explode.

In fact the Italians might have been able to alter the naval balance decisively in their favour if they had used an entirely Italian-designed secret weapon. This was the *maiale*, or pig, a modified torpedo crewed by divers, who would covertly approach major warships underwater and attach mines to them. This weapon would prove a great success, and spectacularly sank two British battleships in December 1941. It had first been developed during the Ethiopian crisis in 1935 to use against the British navy, and could easily have been ready for action in 1940. Instead, it was mothballed almost as soon as the crisis passed, and its development was not resumed until after the war had started. This was a serious mistake by short-sighted senior officers, and one which severely delayed the employment of this secret weapon.

The *Regia Aeronautica*, or air force, was a well funded Fascist creation. Unfortunately, a great deal of this funding had been squandered on a range of newsworthy record-breaking feats, rather than being invested in constructing a balanced, modern air force. The new service had also been influenced by the theories of General Guilio Douhet, the enthusiastic advocate of air power, and this had skewed its development. It had been expanded significantly to support the Ethiopian war, but these aircraft subsequently experienced significant attrition in Spain. As a result, in April 1939 it was revealed that the air force was but a pale shadow of what it had appeared. Its commander, General Guiseppe Valle, had been inflating the number of aircraft on strength by including obsolete and damaged aircraft, in order to secure a larger share of military expenditure. However, its operational strength stood at only 30 per cent of its reported establishment of 3,000 aircraft. This scandal resulted in the downfall of Valle; but this did nothing to rectify the shortage of modern aircraft.

The quality of Italian aircraft stood below that found in the rest of Europe: although Italian industry designed beautiful airframes, it appeared incapable of producing powerful aero engines. As a consequence, all Italian aircraft were underpowered, and many were tri-motor designs because two engines were insufficient. In 1940 Italy had no operational dive bombers until the purchase of German Stukas in August, and it was only after Germany agreed to permit licence production of their aero engines that Italy began to catch up. The Macchi MC 202, first produced in August 1940 with a German engine, proved an excellent aircraft, and one that would do much to restore Italian strength in the air.

The air force also suffered from a lack of training, particularly in navigation and night flying. The experience in the Ethiopian and Spanish fighting proved less beneficial than expected. The war that started in 1940 was fought against modern aircraft operating with the benefits of radio control and radar warning. The belief that fast bombers needed no escort was shown to be mistaken against modern fighters operating under radar direction. The highly manoeuvrable Fiat CR32 biplane was a success in Spain, and the continued use of this design in modern war seemed to be justified. An improved Fiat CR42 biplane was therefore introduced into widespread service in 1939 – only to be revealed as obsolete against modern monoplane designs.

The *Regio Esercito*, or army, was the largest but also the most neglected of the services. It was a large force with an establishment of some seventy-two divisions, compared to the thirty-four divisions of the British army, but it still fell well short of Mussolini's boast of 'eight million bayonets'. This was illusion, however, since as late as January 1942 only 50 per cent of these divisions had their full establishment, while the rest stood at half strength. The majority were marching infantry with minimal firepower and limited mobility. There were only three armoured divisions, two motorized divisions, and seventeen so-called 'self-transportable' divisions. The last were little more than infantry units with some attached motor transport. In addition, all of these Italian divisions were so-called 'binary' divisions, consisting of two infantry regiments rather than the three found in most other armies. This made Italian infantry divisions nearer in size to a British brigade or a German regiment, a point often overlooked by military historians.

It might have been better for the Italians to have fielded a smaller number of better equipped divisions, and the manpower released could have been re-allocated to industry or agriculture. This idea had been advocated by Marshal Italo Balbo, the Fascist Air Minister, in 1933: he proposed a completely mobile force of twenty divisions, equipped with the latest weaponry and trained in amphibious warfare. But the proposal was swiftly rejected by Mussolini and senior army figures: Mussolini was jealous of Balbo and wanted large numbers of divisions to intimidate opponents. The military men also wanted large numbers, to maintain their prestige and their share of military expenditure. It was an opportunity lost, although it is likely that Balbo's complete plan was beyond Italian resources.

The Italian army also had problems with poor or obsolescent equipment in many areas. On the outbreak of war, the army had to curtail a long-planned replacement of its obsolescent artillery, and persevere with some 10,000 antiquated weapons of limited range and striking power. An additional 7,000 artillery pieces were produced during the war, but almost 50 per cent were small calibre – 20mm and 47mm – weapons. They were also in the midst of replacing their standard 6.5mm rifle, which lacked stopping power, with an improved 7.35mm model. They therefore went to war with two different calibres, each requiring its own ammunition, a situation that presented significant supply problems. The Italian soldier was burdened with several other poorly designed weapons, including their light machine gun, grenades, light mortar and landmines. It was not all negative, however, as they had some excellent weapons, notably their 9mm Beretta pistol and submachine gun, though unfortunately this added another calibre of ammunition to the supply lists. They also had a good quality, 80mm heavy mortar, and an excellent 20mm Breda multi-purpose infantry gun. The condition of Italian armour will be discussed in the next chapter.

The training of the Italian army was severely restricted by budgetary and fuel constraints, and often consisted of little more than marching and drill. There was very little live firing practice, which meant that many men fired their weapons for the first time in actual combat. There were also few divisional or larger unit exercises, with the exception of some of the annual manoeuvres, which meant that many officers, NCOs and men lacked experience relevant to battlefield conditions. The relatively small pool of older men who had served in Ethiopia or Spain, experienced a different kind of combat from that faced in World War II. Thus the bulk of the Italian troops that fought in World War II received much of their training at the front, when it was often too late to be of use for many of them.

The Italian army also had a large number of older senior officers and a comparative shortage of experienced junior officers and NCOs. This situation had arisen because older officers had been retained in post at senior levels, instead of being posted to the reserve and replaced with younger men. This problem was exacerbated by the switch to a larger number of 'binary' divisions by increasing the number of senior posts for these older officers. This left few promotion opportunities for younger officers with more open minds and experience of modern warfare, and it reinforced the basic conservatism of the army and its resistance to change and new ideas. It also made the army unattractive to many ambitious younger men seeking a challenging career. In contrast, the ruthless reduction of the German army under the Versailles Treaty removed older officers and made way for younger men with new ideas when it expanded in the 1930s.

In the light of all of this it is hardly surprising that Mussolini baulked at entering a European war in August 1939. This alarming prospect brought him to his senses, and he immediately sought a way out of this predicament. In this he was supported by the entire Italian establishment and by the public at large. He wrote to Hitler reaffirming his commitment, but setting out a long list of requirements considered essential before Italy could enter a general European war. The list ranged from quantities of steel and oil to large numbers of heavy anti-aircraft guns. It amounted in total to 170,000 tonnes of material and would have required 17,000 trains to transport it. It was, Ciano noted, 'Enough to kill a bull'. The tactic proved successful, and Hitler, who still believed that Britain and France would not intervene, let his partner off the hook. He was also fully aware of the state of the Italian armed forces and did not think he would need their assistance.

On 3 September 1939, when Germany invaded Poland and the wider European war erupted, Mussolini was again hugely popular for keeping Italy out of it. But Mussolini was humiliated by this retreat and attempted to disguise Italian neutrality – a reminder of 1914 – by declaring Italy 'non-belligerent', which allowed him to register nominal support for Germany. It was widely anticipated that this new war would develop into a long struggle between evenly matched opponents, as in 1914. This would allow Italy to complete her preparations and enter the war at an opportune moment, which would maximize her contribution to final Axis victory.

Unfortunately for Mussolini this would not be the case. The Germans crushed Poland in one month and conquered Denmark and Norway in two. On 10 May 1940, they launched their Western offensive against Holland, Belgium and France. In only ten days the Dutch had surrendered and the Germans had reached the Channel and cut the Allied armies in two. The incredible success of their new Blitzkrieg forced everyone to revise their earlier predictions. The Italians were no more prepared for war than they had been in September 1939, but circumstances had changed radically since then. It now appeared that they might miss the chance to enter a war already in its closing stages and earn rich spoils at minimal cost. Mussolini declared that Italy needed 'a few thousand dead to be able to attend the peace conference'. On 28 May the Belgians surrendered, and on 4 June the British withdrew the last of their shattered army from Dunkirk. It was clear that France was on the verge of collapse, and indeed Paris fell on 14 June. It seemed to most observers that Britain would soon follow. The temptation became too great to resist, and on 10 June 1940 Mussolini declared war on Britain and an already beaten France. He was no longer dissuaded by the weakness of his armed forces, since he did not expect to do much fighting. There was little dissent among the Italian establishment, which agreed with his assessment. The Italian public were not entirely convinced, but were open to persuasion if military or political success followed quickly.

The fundamental basis for Italian involvement in the war was clearly political opportunism: the entire Italian establishment hoped to gain advantage for itself and for Italy from the current situation. Unfortunately for Italy, this opportunistic attitude was carried over into the conduct of the war itself. This led to a lack of consistency in subsequent planning, with principal objectives and enemies being changed with little regard for the consequences. This produced confusion amongst ordinary Italians, and particularly ordinary soldiers, about the nation's war aims, and they seldom had a consistent or clear idea of what they were fighting for. This contributed to their inconsistent performance during the war, and contrasted sharply with the clear motivations of their Axis allies, Germany and Japan, and their main opponents, Britain and the USA. The ordinary soldier found himself fighting the French, British, Greeks, Soviets, Americans or the Germans, usually with no clear idea of the reasons.

In spite of the vaunted propaganda skills of the Fascist regime, they were often unable to motivate their soldiers satisfactorily; this was in spite of many years of militant propaganda and militarist education in the schools. They had some successes when tapping into existing anti-communism or racism in particular campaigns, but the inconsistency of their overall objectives undermined this. They were unable to justify the war to any significant extent in the vast majority of ordinary Italians.

In the absence of any clear national direction, most Italian soldiers fought for their country from a sense of duty rather than conviction. In addition many officers fought out of a sense of personal honour. This meant that the Italians showed less rancour towards their enemies than their allies, Germany and Japan; they also showed less reluctance to surrender when they had done their duty and the odds were against them. They showed, with a few exceptions, little of the fanaticism demonstrated by their allies, who had been much more thoroughly indoctrinated, and often fought on against the odds even if to little purpose.

In the immediate aftermath of Italy's declaration of war, Mussolini and his senior advisers considered that they would not have to wage a long war, and that their lack of preparedness would not be important. It seemed that the war would last no more than a few months, and in that time Italy's armed forces could probably do enough to obtain something at the peace conference. The Italian War Plan, featured in a secret memo of 31 March 1940, ran as follows:

> Ground front: on the defensive on the Alps... Initiatives only in the unlikely case of a complete French collapse under German attack [*sic*]....
>
> In the east, towards Yugoslavia, first cautious observation. Attack in case there is an internal collapse....
>
> Albanian front: the attitude to the north (Yugoslavia) and to the south (Greece) is related to what will happen on the eastern front.
>
> Libya: defensive posture towards Tunisia, as well as Egypt.
>
> Aegean: defensive.
>
> Ethiopia: offensive to guarantee Eritrea and... Gedaraf and Kassala; offensive on Djibuti, defensive and possibly counter offensive on Kenya.
>
> Air forces: will shadow the activity of the army and navy....
>
> Navy: offensive across the Mediterranean and elsewhere.

There were no plans for immediate action against Britain or France. Instead, Mussolini initiated a hastily organized invasion of France across the Alps, which was intended more to stake a claim to future spoils than to occupy territory.

There were also important economic consequences of the hasty declaration of war. The large Italian merchant fleet could not be warned beforehand, and suffered significant losses when they were caught outside the Mediterranean. It has been calculated that 27 per cent of the Italian merchant fleet, or 3.3 million GRT, was lost. Italy also lost two important sources of national income: foreign tourism, and money sent home by Italian emigrants, particularly from the United States. The British blockade also cut off essential imports of strategic raw materials including coal, oil, steel and rubber. In World War I, Italy had been supplied with these essential materials by her then allies Britain, France and the United States. In the current war only Germany could offer Italy alternative supplies, but Germany herself was desperately short of these materials, particularly oil and rubber. The exception was coal, which Germany supplied to the Italians in large quantities. All of this would have been of little consequence in a short war – but this would not be the case.

The real nature of this war became clear in the autumn of 1940, when the

Germans failed to win the Battle of Britain. It was only then that Mussolini and his military leaders realized that the war might not end soon after all. The British had held out, and although still extremely weak, showed absolutely no sign of surrender. It was only now that they might actually have to fight that Mussolini and his commanders finally began to seriously consider their war plans. Nevertheless, in spite of this unforeseen turn of events, the immediate Italian position remained a strong one. The capitulation of France in late June 1940 left them facing a Britain that was isolated, overstretched, and facing the threat of invasion. The main point of contact between them was in the Mediterranean and Africa, where the Italians possessed numerical superiority and the advantage of a central position. The Italian armed forces should have exploited this advantage to attack the British, but instead, they quickly lost the initiative.

This initial failure originated from a mixture of factors: poor planning and intelligence, poor command, poor performance, and a reluctance to incur losses. There was a lack of clear political direction from Mussolini, who flirted with a wide range of possible options. In this political vacuum, the senior military leaders adopted a largely passive stance, bolstered by inaccurate intelligence that exaggerated British strength. In sharp contrast, the British immediately instituted an aggressive policy of attacking the Italians everywhere, by land, sea and air; this forced the Italians into a reactive mode, and put them firmly on the defensive almost everywhere. There were a few exceptions: in East Africa, where the local Italian commander, the Duke of Aosta, initiated some local offensives to improve his defences; and in North Africa, where intense political pressure from Mussolini eventually prodded the cautious Marshal Rodolfo Graziani into a tentative invasion of Egypt. The results of these minor actions – the occupation of British Somaliland, and the capture of Sidi Barrani respectively – were extremely disappointing in comparison to Italian ambitions.

In the circumstances it would have been prudent for the Italians to concentrate their resources against the British in the Mediterranean and Africa, to maximize results. Unfortunately, Mussolini was anxious for Italian forces to make an impact on every aspect of the war. As a result the Italians found themselves having to stretch their limited resources. In October 1940, for example, the *Corpo Aereo Italiano*, or Italian Air Corps, with 175 aircraft was sent to Belgium to take part in the final stages of the Battle of Britain. This was done chiefly to allow Mussolini to boast about their role in this campaign. The result was that aircraft that might have helped retain air superiority over the Mediterranean or North Africa were sent to Belgium where they contributed little. But this relatively minor distraction was quickly eclipsed by a much more significant diversion of effort, one that would not only completely refocus the entire Italian war effort, but would also expose their military weakness to the world.

In September 1940 Mussolini was brooding about the lack of Italian military success against the British. This stood in stark contrast to German triumphs in Poland, Scandinavia and Western Europe. He was particularly envious of Germany's recent occupation of oil-rich Romania. He badly needed to secure victories to maintain his position in the Axis, and was persuaded by Count Ciano and others that Greece would fall easy prey to Italian aggression. This idea went completely against accurate political and military intelligence, which indicated that the Greeks would oppose any Italian invasion, and that Britain, desperate for allies, would assist them. It also ignored the horrendous difficulties of staging a major offensive across the Albanian mountains in winter; and it completely contradicted the recent demobilization of 600,000 troops, the only source of trained reinforcements to support such an offensive. In spite of this, and in an atmosphere of wishful thinking, Mussolini launched the invasion of Greece on 26 October 1940, without proper preparation and using only the forces already in Albania. The result was, predictably, a complete fiasco.

The Italian plans for this campaign were wholly inadequate. They centred on an attack through mountainous terrain, although the invasion force included only one of six available *Alpini* divisions that were trained and equipped for these conditions. Usually an attacking force requires a superiority of two to one to have any prospect of success, but the invading Italians were in fact the inferior force, with only nine divisions and 125,000 men opposing an initial ten Greek divisions and 180,000 men. The Italians had air superiority, but poor weather largely negated this. This campaign therefore carried the seeds of disaster from the start, though few of those involved raised any concerns. The Italian soldiers sent into Greece so cavalierly would suffer enormously for this act of folly.

After little more than a week of minor advances, the Italians were stopped dead in their tracks. The Greeks quickly transferred troops from the Bulgarian border and called up reserves. The Italians, hampered by the recent demobilization and limited transport capacity between Italy and Albania, were unable to match them. The Greeks soon had a clear superiority of about 250,000 men against 150,000 Italians, and launched a series of counter attacks, starting on 4 November 1940. They quickly routed the outnumbered Italians, and drove them back into Albania. The Italian reinforcements were largely untrained replacements for the men demobilized only weeks earlier, and they arrived at the front piecemeal. Nevertheless, in spite of everything, the Italian soldiers fought on tenaciously and finally succeeded in stabilizing the front. It was, however, too late to save the Italian military reputation by then: they were already the laughing stock of Europe. The Germans were graciously offering to sort things out for them, and the British were planning their own attacks.

The Greek fiasco had exposed Italian weaknesses to the world, and it encouraged an overstretched Britain to take the initiative against them. On 11 November 1940 they attacked the Italian fleet in its home port of Taranto, sinking three battleships for the loss of only two aircraft. This blow effectively removed the threat of decisive intervention in the Mediterranean by the Italian navy in the near future. This was followed, on 9 December, by a British offensive in North Africa (discussed in Chapter 3). This offensive not only expelled the Italians from Egypt, but went on to conquer Cyrenaica, the eastern portion of Libya. This was followed by an offensive against Italian East Africa that began on 19 January 1941, conquered Italian Somaliland in March, and occupied Addis Ababa in April, after some stiff resistance.

This rapid series of disasters had ruthlessly exposed the deficiencies of the Italian armed forces, and effectively ended Italy's independent role in the war. It had a salutary effect on the Italian leadership, who were forced to reassess their priorities and take this war seriously, perhaps for the first time. In Albania, they introduced reinforcements as quickly as the capacity of the local ports allowed, and stemmed the Greek advance in late December 1940. In January 1941 they sent reinforcements, including armoured and motorized divisions, to hold what was left of their Libyan colony. They could do little to help their isolated East African colonies, but flew in some crucial supplies, including fighter aircraft. They also swallowed their pride and accepted German assistance. This new Italian focus on the war provided some of the applied effort that had been lacking in their earlier military planning and helped to restore the situation in the Mediterranean and North Africa. This Italian activity is frequently overlooked in favour of a narrower focus on the German intervention.

It is nevertheless true that this German intervention, quickly following Mussolini's requests for assistance, ushered in a new phase of the war. The introduction of their superior tactics and equipment reversed most of the recent Allied successes and brought a new equality to the contest. In this new phase of the war, Italy no longer waged her own independent campaigns, but fought alongside her German allies. In these circumstances, Italy finally recognized the vital importance of the North African campaign. The rapid German occupation of Greece and Yugoslavia in April 1941 released Italian resources for redeployment to North Africa.

Mussolini had rushed the Italians into World War II in the full knowledge that they were unprepared, but in the hope that the war would be short. Unfortunately this proved not to be the case, and the Italians found themselves involved in a long, face-to-face struggle with a powerful British opponent. They now had the promise of support from a powerful, if not entirely reliable, German ally. The main theatre for this conflict would be North Africa, where mobile forces and especially armoured divisions had the advantage. What sort of armoured forces did Italy have ready for this conflict?

2
The Birth of the
Armoured Divisions

In the inter-war period military theorists attempted to learn the lessons of World War I, and in particular to assimilate the new weapons that emerged from that conflict: the aircraft and the tank. The tank had been used during the war to penetrate enemy defence systems of barbed wire, trenches and machine guns, in direct support of the infantry. In the post-war period ideas about the future potential of the tank blossomed, and there were important developments in the area of military mechanization across Europe. As a result, Britain, the nation that had invented and introduced the tank, was also first to develop the concept of the all arms armoured division, incorporating infantry, artillery and tanks, in 1927. This force was designed to break the stalemate of trench warfare and restore mobility to the battlefield.

The further development of this pioneering all arms armoured division was to be stillborn, however, as this basically sound concept was submerged in heated debate about the best use of tanks, a debate that was never resolved. The result was that tanks were compartmentalized into two mutually exclusive roles, and the British ended up with two different kinds of tank to match these roles: a heavily armoured but slow infantry tank designed to operate in the close infantry support role in army tank brigades; and lightly armoured but fast light and cruiser tanks designed to operate in the reconnaissance and exploitation role formerly filled by the cavalry in new armoured divisions. The latter were heavily dominated by tanks, and although they had some infantry and artillery attached, they could not be described as balanced all arms formations. This cost the British their early lead in the tank field to an eager competitor: Germany.

In World War I, Germany had been a latecomer to the use of tanks and had been on the receiving end of this new weapon. In the wake of defeat, however, the Germans worked hard to learn the lessons, including the potential of the tank in future warfare. In this process they drew heavily on early British experience of the all arms armoured division, but managed to avoid their subsequent errors. The Germans were therefore able to develop an armoured division, based on the tank but with a balance of all arms, and provide suitable tanks to equip it. This was the panzer division that would provide the engine for the Blitzkrieg, which brought the Germans such

30

success in the early part of the war.

This story of contrasting development in Britain and Germany is well known, but where Italy stood in the development of armoured divisions and tanks is less well known. The Italian army had no prominent advocates of armoured warfare, to compare with Guilio Douhet in the sphere of air warfare. In World War I it had experienced trench warfare in the mountainous areas of north-eastern Italy, where tanks appeared to have a very limited role. It had also retained a higher percentage of older officers post-war than any other army in Europe, which reinforced its natural conservatism. This combination of factors made the development of armour much slower than elsewhere. On the other hand, this meant that development was undertaken firmly in the context of infantry support, and so it avoided some of the wilder flights of fancy of the British enthusiasts.

The origins of Italian interest in the tank lay, like those of other armies, in the carnage of the Western Front. Captain Alfredo Bennicelli, an officer serving in France, had closely observed the operations of French tanks since early September 1916. Early in 1917, he persuaded the Italian army to import a French Schneider tank for tests, and these were sufficiently impressive to cause them to order further studies; late in 1917 they acquired another twenty Schneider tanks and 100 Renault FT17 tanks from France. In the wake of defeat at Caporetto in November 1917, however, this ambitious programme was abandoned, and it was not until May 1918 that more French tanks arrived in the shape of three Renault FT17s and a single Schneider. The first experimental Italian tank unit was the *Reparto speciale di marcia carri d'assalto*, or Special Detachment of Assault Cars, formed in the summer of 1918 with the few French tanks available. The newly promoted Major Bennicelli arranged demonstrations of the new Renault FT17s, and this prompted the army, denied further supplies from France, to initiate production of its own version.

This licence-built Renault FT17 was known as the Fiat 3000 and had an improved engine and transmission. However, an initial order for 1,400 vehicles for delivery by 1921 was reduced to 100, following the end of the war in 1918, and in fact the new tank did not enter service until 1921, too late to see any action. It weighed 5.5 tonnes, had a speed of 24kmph (15mph), and carried two machine guns. This first purely Italian-designed tank was the Fiat 2000, a speculative private venture by the company, but which proved distinctly inferior. It was little more than a large armoured box, with a very low speed and a few machine guns, and very few were built.

The Fiat 3000 was the only Italian-built tank for many years, and it formed the basis for all initial Italian armoured doctrine. This focused largely on theory and experimentation, due to a shortage of actual armoured vehicles. In this period the purpose of tanks was to provide close support for the infantry and nothing more. The only organized tank units were small, and designed to support infantry units during the assault; in this context the tank would eliminate enemy barbed wire and machine guns, and allow the infantry to penetrate enemy defences. But although the Italians were using tanks operationally, they had not yet developed any official doctrine for their employment; instead individual commanders made their own pragmatic decisions, based on supporting the infantry.

In November 1918 the Italians formed the *Batteria autonoma carri d'assalto*, or Independent Battery of Assault Cars, with a single Fiat 2000 and three Renault FT-17s. It was formed too late to participate in World War I, but it had the distinction of being the first Italian armoured unit to fight in North Africa. It was sent to Libya in 1919 to fight the local tribes and restore control lost during the war. On 23 January 1923 the Independent Battery of Assault Cars was reconstituted as the *Reparto Carri Armati*, or Tank Detachment, with a strength of 286 officers and men. This unit gradually increased in size as more tanks became available, until in 1927 it became the *Reggimento Carri Armati*, or Tank Regiment. It consisted of five company-sized battalions of twenty tanks and 100 men each, equipped with the original 100 Fiat 3000 tanks produced during 1918–21.

It was Colonel Enrico Maltese, Commander of the Tank Detachment 1924–26, who made the early running in the development of Italian armoured doctrine. In 1924 he wrote an introduction on tanks for the Central Military School at Civitavecchia, which was based firmly on existing practice. There were, nevertheless, some elements of innovative thinking, including the first mention of the concept of the self-propelled gun. Maltese also set out the classification system for future Italian tanks into *pesante, medi e leggero* – heavy, medium and light. In 1925 a manual on the employment of tanks, published under the auspices of Maltese, proposed the use of light tanks as scouting vehicles for cavalry units, even though Italy had no such tanks at the time. In 1927, an article by Maltese dealt with anti-tank defences, including artillery, mines and anti-tank rifles. In 1928 the infantry manual considered the use of artillery and ground-attack aircraft to deal with enemy anti-tank defences, and advocated the dispersed deployment of tanks in the assault phase to prevent damage by enemy artillery. It ignored, however, the possibility of using tanks against other tanks.

In comparison with developments in Britain and Germany, Italian progress seems insignificant; but it must be placed in context. In the 1920s Italy still foresaw her main potential enemies as Germany, Austria, Yugoslavia and France, with the emphasis on the first three. This meant a concentration on their Alpine frontiers, where the mountainous terrain severely restricted the possibilities for mobile warfare. It also meant a concentration on defence against these powers, in line with a largely passive foreign policy. In this strategic context the role of armour was very much to support the infantry. The development of the Tank Regiment and these cautious forays into the development of armoured doctrine provided Italy with a small but solid basis for future expansion.

In the 1930s, Italy adopted a more aggressive foreign policy, which transformed the attitude of the Italian armed forces: they now faced potential demands for offensive military action against other states, which forced them to reassess their current defensive posture. They now had to develop the means to undertake offensives, and a process of modernization was initiated that would result in major developments in Italian military doctrine and equipment during this decade. Thus the Italian army moved gradually towards an emphasis on offensive war based on manoeuvre and mobility. This transition was also influenced by developments elsewhere, with the Germans in particular placing an increasing emphasis on the offensive. This brought about the first steps to the development of the concept of modern mechanized warfare, and the idea of decisive war involving strategic manoeuvre. This would include significant changes in the role of armour.

The first stage in this process, the concept of the *Divisione Celeri*, or Fast Division, would ironically distract the Italian army from the development of true armoured divisions. This *Celeri* division consisted of a combination of *Bersaglieri*, or sharpshooters, and mounted cavalry, supported by fast tanks. The former were light infantry formed in 1836 as an élite corps, distinguished by black cockerel feathers in their helmets and a rapid marching style. It was the *Bersaglieri* and cavalry that had led the pursuit of the defeated armies of the Central Powers after the breakthrough at Vittorio Veneto in 1918. They remained the key offensive elements of the Italian army at this time, and it made sense to utilize their élan in any offensive military formations. The *Bersaglieri* would later supply infantry for the motorized and armoured divisions, although the cavalry would eventually be converted to crew armoured cars. The new *Celeri* concept, however, represented a counterpoint to the early emphasis on the combination of tanks and infantry to break through enemy defences. It also incidentally offered a justification for the mounted cavalry, whose continued existence was under threat at this time.

This new concept was developed by General Ottavio Zoppi, Inspector General of Infantry 1933–35, who had fought in Libya against the local tribes immediately after the war, and who published *I Celeri* in 1933. He sought an alternative to trench warfare by infusing the troops with the aggressive spirit embodied in the élite *Bersaglieri* and cavalry. They would be combined in units supported by tanks and aircraft which would break through enemy defences and envelop and destroy the enemy. In reality this new formation would prove a doctrinal cul-de-sac of limited use during World War II, and a diversion of valuable resources, particularly scarce tanks, from the development of all arms armoured divisions. It was, however, very important in inspiring change and in breaking a defensive mindset that had been in place since 1918. Its demand for aggressive spirit was particularly designed to appeal to the Fascists, who saw this spirit as the core of their new Italy.

This new doctrine required fast tanks to work alongside the cavalry and the motorcycle-mounted *Bersaglieri*. In 1929 Italy purchased four Carden Lloyd Mark V tanks from Britain, and in 1933 produced the first of its own version, the *Carro Veloce* CV33, or Fast Tank (it would later be renamed the *Carro Armato* L3/33). This was a 3-ton light tank with a petrol engine providing a top speed of 15kmph (9mph) across country and an endurance of six hours. It had an armament of two 6.5mm Fiat machine guns in the front hull, and a crew of two. It had 13.5mm of armour at the front and rear, 8.5mm at the sides and 6mm on the top and underside. It was relatively inexpensive to produce, a huge advantage from the Italian viewpoint, and could therefore be built in large numbers. This allowed the Italians to experiment with the deployment of large formations of tanks and test them in a wide variety of roles including flame-throwers, bridge-layers and so on. On the other hand, the CV33 had no rotating turret, was thinly armoured, and armed only with machine guns. In 1935 it was rearmed with two 8mm Breda machine guns in the front hull; this version was known as the *Carro Veloce* CV35, and later as the *Carro Armato* L3/35.

In 1933, three groups of CV33 tanks were formed to support the three new *Celeri* divisions under the command of Colonel Gervasio Bitossi. He was a cavalry man by origin, who was largely left to establish his own policy for their employment. He envisaged the role of the fast tank as introducing

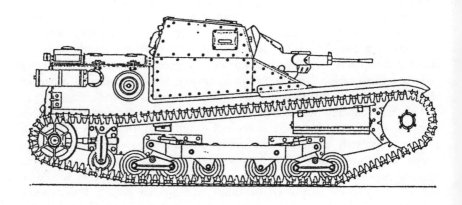

L3/35 light tank. (Ian W. Walker)

motorization into the cavalry without interfering with its traditions, and in the interim supporting the horsed cavalry in action. The training for these new units, although linked to the *Celeri* divisions, in practice differed very little from that of the Tank Regiment. In both cases tanks were to be deployed in a supporting role rather than independently or as the main weapon, and always as an offensive weapon in the attack or counterattack. It was specifically prohibited to use the tank in a defensive role or in defensive positions. The idea of tanks encountering other tanks remained absent.

In 1934 the Italian army was prompted to further action by the emergency mobilization that followed the attempted Nazi coup in Austria, and by subsequent preparations for an attack on Ethiopia. This led to the rapid creation of a large number of tank units equipped with the ubiquitous CV33, the only modern armoured vehicle widely available at the time; these were dispatched to accompany the infantry and cavalry involved in the Ethiopian invasion force. In 1934 Colonel Sebastiano Visconti Prasca published *La Guerra Decisiva*, which advocated a decisive war of movement, involving maximum use of supporting arms to assist the infantry and cavalry. He envisaged the tank as the main means to open up an enemy front for the infantry and cavalry, although it remained a supporting arm, alongside artillery and aircraft, rather than the primary means of attack. He also advocated the idea of balanced combat teams, although these remained based on the infantry. This concept offered a significant step forwards from the doctrine of the previous decade, since it reflected the new aggressive stance of the political leadership and its increasing emphasis on militarism; and it would soon benefit from practical experience in Ethiopia and Spain. Thus a war of mobility was gradually becoming official doctrine. The 1935 manual stressed the need for boldness, initiative and a decisive victory in a new war of movement.

In 1935 many countries were already developing the next generation of medium tanks, with turret-mounted guns offering all-round traverse; but Italy lagged behind. The main reason was that they already had more tanks, with 2,500 CV33s, than any other power. This had allowed them to employ them *en masse* – although it also had important disadvantages. First, they were all one type, which restricted their usefulness for experimentation with different tactical roles. More crucially, the presence of so many existing tanks discouraged the introduction of new models; the army already had a full inventory and was not anxious to order more of these expensive items. In 1935 the Italians had really only just made the first moves towards mechanization and the development of armoured divisions. They had fallen behind many other powers, and still had a long way to go. It was during the five pre-war years that Italian doctrine, tank design and unit development finally made important strides forwards. This came about through a mixture of increased political ambition, theoretical flexibility, practical testing in manoeuvres, and the direct experience of combat.

The campaign in Ethiopia in 1935–36 provided the first practical combat experience of the doctrine and the tanks themselves. In April 1936 the 'March of the Iron Will' on Addis Ababa involved an advance of 200 miles (320km) by a powerful motorized column of 12,500 men and 1,785 vehicles, supported by light tanks, artillery and aircraft. It was largely unopposed, since the Ethiopians had already been beaten, but significantly it was completed across difficult terrain and in bad weather in only ten days, an achievement that vividly demonstrated the offensive potential of motorized forces in securing bold advances.

On 15 December 1935 the design shortcomings of the CV33 light tank were ruthlessly exposed in a disastrous engagement at Dembeguina Pass in northern Ethiopia. An Italian forward observation post at Mai Timkat, held by 1,000 Eritrean native soldiers and nine CV33 light tanks under Major Criniti, was attacked by 1,000 Ethiopians, while another 2,000 circled behind them. The Italians sensibly withdrew towards their main positions at Selaclaca. They reached Dembeguina Pass at midday to find it held against them by the Ethiopians, who had circled around to occupy the surrounding hills. The isolated Criniti had little choice but to try to force the pass. He organized his force for the attack with the light tanks in the lead, and his infantry, with himself on horseback at their head, close behind.

It was a bold gamble that almost succeeded, until the rough terrain blocked the progress of the tanks; Criniti was wounded and two officers killed. The Ethiopians counterattacked and the Italians rallied around their stranded light tanks. The pursuing Ethiopians now entered the fray and the exposed Italian infantry came under heavy fire from all directions. The light tanks with their fixed machine-gun mountings were unable to protect the infantry, who were slaughtered. The isolated tanks were then exposed to close-quarter attack by Ethiopians who approached from the rear and disabled their tracks and machine guns. They were rendered useless and their crews killed.

The Ethiopians then ambushed an Italian relief column, including another ten CV33s, by rolling large boulders in front of and behind them. The Italians were trapped, and once again, first the infantry and then the immobilized tanks were picked off. A few tanks attempted to bypass the roadblock, only to slip down a steep roadside embankment and overturn. Another two isolated tanks resisted fiercely until they were destroyed by the Ethiopians setting light to their fuel. This desperate stand nevertheless allowed a remnant of the Italian column to escape. The actions at Dembeguina Pass highlighted the need for tanks equipped with rotating turrets for all round fire and for improved coordination with the infantry.

In the European context the lessons of the Ethiopian fighting, where the Italians conquered through the application of superior technology, were of limited relevance. The experience gained nevertheless led to important changes. The defeat at Dembeguina Pass led to the immediate issue of revised instructions for the use of tanks, emphasizing the need for reconnaissance and for closer coordination with the infantry, particularly in close terrain. They also suggested, rather gratuitously, that crews should not abandon their vehicles unless absolutely necessary. More importantly, the army finally instituted plans for tanks with rotating turrets to rectify the main problem with the CV33.

The experiences of this war also influenced the development of Italian military doctrine. In 1936 General Alberto Pugnani published a report that advocated the increased use of motor vehicles, including tanks based on Ethiopian experience. The 1936 manual incorporated instructions on the employment of the new *Celeri* divisions, advocating the use of their mobile elements – cavalry, motorcyclists and tanks – in open warfare, and their static elements, infantry and artillery, in positional war. This concept offered a potential blueprint for the future employment of an all arms armoured division, which only required the development of such an armoured division. At a more general level, these ideas increased the emphasis on offensive warfare and on motorization in the army. The missing element was the concept of mechanization, the use of tanks as a main weapon in large mobile units in offensive war.

A significant development for the future took place in Libya at this same time. A new combined *Reggimento Misto Motorizzato*, or Mixed Motorized Regiment, was set up there as part of a reinforcement for this colony in the wake of the Ethiopian conflict. It was commanded by Colonel Bitossi, who had formerly commanded tanks in the *Celeri* divisions. The new unit consisted of a combination of motorcyclists, motor machine-gun units, infantry and tanks, and provided an important model for tactical experimentation with combined arms. The dedicated and far-sighted Bitossi trained them hard to work together, and emphasized operations in rough desert terrain. He urged his men to go beyond current doctrine and existing vehicle designs in their employment of tanks. He recognized that the CV33 was an interim design and that armoured tactics should be designed to fit potential new medium tank designs. This unit, although only temporary, was the first truly mechanized unit in the Italian army and it pointed to the future.

The increased emphasis on motorization and offensive warfare would be reflected in the commitment of Italian forces in the Spanish Civil War. In October 1936 the first Italian units to arrive in Spain were more thoroughly motorized than the army at home, and were later supplied with tanks. They were drawn from a mixture of volunteers and regular army men, released from active service. They were initially intended to serve as instructors for the Spanish Nationalists, but were soon formed into the Italian *Corpo*

Truppe Voluntarie (*CTV*), or Corps of Voluntary Troops, to be employed as front line troops in direct support of the Nationalists. On 26 January 1937 the first tank unit, consisting of thirty-one CV35 tanks, arrived to join them.

In early 1937 General Mario Roatta, the *CTV* commander, proposed a practical trial of the new concepts of motorization and the decisive offensive. He would use three columns of motorized infantry, artillery and light tanks to capture Malaga. The men lacked training and their equipment was in poor condition, but they faced only weak opposition. The attack commenced on 5 February with the three columns breaking through the enemy front with armoured cars and tanks in the lead. They advanced rapidly towards the coast, showing little concern for their exposed flanks, and occupied Malaga on 7 February ahead of their footsore Spanish allies. They subsequently pursued the retreating enemy along the coast until 14 February.

The success of this operation persuaded Roatta to try to repeat it on a much grander scale against Madrid. In March 1937 he planned an offensive north of Madrid using the whole *CTV*, three Blackshirt divisions and the motorized *Littorio* Division from the regular army, commanded by General Annibale Bergonzoli, with 2,000 lorries, 200 artillery pieces and eighty CV35 light tanks. Unfortunately they had very few anti-tank or anti-aircraft guns, and they would face formidable opposition in both these categories. They would be supported by the entire Italian air contingent in Spain. The proposed offensive involved an advance of 30 miles (50km) from Siguenza to capture the town of Guadalajara and achieve a partial encirclement of Madrid. Two Blackshirt divisions would penetrate the Republican front, while a third and *Littorio* would exploit the thrust towards Guadalajara. The Spanish Nationalists to the south of Madrid would simultaneously launch an attack northwards to prevent the Republicans using their reserves against the Italians.

The offensive opened on 8 March 1937 with a heavy artillery barrage, and achieved complete surprise. The Blackshirts broke through the Republican front, and their spearheads reached Trijueque and Brihuega by 13 March, two thirds of the way to Guadalajara. But this rapid advance was somewhat misleading, since a number of things were already going wrong. First, the weather had deteriorated, with alternating rain, sleet, ice and fog, and had grounded the Italian air support, which was based on temporary airstrips. In contrast the Republican air force, which included large numbers of Soviet aircraft piloted by trained Soviet aircrews, operated from all-weather airfields. Second, the Italians had exposed their flanks during their rapid advance, and were slow to bring up their reserves. Moreover, the Republican forces around Madrid were much stronger than at Malaga, and had well-trained reserves available. They were commanded by trained Soviet advisers, and their armament included large numbers of Soviet medium tanks. Also, the Nationalist diversionary attack in the south had not taken place, which allowed the Republicans to release their reserves against the Italians. The situation was ripe with the potential for disaster.

On 13 March, the arrival of Republican reinforcements at Brihuega blocked any further Italian advance, and there followed four days of fierce fighting around the town, during which several key positions changed hands several times. At midday on 18 March the Italians were completely exhausted and the Republicans launched their counter-attack, using three fresh divisions, artillery and seventy medium tanks equipped with 45mm guns, supported by 100 aircraft. The main weight of this attack fell on an exhausted and badly overstretched 1 Blackshirt Division, which quickly collapsed. In contrast the regular *Littorio* Division resisted strong Republican attacks for nearly two hours, and launched a powerful counter-attack with heavy artillery support. They penetrated the boundary between two Republican units, and briefly menaced the rear of those attacking the Blackshirts. The collapse of the latter, however, exposed their own flank and placed them in imminent danger of encirclement. In spite of this it was only when Bergonzoli was ordered to withdraw that *Littorio* finally retreated. But the Republicans failed to follow up the Italian withdrawal immediately, and this allowed them to rebuild their front at Argecilla. A series of subsequent Republican attacks on these new positions were repulsed by *Littorio*, and the Italian front stabilized.

This Italian attempt to encircle Madrid had been too ambitious and had failed disastrously, but it had not been due to cowardice. The Italians had suffered from poor intelligence, poor planning, and a lack of anti-tank and anti-aircraft guns, and had lost air support at a critical stage. Many of the Blackshirts were inexperienced and had suffered accordingly. The Italians lost 400 killed and another 500 missing or taken prisoner, and 800 rifles, twenty-five artillery pieces, sixty-seven lorries and most of their tanks. The losses had fallen mainly on the Blackshirts, especially 1 Blackshirt Division. In contrast the regular *Littorio* Division had performed well, and had suffered fewer losses. The significance of this battle has been exaggerated by propaganda both at the time and since, which has portrayed it as a struggle between Fascism and socialism. The European Left were particularly eager to represent it as a sign of the imminent demise of Italian Fascism. In fact, the reformed and reorganized *CTV* went on to fight very successfully against the Republicans for two more years, and they played a significant role in the subsequent conquest of the Basque provinces and Catalonia. They would not repeat the sort of rapid and exposed advance, without prior recon-naissance, that had brought disaster at Guadalajara. Instead they undertook more closely co-ordinated advances using all arms in close combination and with greater regard for enemy strength.

In July 1937, while fighting still raged in Spain, the first integrated armoured unit was formed back in Italy, as 1 *Brigata Corazzata* or Armoured Brigade. It had been formed as a result of recent experience in Spain, and consisted of 5 *Bersaglieri* Regiment, three battalions of light tanks, and a light mechanized group. It was the first unit to involve a balanced combination of infantry, artillery and armour, and represented the basis for future mechanized warfare. It drew on a number of units employed in previous mechanization experiments, and was organized as an 'instrument of high penetrating capacity designed to open a breach in a solid enemy line'. It was still rather small to operate independently, but could be reinforced with supporting units for manoeuvres against enemy flanks, or used in co-operation with other mobile divisions. This new armoured brigade was tested during the 1937 manoeuvres alongside the *Celeri* and motorized infantry divisions. The result was a renewed emphasis on the need for closer co-operation between tanks and other arms, and the need for a higher proportion of these other arms within the armoured unit itself. In short, the armoured brigade was recognized as a step in the right direction, but it was felt that a larger all arms unit was required. This was the germ from which the armoured division would soon grow.

The combat experience in Spain and the 1937 manoeuvres brought renewed demands for improved tanks to replace the CV35, particularly medium and heavy tanks with rotating turrets. The development of a medium tank was already under way, but progress was slow because time, money and industrial capacity were all extremely limited. The army had accorded no particular priority to tank development at a time when the replacement of essential infantry and artillery equipment seemed more important. In consequence it took nearly three years from original design through to production of the first Italian medium tank, the *Carro Armato* M11/39, in 1939. In addition, it quickly became apparent that this long-awaited model would be little more than an interim design, and the first useful medium tank would not appear until 1940.

A similar lack of priority delayed the introduction of the first true anti-tank gun, even though combat experience in Spain had demonstrated the vital need for such a weapon to oppose enemy medium tanks. In the absence of a suitable indigenous design the Italians adopted the Austrian Bohler 47mm, which proved highly effective on its introduction in 1937. It would later be adopted as the principal weapon for the M13/40 medium tank, and would be described by the Italian tank commander, Enrico Serra, as 'a little jewel'. It stood comparison with contemporary guns with an ability to penetrate 43mm of armour plate at a range of 550yd (500m). The German 37mm gun could penetrate 38mm of armour at 500yd (460m), the American and Japanese 37mm guns 25mm at 1,000yd, and the British 2pdr gun 53mm at 500yd. Unfortunately this new weapon was to have no successors to respond to increases in armoured protection, and it gradually fell behind as new anti-tank weapons with increased calibre and penetration were introduced by others.

The consequence of the Ethiopian and Spanish wars, and the increasing closeness between Italy and Germany, was to reduce any potential threat from the north. Instead, growing tensions with Britain and France increased the threat from these powers in the Mediterranean and Africa; in particular the new Italian empire in Africa represented a major investment for Italy, as it required protection from attack. As a result, the Italian army was forced to reassess its potential opponents in a future war, and to adjust military plans accordingly. The possibility of facing opponents in the more open terrain of North Africa could only reinforce the increasing emphasis on mobile warfare.

In the construction of a modern, mechanized army Italy was able to build on the base provided by a small but effective automobile industry. In 1939 this industry produced a total of 71,000 vehicles, although only 12,000 of these were commercial types most useful to the military. In 1939 there were some 372,000 vehicles of all kinds on Italian roads. The comparatively modest scale of this industry did, however, place constraints on Italian ambitions to construct a fully mechanized army, since it limited the pool of trained or experienced civilian drivers and mechanics that could be called up for the army. This meant that the army had to train a large proportion of the drivers and mechanics that it required – indeed, it was a common complaint from officers in the armoured units that new tank drivers had often not driven any sort of vehicle before. In spite of this, the Italian automobile industry provided an essential backdrop to the development and equipment of armoured divisions.

In 1938, the combat experience in Spain and the manoeuvres with 1 Armoured Brigade, renewed the debate about the use of tanks. General Edoardo Quarra, commander of the Tank Regiment from 1933 to 1936, urged the use of tanks *en masse* with artillery and infantry support both to break through enemy positions and to exploit thereafter. Practical experience in Spain had proven that small groups of tanks lacking artillery and infantry support were both less effective and more vulnerable in these roles. This required a larger formation, with more tanks, a substantial motorized infantry element, and dedicated artillery units, preferably self-propelled to keep pace with the tanks. The current Italian armoured brigade had no integral artillery and only two battalions of lorried infantry, and so remained little more than a support unit that had to operate with infantry divisions. General Carlo di Simone, commander of 2 Armoured Brigade, formed in 1937, also advocated a larger armoured unit, but was reluctant to form a full-scale division in the absence of medium tanks and fully motorized artillery. He suggested the use of more anti-tank guns as a stopgap while awaiting the arrival of medium tanks. He envisaged an increase from 120 to 210 tanks, and the addition of a third infantry battalion and two groups of self-propelled artillery. He also suggested the mechanization of all infantry elements using armoured personnel carriers, and the direct assignment of a squadron of ground-attack aircraft to the unit. The ideas advocated by these men and others were far-sighted and on a par with those expressed across Europe. Unfortunately, they proved beyond Italian capabilities at this time.

In May 1938 a British tank officer, Lieutenant David Belchem, found himself, perhaps surprisingly, posted to an unnamed Italian armoured regiment. In spite of increasing ties between Italy and Germany, he developed close relations with his Italian hosts and made some interesting observations. He noted that their morale was high and, surprisingly, recorded a degree of antipathy amongst Italian officers towards their German allies. He also noted the poor quality of their equipment and their lack of formation training, and made the following specific observations:

> ... [I was] appalled at the age and inadequacy of the equipment with which the Italian units were supposed to prepare for war. This consideration has not, to my knowledge, been sufficiently empha- sized: Mussolini sent men into action utterly ill equipped, untrained in mobile armoured operations, and often lacking in competent assured leadership. How could they be expected to prevail?

The unnamed colonel of this regiment made an interesting observation to Belchem during his stay, when he confessed: 'You know, if only we could combine Italian fighting guts with the backing of British money, we could sweep through Europe!' This was a frank admission of the Italian lack of resources both generally, and in the armoured formations in particular.

In late 1938, manoeuvres with the two new armoured brigades, practical experience in Ethiopia and Spain, and theoretical discussion, all combined to produce a fundamental shift in Italian military doctrine towards the introduction of a policy of mechanization. On 28 October this was introduced by General Alberto Pariani as *guerra di rapido corso*, or 'high speed mobile warfare', and reflected many of the same developments witnessed elsewhere in Europe. It stated for the first time that tanks in large armoured formations should be the primary offensive weapon, and that other arms would support the tanks, rather than vice versa. It emphasized the use of tanks *en masse*, and wherever possible in flank attacks, with direct assault only as a last resort. It would now be the role of the artillery and anti-tank guns to protect the tanks against enemy armour. The new armoured formations would employ manoeuvre and the indirect approach to attack the enemy in his weaker flanks. They would use the maximum mass of tanks and artillery available to break through the enemy line, and employ their armoured and motorized infantry forces to exploit this breach.

There remained flaws in this doctrine, however, including no direct consideration of the problem of tank-versus-tank encounters. It was envisaged that tanks would attack enemy artillery, but if they did so directly the results could prove disastrous. In spite of these minor failings, it was clear that the Italian army had finally grasped the concept of the armoured division, somewhat later than most but perhaps more fully than some. There remained considerable debate about the details of the policy, but all were now agreed on the need for an all arms armoured division with the capacity for independent action. They also accepted that it should be employed not only to break through enemy positions, but also in the exploitation phase to disrupt and encircle the enemy. This consensus had taken the military employment of armour far beyond its original infantry support role. The use of armour in Italy had entered an entirely new phase. The practical implementation of this move towards mechanization would, however, be limited in extent by Italian industrial capacity. The new policy was therefore on a smaller scale than in other European armies. It would be constructed around a single *Corpo d'Armata Corazzato*, or Armoured Corps, which would consist of two newly created armoured divisions and two existing motorized infantry divisions. This force would be supported by a *Corpo d'Armata Celere* or *Celeri* corps, made up of the three existing *Celeri* divisions. Together, these two corps would form the élite Army of the Po, entrusted with the defence of Italy's key industrial heartland. Their commander would be General Ettore Bastico, a *Bersaglieri* and intellectual staff officer and a leading exponent of the new mechanized warfare, who had commanded the *CTV* in Spain in the aftermath of Guadalajara. This new force would provide Italy with a mechanized force equal, on paper at least, to any at the time. Its weakness lay in the *Celeri* corps, which would be unable to deal with conventional armoured divisions or to serve outside Europe.

The new armoured divisions proposed for this mobile corps would be formed around the core of the two armoured brigades set up in 1937. They would consist of an almost equal balance of infantry armour and artillery, with a regiment of each. The armoured regiment of 140 tanks was intended to have four battalions of medium tanks for use in the exploitation phase or against hastily prepared defences, and one battalion of heavy tanks for use against strongpoints or prepared defences. The supporting infantry would consist of a *Bersaglieri* regiment with two battalions of lorried infantry and one of motorcycle infantry, and a company of armoured cars. The artillery regiment would consist of two groups of artillery, a company of anti-tank guns and two batteries of 20mm AA guns. It was a thoroughly modern concept, but its potential was undermined by poor equipment; it had no medium or heavy tanks, and had to make do with the miserable CV35. This would remain a fundamental weakness of the armoured division until almost a year after the outbreak of war. In addition the continued use of motorcycles instead of lorries by one *Bersaglieri* battalion echoed the tradition of bicycle troops, rather than reflecting the needs of modern war. In addition, most of the artillery used in these divisions remained non-motorized and often dated from World War I. The concept of the modern armoured division had therefore been adopted by the Italians, but its practical expression fell somewhat short.

The structure of the Army of the Po was an ambitious goal for the Italians, especially immediately after the Munich crisis, when war appeared closer than ever before and the army was simultaneously expanding to near its wartime strength. It was necessary to devote time and resources to setting up the units to equip this force in a relatively short period. The first priority was to complete one *Celere* and two motorized infantry divisions, and create a first armoured division from existing cadres. The armoured division would form around the core provided by an existing armoured brigade. The first Italian armoured division, 132 *Ariete* (Ram) Armoured Division, created from 2 Armoured Brigade, was established on 1 February 1939 under General Di Simone. It was based at Verona and consisted of the 132 Armoured Regiment, 8 *Bersaglieri* Regiment and 132 Artillery Regiment and attached units. It was quickly followed on 20 April 1939 by 131 *Centauro* (Centaur) Armoured Division under General Giovanni Magli, created from 1 Armoured Brigade; it was based at Siena and consisted of 131 Armoured Regiment, 5 *Bersaglieri* Regiment and 131 Artillery Regiment. The new divisions initially retained the commanders of their component brigades to ensure continuity.

The formation of the new units progressed more slowly than expected, due to the lack of sufficient vehicles and the shortages of manpower during the sudden expansion to wartime establishment. The peacetime core of an Italian division was normally a training organization manned at 50 per cent of wartime establishment for a two-year period, and only filled out with reservists during mobilization. In spring 1939 the two new armoured divisions were built up to 80 per cent of their strength in the wake of the German occupation of Prague and in preparation for the invasion of Albania. This expansion brought large numbers of reservists into the units, and few had any experience of armoured operations. The peacetime training of the new armoured divisions was also disrupted by shortages of funds and fuel. In the midst of the process a budget shortfall led to a 50 per cent reduction in orders for desperately needed medium tanks. The armoured divisions were assigned only enough fuel for 300km (200 miles) of operations, which would just about allow them to reach the Alpine frontier. In Libya there were no fuel depots at all, although it seemed increasingly likely that armoured divisions would need to be deployed there.

In April 1939 the Spanish Civil War ended, drastically reducing Italian military expenditure and releasing a pool of experienced men. A large number of officers rejoined their old units and disseminated knowledge of what they had learned in Spain. In the same month the Italians launched an almost bloodless invasion of Albania, which exposed some major weaknesses. For example, a whole range of equipment and clothing was revealed to be flawed. There were also severe deficiencies in Italian supply arrangements, which barely functioned across the short Adriatic crossing. The brand new *Centauro* Armoured Division participated, but failed to distinguish itself, with its obsolescent ten- and twenty-year-old tanks prone to breakdowns in the mountainous terrain. It was fortunate that the Albanians offered little opposition and had no anti-tank weapons, or a disaster might have ensued. If it had not been for air drops of fuel the Italian motorized units might have been stranded altogether. The *Centauro* had learnt a number of hard lessons, but at least had the distinction of being the first Italian armoured division to be deployed operationally.

This deployment also raised the urgent need to replace *Centauro* in the Army of the Po. The Italians therefore decided to convert the regular army division previously deployed in Spain into an armoured division, the 133 *Littorio* (from Lictor, meaning an 'ancient Roman official') Armoured Division. It was based at Parma, and consisted of the 133 Armoured Regiment, 12 *Bersaglieri* Regiment and 133 Artillery Regiment and attached units. It was commanded by General Bitossi, one of the original armoured pioneers, who had led *Littorio* during the latter stages of the fighting in Spain. Its motto was '*A Colpo Sicuro*' or 'To make sure'. In 1939 the Italians also briefly considered converting their *Celeri* divisions into armoured divisions. They sought out officers with tank experience for this purpose, but in spite of a shortage of these, it was the shortage of tanks that effectively prevented the formation of further armoured units.

In the 1939 manoeuvres the Italians employed the entire Armoured Corps for the first time, although a great deal of effort was devoted to training *Littorio* for its new role. Inevitably the main issue was that of the useless L3/35 light tanks and their replacement with newer and heavier medium tanks. Bitossi of *Littorio* and Colonel Ugo de Lorenzis, commander of 133 Armoured Regiment, strongly supported these views. The diligent Bitossi urged his officers to try to think in terms of new tanks during these exercises and emphasized the importance of close co-operation between infantry and tanks. This reflected the experience of this Spanish veteran, who appreciated that Italy was still far from ready for the sort of modern war that erupted in September 1939.

The Italians studied closely the German employment of armour during the Polish campaign and their new Blitzkrieg, and this convinced them of the importance of anti-tank guns, and particularly of placing them well forward; they realized that ideally they should be self-propelled in order to keep pace with tanks and motorized infantry. They also accepted that anti-tank guns rather than tanks were the best weapon to fight enemy tanks. The Germans sent Major Eugenio Midolla to Italy to lecture on the subject; he flatteringly drew comparisons to the Italian *guerra di rapido corso* in style and concept, if not in actual execution. He also stressed the vital importance of thorough training, good equipment and an aggressive spirit for success. In many of these areas the Italians had deficiencies that prevented them from attaining the high standards set by the Germans. The Italians were therefore very much aware of many of the key lessons being demonstrated in Poland; the problem was that they lacked the means to put these ideas into practice.

In late 1939, the Italian army finally received the first of its long-awaited new medium tanks, the *Carro Armato* M11/39. This was an 11-ton medium tank with a diesel engine providing a top speed of 14kmph (9mph) across country, and an endurance of ten hours. It had an armament of one 37mm cannon in the front hull, and two 8mm Breda machine guns in a rotating turret, and a crew of three. It had 30mm of armour at the front, 14.5mm at the sides and rear, and 6mm on the top and underside. It had been designed to address the problems encountered in Ethiopia, with turret-mounted machine guns offering all-round protection against infantry, and a hull-mounted cannon for use against other vehicles or fortifications. It was a good design in 1937, but its prolonged development meant that it was obsolescent when it finally reached the troops in 1939; as a result of progress in tank design elsewhere and recent developments in armoured doctrine, what was now required was a medium tank equipped with a turret-mounted cannon capable of dealing with infantry, artillery and other vehicles.

It would be another year before such a vehicle came into service, in the shape of the *Carro Armato* M13/40. Although developed directly from the M11/39, this proved to be a vastly improved design, and it showed that Italian designers were capable of producing competent designs broadly in step with developments across Europe. It was a 13-ton medium tank with a diesel engine providing a top speed of 14kmph (9mph) across country, and an endurance of twelve hours. It had an improved armament of one turret-mounted, 47mm Bohler cannon, and no fewer than four 8mm Breda machine guns: two in the front hull, one mounted coaxially with the cannon, and one mounted on the turret for anti-aircraft defence; and it had a crew of four. It had 30mm to 40mm of armour at the front, 25mm at the sides and rear, and 14mm on the top and underside. It could also carry a radio, but usually only the tanks belonging to unit commanders actually had these. When this design first appeared in 1940, it bore comparison with most contemporary designs; unfortunately, as a result of extremely slow

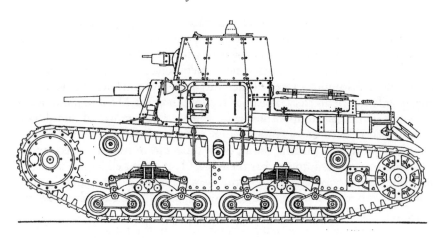

M11/39 medium tank. (Ian W. Walker)

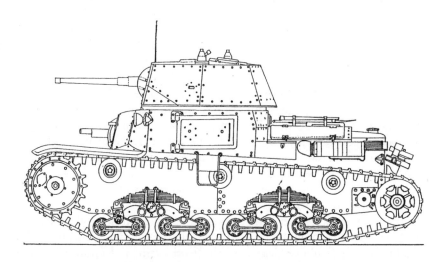

M13/40 medium tank. (Ian W. Walker)

production, this M13 did not enter widespread service until the second half of 1941.

In the end this model would provide the backbone of the Italian armoured divisions throughout the war. It has been almost universally condemned as worthless, but this is unfair. It was prone to mechanical breakdown, particularly in the desert, but so were many British tanks. More seriously, its armour plate was extremely brittle and had a tendency to split when hit by heavy anti-tank shells. It had one important advantage over contemporary British tanks: its 47mm gun could fire both armoured-piercing and high-explosive shells, which allowed it to engage infantry and artillery targets as well as tanks. The contemporary 2pdr gun mounted in British tanks had only armoured-piercing shells and was therefore unable to engage infantry or artillery. The poor reputation of the M13/40 has much to do with invidious comparisons with some of the more advanced tank designs that it faced in subsequent years. It suffered unduly from the Italian failure to produce a suitable successor in time and in numbers. As a result, although marginally improved as the M14/41, it remained largely unaltered in front-line service throughout the war. Elsewhere new tanks entered service, and the Italian medium tanks faced increasingly powerful opposition, with better armour and better guns.

The Italians had produced a heavy tank design, the *Carro Armato* P40, as early as late 1940. It was a 26-ton, heavy tank with a diesel engine providing a top speed of 25kmph (16mph) across country, and an endurance of twelve hours. It had the excellent main armament of one turret-mounted 75mm cannon, but only one 8mm Breda machine gun mounted coaxially; it had a crew of four. It had 50–60mm of armour at the front, 40mm at the sides and rear, and 20mm on the top and underside; in many respects it stood comparison with the German Panzer IV. Unfortunately the Italians were unable to introduce the P40 into service before the Italian collapse in September 1943. The first prototype was not produced until early 1942, a whole year later – a ridiculous timescale! If Italian industry had been able to bring this model into service either in late 1941 or during 1942, it might have made a considerable difference to the performance of her armoured divisions; it would not have transformed them into war winners, but it might at least have given them a fighting chance. Instead the Italians were forced to persevere with their increasingly obsolescent M13s against enemy tanks with superior capabilities.

At the time of the Italian entry into the war, on 10 June 1940, the army had three armoured divisions: *Centauro* Division under General Magli; *Ariete* Division now under General Carlo Vecchiarelli; and *Littorio* Division under General Bitossi. The basic structure is illustrated in Table 3 opposite, consisting of an armoured regiment, an artillery regiment and a *Bersaglieri* regiment, and a complement of around 7,500 officers and men. The armoured regiment was made up of three armoured battalions, on paper one heavy and two medium, although most were still equipped with obsolete L3/35 light tanks, 184 in total. The new M13/40 would not become available in sufficient numbers until 1941, and until then the armoured divisions had only a few medium tanks and had to make do with their useless L3/35s. The artillery regiment consisted of two battalions with a total of twenty-four 75mm field guns. The *Bersaglieri* regiment was

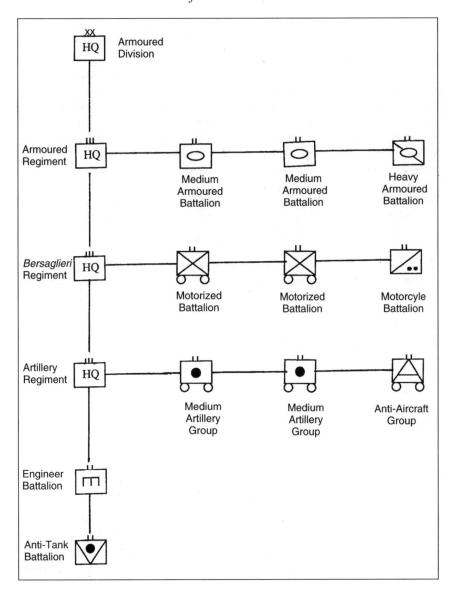

Table 3

Basic Structure of Italian Armoured Division 1939

composed of three battalions, two motorized and one on motorcycles. So how did this basic formation compare to other contemporary armoured formations?

The Italian armoured division was weaker in almost every respect than its German counterpart, the panzer division, which even in its reduced post-1940 state was a much more powerful formation. It had a larger complement of 15,600 officers and men, and superior equipment and weaponry in virtually every category. A typical panzer division had around 105 panzers, and ten of these carried powerful 75mm guns. It had fifty artillery pieces from 75mm upwards, and thirty-nine anti-tank guns, excluding additional 88mm anti-aircraft guns that could be used in this role. In addition it benefited from better training and better command and control systems, including the German philosophy of mission command. In short, the panzer division was not only larger in size, but it carried a much bigger punch than any similar unit.

The British armoured division was variable in size but had, typically, two or three armoured brigades. In its two-brigade form it had a complement of 10,700 officers and men, and was generally somewhat better equipped than its Italian counterpart. It was, however, a less well-balanced formation, with twice as many tanks, at 340, but less infantry and artillery, with only two infantry battalions and only sixteen 25pdr guns in its support group. It was a powerful force when its brigades operated together, although it *was* deficient in infantry and artillery, especially when its brigades operated independently, as was frequently the case. In comparison to the typical British armoured division, the Italian equivalent had more infantry and artillery, but far fewer tanks. An Italian armoured division was broadly equivalent to a British armoured brigade in tank strength, but had the advantage of integrated infantry and artillery.

Such comparisons are, of course, no more than crude equivalents based on theoretical establishments. In practice, the individual components of all military formations varied considerably, in numbers and equipment, from their paper establishments. They can be flexible in the first place, like the alternative two- or three-brigade combinations for British armoured divisions. They can be reinforced or reduced by the addition or detachment of various sub-units. The impact of casualties or breakdowns will cause units to fall below, sometimes far below, their original establishments. The different sizes of formations involved in combat, and the fact that these sizes will fluctuate over time, should be borne in mind in any consideration of battlefield engagements. A division on paper might on occasion have fewer men than a regiment or even a battalion, and this will reduce its performance correspondingly: in many accounts, mention of a particular unit conjures up an impression of it in all its might, when it may have been reduced by losses to a mere remnant of this original state.

In addition, relatively small changes in equipment can make an immense difference to the striking power of an otherwise unchanged unit. A battalion of M13/40 medium tanks with 47mm guns carries far more offensive power than a similar unit of L3/35 light tanks with only machine guns, even if it has more of them. The introduction of only eight of the formidable Italian 90mm anti-aircraft guns, the equivalent of the German 88mm, into a formation will enhance its overall anti-tank capability out of all proportion to these small numbers, by increasing substantially the range at which enemy tanks can be destroyed. The introduction of twenty *Semovente da 75/18* self-propelled guns provided a response to the increased armour and firepower of enemy Grant and Sherman tanks, where none had previously been available.

The Italian armoured division of 1940 represented a well-balanced force of all arms, designed to operate together under a single command. It had the potential to operate in an extremely flexible way using its combination of armour, infantry and artillery. It was still weak in armour, with its inferior light tanks, and this would remain the case until 1941; and it was also weaker than it might have been in artillery and anti-tank guns, although these deficiencies would be remedied through wartime experience. It is important, however, to be clear that it remained, even at full strength, smaller than its British or German equivalents, a point seldom made clear in wartime accounts.

In the month prior to 10 June 1940 the three Italian armoured divisions were all mobilized to full wartime strength. The *Ariete* and *Littorio* Divisions remained with the Armoured Corps in the Po Valley to defend Italy's northern borders; the *Centauro* Division remained in Albania to watch Greece and Yugoslavia. The wholly defensive posture for these élite mobile formations was not in line with the doctrine of offensive war, but it matched initial Italian political intentions to await suitable opportunities to snatch an easy prize before the imminent peace conference. After the declaration of war, *Littorio* was sent to support the hastily organized attack on France across the western Alps. Unsurprisingly, their puny light tanks made no progress in difficult terrain, and suffered heavy casualties to French fortifications equipped with heavy artillery. Only the French surrender prevented their complete immolation.

In 1940 *Ariete* was spared from this fate, because it had been stationed behind the front to exploit a breakthrough that never came. In January 1941, in the wake of Italian defeat at the hands of the British, *Ariete* became the first Italian armoured division shipped to North Africa. It was still largely equipped with L3/35 light tanks, although one of its armoured battalions had the new M13/40 medium tank. It would thereafter fight alongside its new German allies in almost every battle right up to El Alamein in November 1942.

The *Littorio* Division was slowly re-equipped with medium tanks while it remained in northern Italy to watch Yugoslavia. On 11 April 1941, they participated in the Italian invasion of Yugoslavia, driving through Istria into central Yugoslavia and reaching Trebinje on 17 April. They had covered over 300 miles (500km) to link up with *Centauro*, which had driven north from Albania. This was the task that Italian armoured divisions had originally been designed for, and *Littorio* performed it well. It was admittedly undertaken against light opposition from the Yugoslavs who were already dissolving under the combined pressures of German Blitzkrieg and internal collapse. In January 1942 following re-equipment and retraining, *Littorio* was sent to North Africa to join *Ariete*. This virtually recreated the original armoured corps on North African soil, since the motorized infantry divisions were also there. Unfortunately they were all badly below strength and would never operate together in the way originally envisaged. The closest that they came was during the futile Axis attack on Alam Halfa in August 1942, when *Ariete* and *Littorio* Armoured and *Trieste* Motorized Divisions operated under the Italian XX Corps. The *Littorio* was subsequently destroyed at Alamein.

In May 1942, the 1939 proposal to form a fourth armoured division was revived. The career of *Ariete* in North Africa had already more than demonstrated the validity of the armoured division concept. In contrast the three *Celeri* divisions, although employed in Yugoslavia and Russia, had been shown to be deeply flawed. Although mobile enough, they lacked the armoured punch necessary to tackle enemy defences or armoured units. It was therefore proposed to convert the 2 *Celere* Division into the 134 *Freccia* (Arrow) Armoured Division. The proposal never actually got off the ground, however, simply because Italian industry was unable to produce sufficient medium tanks. It barely managed to replace the losses suffered by the three existing armoured divisions. It could not produce the 150 extra required to equip another full armoured division and as a result the *Freccia* Division never left the drawing board.

The *Centauro* Division was the last of the three armoured divisions to reach North Africa, but it saw plenty of action before then. On 28 October 1940, *Centauro*, still in Albania, participated in the ill-fated Italian attack on Greece. It was tasked with the capture of Ioannina in Epirus with 4,037 men and 163 L3/35 light tanks. Its lead elements under Colonel Solinas advanced, through pouring rain and thick mud, for two days until they reached the swollen Kalamas river, 15 miles (24km) inside Greece. They had, however, lost contact with the rest of the division in the process and were unable to cross the raging torrent. They launched some unco-ordinated attacks against the well-constructed Greek main defensive positions, which were all repulsed. They held on, although increasingly isolated, until Greek counter-attacks on 16 November routed Italian forces to the north and forced them to withdraw to avoid being cut off. In the process they had to abandon their few remaining tanks, which had broken down or become stuck in the mud. On 9 December they were sent into reserve to reorganize and re-equip with medium tanks.

In spite of this setback, the restored *Centauro* went on to support the reconstructed Italian front in Albania. They took part in a number of counter-attacks against the Greeks, but the mountainous terrain restricted their mobility and forced them into frontal assaults on well-defended positions. This was not the most effective employment for an armoured division, and they were unable to achieve a breakthrough. In late March 1941 they were withdrawn north to participate in the Yugoslav campaign. On 11 April, they advanced into Yugoslavia from northern Albania against disintegrating opposition, with the intention of linking up with *Littorio* advancing south. On 17 April they completed this task successfully, after crossing 100 miles (160km) of mountainous terrain, near Trebinje in Dalmatia. Thereafter *Centauro* was shipped home for reorganization and refitting, before it was finally transported to North Africa in November 1942. It arrived too late to join its sister divisions, *Ariete* and *Littorio*, which had been all but destroyed at El Alamein earlier that month. They took part in the final battles in Tunisia before being disbanded in April 1943.

The arrival of *Centauro* in North Africa at the end of 1942 was nevertheless a significant event, because it meant that all three of the Italian armoured divisions had been deployed to this important theatre. It was, arguably, the most critical theatre for the Italians, in spite of the deployment of larger numbers of Italian troops in support of the German campaign against the Soviet Union. It was where they defended the last remnants of their colonial empire, and where, indirectly, they were best able to defend the homeland itself. In 1943, the collapse of Axis resistance in North Africa led inexorably to the invasions of Sicily and Italy. It was a place with immense scope for the application of the *guerra di rapido corso,* and where Italy's armoured divisions might have most impact on the war. It is to this North African theatre that we must now turn to assess the opportunities and challenges it offered for armour, and the impact of the Italian armoured divisions on the fighting that raged there between June 1940 and May 1943.

3

Baptism of Fire

The North African desert would offer the greatest scope for the Italian armoured divisions during World War II. On the southern shore of the Mediterranean stood the Italian colony of Libya, with British-occupied Egypt to the east, and the French protectorate of Tunisia to the west. The bulk of the fighting took place in a narrow strip 50–100 miles (80–160km) wide along the coast in its eastern province of Cyrenaica and the Western Desert of neighbouring Egypt. It was bounded to the south by the wide expanses of the Sahara Desert, which would not support the passage of heavy vehicles. In this vast region there were only a few isolated points of human habitation, almost all situated on the coast. There was little agriculture, except in the hills of the Jebel Akhdar in western Cyrenaica, only a single tarmac road along the coast, and, in Egypt, a single-track railway. There were few significant natural features of any kind, with the exception of the Jebel Akhdar and the Qattara Depression, and a steep escarpment dividing the coastal strip from the inland plateau, which could only be ascended or descended by vehicle traffic at a few key points. In this largely featureless terrain, small alterations in ground level might offer wide views over the surrounding area, or welcome concealment. In North Africa, small rises or depressions of a hundred or so feet that would have gone unnoticed elsewhere, were fiercely contested: they were key features that men struggled to hold or capture, and around which many men died.

This desert has often been described as ideal terrain for mobile warfare, precisely because it presents few obstacles to manoeuvre. In fact it represents some of the most unforgiving terrain on earth, particularly for vehicles and machinery of all kinds. In contrast to expectations, it does not consist entirely of flowing sand dunes, but rather of large areas of exposed rock with a light covering of dusty sand. This gives a rough, stony surface that is extremely tough on both wheeled and tracked vehicles, and causes severe wear and tear to vehicle tyres and suspensions. The surface coating of fine dust, if disturbed by the wind or vehicle movements, penetrates every bit of machinery, clogging filters and moving parts, and blocking fuel lines; and it penetrates the eyes, noses and mouths of the men, too. There are also occasional areas of softer sand and salt marsh, both of which are truly impassable to vehicles, although these areas are relatively few and scattered.

The desert is therefore not the ideal place to operate the highly complex vehicles or machinery necessary in mobile warfare, and presents tremendous challenges to anyone who attempts it. In these circumstances the sturdiness and reliability of all kinds of equipment is an important aspect of success.

Furthermore the desert climate is unforgiving to both men and machines: in summer the midday temperatures can rise as high as 130 degrees, turning vehicles into searing ovens and overheating their engines; while at night the temperature drops significantly. The intense heat often forced tank crews to keep their hatches open, even during fighting, with an increased risk of death or injury. Also, the heat haze during the middle of the day can conceal dangers or produce imaginary dangers in the form of mirages. In summer the sand can be stirred up by hot winds into blinding sandstorms, which make movement difficult and sometimes prevent any movement at all. The same effect can be caused by vehicle movements, obscuring the vision of drivers and gunners, with the consequent risk of accidents. In winter, while temperatures are mild during the day, at night they can drop below zero. In winter there are also sometimes heavy rainstorms, which wash away desert tracks, flood normally dry wadis, and transform the sand into mud that could trap heavy vehicles.

The open expanses of the desert also present problems of navigation and communication for mobile armies. The lack of easily identifiable landmarks such as towns, mountains or rivers, means that it is very difficult to locate your position most of the time. In the days before GPS, men were forced to navigate using a compass and celestial observations of the sun, moon and stars, almost as though they were at sea. This was a particular problem for the Italians who had very few vehicle compasses, and whose ordinary compasses were affected by the proximity of the steel vehicle hulls. This meant that Italian tank commanders were often forced to halt and leave the safety of their vehicle in order to take compass readings. This procedure inevitably slowed their progress in the open desert, while failure to do it meant they might stray off course without realizing it.

In the desert, communications are obviously vital for mobile operations, involving rapid movements and frequent changes in orders, and it is therefore essential for mobile forces to receive orders and intelligence from headquarters quickly, and for them, in turn, to be able to report back as swiftly. This obviously cannot be done through land lines during mobile operations, although these were used in fixed positions at Tobruk and Alamein. It was occasionally possible to use messengers or air drops to pass instructions, but these methods were slow and unreliable. The key to mobile communications in the desert was the radio, which allowed the rapid exchange of information required and, atmospheric conditions permitting, could reach anywhere. Unfortunately, despite the pioneering work of Marconi, the Italians had difficulties in this respect, with very few reliable

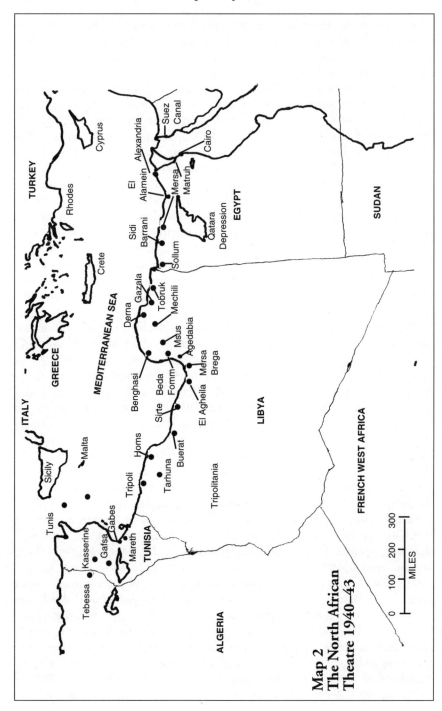

Map 2
The North African
Theatre 1940–43

vehicle radios available; in their armoured units it was often the case that only the vehicles of the company commander and upwards had a radio. This meant that the company commander had to communicate with the rest of his tanks through visual signals, which often meant exposing himself to enemy fire. In addition, visual signals might not be seen in the dust, haze, smoke and confusion of battle, especially from other enclosed armoured vehicles with small vision slits.

The widespread use of radio meant that most messages had to be encoded against enemy interception, and each side tried to break the other's signals, while safeguarding their own. In 1940 the British had the advantage, but this early lead was lost with the arrival of German radio intercept units, and improvements in Italian codes. There followed a contest between local radio interception and code-breaking teams, which provided each side with partial insights into enemy intentions. There were also significant gains and losses at the more strategic level. In September 1941 the Italians stole a code from the US Embassy in Rome, which provided access to the reports of Colonel Fellers, their attaché in Cairo. These reports contained detailed information on the strength and intentions of the British in North Africa, which Rommel used to inform his operations right through the war until mid-1942. The real winners at this higher level, however, were the British, who broke the German Enigma machine cipher in 1940. This Ultra intelligence supplied an increasing amount of information on Axis strengths and intentions, and by 1942 an unprecedented insight into every aspect of Axis operations. It enabled them to intercept increasing numbers of Axis supply ships, most of which would otherwise have been missed, and it would prove very important to ensuring final Allied victory. The Germans suspected that the Allies had access to secret information, but blamed this on the Italians' poor radio discipline and insecure ciphers. Ironically, they never suspected for a moment that their own highly advanced Enigma machine ciphers were responsible.

A mobile army needs large amounts of food and water and ammunition and fuel to operate effectively, but the desert offers few supplies of any kind. There are almost no crops or herds of domestic animals, no munitions factories or petrol stations, and little enough water. In short, there is nothing for foraging troops except what they can capture from the enemy. This means that virtually everything necessary for a mobile army to operate effectively must be transported from elsewhere and brought to where it is needed. This places enormous restrictions on mobile warfare, since, while a mobile army can operate for short periods without food and sometimes even without much water, it is virtually useless without fuel and ammunition. This makes logistics and supply vitally important.

This basic problem was exacerbated by the immense distances involved, and the poverty of transport facilities. The distance by sea from Italy to

Libya is significant, but can be surmounted relatively easily with adequate shipping, and this route did not in fact represent a significant problem during the war, with the Italian navy and air force maintaining an excellent record of successfully transferring more than 90 per cent of supplies to North Africa. It is important to remember this fact, since the Italians have been unjustly blamed, not least by Rommel himself, for a failure to transport sufficient supplies to the Axis forces. However, they only fell significantly below this impressive performance for two limited periods of time, namely September to December 1941 and August to December 1942. On these two occasions, British forces based on Malta and directed by Ultra intelligence, were able to significantly reduce the amount of Axis supplies reaching North Africa. This provided an additional hindrance to Axis operations during these periods, and further restricted their freedom of movement. It was not, however, primarily enemy action that constrained this important supply route during the war.

The real problem of the sea route to North Africa was the limited capacity of the Libyan ports, which fatally restricted Axis supplies at all times. The largest, Tripoli, could only accommodate a maximum of five large cargo vessels or four troop transports at any time, and had a maximum unloading capacity of about 45,000 tonnes per month. In comparison, the next in size, Benghasi, which was often subject to bombing, could only manage three cargo vessels or two troop transports, and 24,000 tonnes per month; and Tobruk managed a similar number of ships but a mere 18,000 tonnes per month. These tonnages represent what was feasible in ideal conditions, and take no account of the effects of Allied air attack, which could reduce them significantly. This stark situation imposed strict upper limits on supply deliveries. The requirements of the Axis forces varied significantly depending on their overall numbers, and whether they were in action or not. It has been calculated that an average Axis division required approximately 10,000 tonnes per month, and with between seven divisions in late 1941, and twelve in late 1942, the Axis forces therefore needed between 70,000 and 120,000 tonnes per month. In general, the requirements of the Axis forces operating in North Africa exceeded the capacity of the ports to supply them, at times by a significant margin. If the Italians have a fault in respect of logistics, it lies in a failure to increase the capacity of Tripoli and other ports before the war.

The logistical problems were further compounded at the landward end. The distance from Tripoli to Benghasi in Cyrenaica was about 600 miles (970km), and to Alamein in Egypt it was more than twice that, at around 1,200 miles (2,000km). Along this entire route there existed only a single tarmac highway and, in Egypt only, a single-track railway which could be used to transport supplies. In comparison, the distance from the Polish border to Moscow was only 600 miles and there were many roads and railways along this route. This meant that almost all supplies intended for the Axis forces at the front had to be moved by large numbers of lorries travelling between Tripoli and wherever they were required. This was a massive logistical undertaking and a huge drain on already scarce resources of fuel. It has been calculated that a third of all fuel landed was consumed transporting supplies to the front, which left only a fraction for combat operations. The severe desert conditions also placed a strain on the lorries involved, and as many as a third might be undergoing maintenance at any time and hence unavailable to transport supplies. In transit the supply traffic was also exposed to air attack on their single easily targeted route.

All of this effectively meant that Axis forces in North Africa led a hand-to-mouth existence for much of the time. They seldom had the luxury of sufficient supplies for all their needs, except perhaps during the infrequent lulls in the fighting; it was usually a case of struggling to meet sometimes basic needs, and more often, especially during periods of intense operations, simply a case of doing without many non-essentials. It was even, on occasions, a case of running short of critical supplies of fuel or ammunition. In response to this general poverty, Axis troops quickly developed an instinct for exploiting any potential source of supplies, and particularly the plentiful resources available to their opponents. They frequently not only ran their vehicles on captured fuel and fed their men on captured rations, but also travelled in captured vehicles, used captured weapons and, on occasions, donned items of captured uniform. This was undoubtedly an admirable expedient, but it revealed the basic inadequacy of Axis logistics in this theatre.

The logistical difficulties were so fundamental that it might sometimes have looked as if a conquest of Egypt was never a realistic possibility; however, this is probably an exaggeration. The North African campaign demonstrated that small but well-directed and well-trained forces could defeat much larger but poorly directed and trained forces, and in these circumstances it was always possible that small Axis forces, if their supplies were adequate, might conquer Egypt. Indeed, there were probably at least two occasions when this was distinctly possible. The first of these was in June 1940, when Italian mobile forces might have exploited previously stockpiled supplies to reach Alexandria or Cairo, a relatively short distance from the Libyan frontier. They failed to do so because of a lack of mobile forces and a lack of preparation, and the task proved beyond their poorly trained and equipped marching infantry. The second was in July 1942, when already overstretched and exhausted Axis units reached El Alamein and might have bluffed their way to Alexandria and Cairo. If they had managed this, they could have exploited their superior ability to manoeuvre to push back numerically superior but often panicky British forces. Instead, General Claude Auchinleck's determination to stand firm ensured that this did not happen. In most other circumstances the Allied superiority in numbers and supplies set the odds firmly against the Axis. It is perhaps best to say that this was a campaign that the British could lose rather than one that the Axis could win.

It was in the unforgiving arena of the North African desert and at the end of an attenuated supply line that the Italian armoured divisions would be tested during World War II. On 10 June 1940, however, when Mussolini declared war on Britain and France, none of Italy's armoured or motorized divisions were stationed in North Africa and there were no plans to send them there: they were retained for possible employment against France, Yugoslavia or Greece. Marshal Italo Balbo, the Italian commander in Libya, had only a few ancient light tanks in his otherwise non-motorized army, and he urgently requested armoured units to support Mussolini's proposed invasion of Egypt. On 28 June, however, he was killed by friendly fire without having secured anything, and his successor, Marshal Rodoffo Graziani, initially failed to secure any armour. He was a cautious man, whose main successes had been achieved in campaigns against tribal opponents in Libya and Ethiopia. In spite of intense pressure from Mussolini, he was reluctant to advance into Egypt without armoured support against what Italian intelligence believed were more powerful British forces. And although they had greatly overestimated the strength of British forces at this time, the latter, although much smaller than reported, were better trained and fully motorized.

In the end, a few armoured units equipped with M11/39 and M13/40 medium tanks were sent to North Africa. They were drawn from units initially formed to re-equip the three armoured divisions, and had no training or experience of co-operation with infantry or artillery, and had never functioned as part of any larger formation. On 13 September 1940, Marshal Graziani finally launched his long-anticipated invasion of Egypt with these armoured units in support. He advanced by slow stages, at the speed of his marching infantry, until he reached Sidi Barrani about 50 miles (80km) into Egypt. He was harassed by highly mobile British forces during this advance, but faced no serious opposition. He then halted to rest, construct defensive positions and bring forward supplies for the next stage of the invasion. In fact the Italians would remain in these positions until struck by the British counter-attack in December 1940.

The encounter between the Italians and the British in the winter of 1940–41 – the epic story of General Archibald Wavell's 30,000 – is now the stuff of legend. It was a tale designed to boost British morale during an otherwise bleak winter, when Britain faced the might of the victorious Axis alone. It was certainly the first undeniable British victory of the war on land: the Royal Navy had sunk the battleship *Graf Spee* in December 1939, and the RAF had triumphed in the Battle of Britain in September 1940, but in comparison, the British army had experienced a series of defeats and withdrawals in the face of the apparently unstoppable German army. In this context Wavell's success in North Africa was a gift that was naturally exploited to the full by British propaganda. It reassured the British public that their army could advance as well as retreat, and it provided evidence for still sceptical American and neutral observers that Britain was not finished yet. The newsreels showing long lines of ragged and beaten Italian prisoners made a significant contribution to British prejudices about Italian cowardice and military incompetence. The actual campaign undoubtedly produced evidence of both, but it also witnessed instances of heroism and self-sacrifice.

The propaganda value of this victory of 30,000 British over 300,000 Italians has served to obscure a number of significant facts, and it is only when we look beneath the surface that we begin to see that things were not as clear cut. In fact the British never faced the whole Italian force at any time, but exploited their superior mobility to defeat a series of smaller Italian forces one at a time. In addition, the large Italian force of fourteen divisions, five of them stationed forward in Egypt, was far from the best that Italy had to offer, consisting almost entirely of poorly trained and equipped marching infantry conscripts. It included three divisions of Blackshirt militia that were little more than a scouting organization for Fascist Party members. It included no armoured or motorized divisions, but only a couple of *ad hoc* tank units, equipped mainly with obsolete light tanks and a few medium tanks. The whole force was entirely unsuited to mobile desert war, and ill-equipped to face Italy's most powerful enemy. In contrast, the British had a professional, well-trained, and relatively well-equipped force, consisting of three regular army divisions, two infantry and one armoured, with 175 light tanks, seventy-three cruiser tanks and fifty Matilda II infantry tanks. The hull armour of the latter would prove impervious to almost every Italian gun available at the time. This force was completely motorized, which enabled it to move freely across the desert to surround and destroy isolated Italian units individually.

The sole advantage that the forward Italian forces in Egypt had was their superior numbers, with six divisions and a small armoured group. However, they managed to discard this ace by dispersing their forces amongst a number of defensive camps that were unable to support each other. The Italian camps were well defended with artillery and mines, but had only a few anti-tank guns, and no mobile forces to link the individual camps. The small Italian armoured group present was insufficient to fulfil this task and would, in any case, be destroyed in the earliest phase of the fighting. The morale of the Italian forces had been undermined by more than two months of tedious defensive duties and by news of defeat at Taranto and in Greece. They had experienced numerous scares in the form of British raids and naval bombardments, but nothing more threatening; they had become accustomed to such activity and had ceased their own patrols. In the early morning of 9 December, the British troops involved in their counter offensive were able to approach the Italian positions almost completely undetected. It is not intended to discuss the subsequent British counter offensive in detail here, but to focus on those few engagements that involved Italian armoured units.

Nibeiwa

The initial British assault would fall on Nibeiwa Camp, where the only available Italian armoured unit was based, and it achieved complete surprise. The *Raggruppamento Maletti*, or Maletti Group, under General Pietro Maletti, was an *ad hoc* formation consisting of 2,500 Libyan soldiers and 2 Armoured Battalion, with thirty-five M11/39 medium tanks and thirty-five L3/35 light tanks. It was earmarked for early destruction in the assault, which commenced at 05:00hr with what appeared to be no more than another raid on the eastern side of the camp. At 07:00, however, forty-eight Matilda tanks suddenly appeared from the opposite side of the camp. They struck twenty-three unmanned M11/39 tanks of the Maletti Group, which had been deployed to guard the unmined entrance to the camp. The Italians were caught completely off guard and many did not even reach their tanks, including General Maletti, who was killed emerging from his dugout. They were slaughtered and their vehicles destroyed by the British in less than ten minutes. The Italian artillery fought on valiantly, firing on the Matildas and recording many hits, some at point-blank range – but none penetrated their 70mm of armour. The remaining Italian tanks were captured intact, and the Libyan infantry, left practically defenceless, quickly surrendered. The British had captured Nibeiwa and destroyed the only front-line Italian armoured unit in less than five hours.

The swift destruction of the Italian armour condemned the rest of the Italian forces in Egypt. They consisted entirely of immobile infantry formations that were isolated and destroyed piecemeal by the mobile British forces before they had a chance to organize their defences. The British proceeded to mop up the remaining Italian forces at Sidi Barrani before moving on to conquer the Libyan ports of Bardia and Tobruk in succession. The British were even able to swap their own forward infantry divisions to release the 4 Indian Division to launch an offensive in East Africa. By 22 January 1941, the British had destroyed nine Italian infantry divisions and captured over 100,000 prisoners for minimal losses to themselves.

Mechili, January 1941

It was not until the British reached Mechili that they encountered the sole surviving Italian armoured unit in North Africa. The *Brigata Corazzata Speciale*, or Special Armoured Brigade, was set up in November 1940 under General Valentino Babini. It consisted of fifty-seven M13/40 medium tanks from 3 and 5 Armoured Battalions, originally intended to equip the *Centauro* Armoured Division, three *Bersaglieri* battalions, and an artillery regiment with 75mm guns. It was the first Italian armoured unit, including all arms, armour, artillery and infantry, to fight in North Africa. It should have had 120 M13 tanks, but eighty-two of these had just arrived at Benghasi, and required ten days acclimatization before they became operational. In spite of its weakness, this unit seemed to offer the only chance of stopping the British armour and saving 60 *Sabratha* Infantry Division, holding positions on the coast near Derna, from being isolated and destroyed. It sat in defensive positions around the small fort at Mechili, with its tanks dispersed and its infantry and artillery dug in.

On the night of 22 January, 4 British Armoured Brigade advanced through unknown and badly mapped country in moonlight. It was entirely ignorant of the presence of Babini's Armoured Brigade and arrived at Mechili the next morning in a completely disorganized state. If Babini had been aware of this he might have inflicted a severe defeat on this force; but instead, the British were allowed time to reorganize. They had about fifty cruiser and ninety-five light tanks, although not all of these were at the front. They were ordered to attack Babini, who had now been spotted, but required considerable reorganization and would not be ready to attack until the next day. On the other side, Babini had also been ordered to attack and prevent the British from enveloping the *Sabratha* at Derna. The Italians, due to their relative newness and lack of radios, took some time to respond to this order, and were not ready until the next day, either.

On the morning of 24 January, the opposing forces finally clashed around Mechili. The British sent their light tanks on a series of probing attacks, which, somewhat to their surprise, met a strong counter-attack by a company of twelve Italian M13s that approached firing their guns on the move. The Italians quickly scored hits and destroyed a number of British light tanks in an encounter where they, for once, had the advantage. The 47mm guns of their M13s outranged and outgunned the machine guns of the British light tanks. The latter quickly turned tail and fled at full speed, calling for support, which was slow to arrive. The British cruiser tanks were, apparently, unwilling to believe that Italian tanks presented any sort of threat. By mid-morning the losses stood at two M13s against two British cruisers and six light tanks. In the end more British cruiser tanks arrived, catching the Italian M13s on the skyline and destroying seven in a matter of minutes. The action ended at 13:30hr, when the Italians withdrew from the field.

On 25 January, the initial Italian success briefly encouraged hopes that this might be the first sign of a change in Italian fortunes. Unfortunately the twenty-four-hour delay in launching the Italian attack meant that any opportunity to do so had already been lost. A depressed Graziani refused to send any reinforcements, and without them Babini's armoured thrust could be no more than a delaying action. In the evening, intelligence falsely reported 150 British tanks on the Italian desert flank, and this alarming news prompted Babini to withdraw the next day. In any case, severe pressure on *Sabratha* at Derna made this the only reasonable course. If the Italians had stood firm they would eventually have been cut off and destroyed. On 26 January, 7 British Armoured Division converged on Mechili from north and south – but the Italian withdrawal went ahead without loss during the night. The exhausted British failed to press their attack and lost a golden opportunity to destroy Babini's Brigade and isolate *Sabratha*. They were soon to be granted a second bite at this cherry.

Beda Fomm

On 5 February a British combined force, including tanks, artillery, infantry and anti-tank guns, crossed the desert and reached Beda Fomm ahead of the Italians retreating along the coast road. They quickly set up an ambush to cut off the Italian forces retreating south towards them from Benghasi. The Italian 10 *Bersaglieri* Regiment were first to encounter this roadblock, whose presence was a complete surprise. They were badly shot up, but in spite of heavy casualties, attempted to break through the British force; but without the support of artillery or tanks, they failed. The Italian armour of Babini's Brigade were north of Benghasi providing a rearguard against 6 Australian Division. As the day wore on, more and more Italian units arrived in front of the British roadblock and crowded together in complete chaos. A few units launched their own desperate but futile attacks against the British. The Italian commander, General Annibale Bergonzoli, who had commanded *Littorio* at Guadalajara and more recently attempted unsuccessfully to hold Bardia and Tobruk, hastily organized them into *ad hoc* assault groups, and threw them against the blockade. But in their haste to break through, the Italians neglected to reconnoitre the British positions, and on the basis of casualties suffered, had an exaggerated idea of their strength. This was not a satisfactory basis for a successful counter-attack on prepared positions. The Italians nevertheless applied immense pressure on the isolated and weak British, who desperately held on while issuing increasingly urgent requests for armoured support. In late afternoon, 4 Armoured Brigade arrived on the Italian left flank and severely punished their close-packed forces.

The arrival of 4 Armoured finally brought Babini's Brigade south with its sixty M13s. They were needed by Bergonzoli, who now planned a holding action on the road while outflanking the British through the desert to the east. At 08:30hr on 6 February the attack commenced without prior reconnaissance or co-ordinated artillery support; the Italians were therefore unaware that the British had reinforced their positions with twenty-two cruiser and forty-five light tanks, well concealed in hull-down positions. The Italian tanks also advanced in single companies at intervals, rather than in a single mass. Thus the leading company of ten M13s were completely surprised when they crested a small rise to find British cruisers waiting for them. They halted to return fire before attempting to withdraw behind the crest, but the British destroyed eight of them before they could do so. The British then engaged a second wave of Italian M13s, destroying another seven without reply. It was only at this point that Italian artillery finally came into action, shelling the area. The Italians now converged on the British roadblock under cover of their artillery. In reply, the British brought more cruiser tanks into action and increased their own artillery fire. In a well rehearsed drill the British cruisers struck the Italians in the flank, and a further eight M13s were knocked out. The Italians, who lacked the radios necessary for this kind of close control, were unable to respond effectively: they were left to react to British movements, and were unable to inflict any significant casualties in reply. They showed great determination, but were fighting at a clear disadvantage. In spite of this, they came very close to breaking the British blockade; only quick action by a combination of British tanks and artillery prevented this.

In the afternoon Bergonzoli prepared a more co-ordinated attack involving a combination of tanks and artillery. This renewed assault on the extremely stretched British brought things to a crescendo at 15:00hr, and it was only the opportune arrival of British armoured reinforcements on the Italian desert flank that forced them to withdraw. At nightfall Bergonzoli abandoned his plans to outflank the British in favour of an attempt to infiltrate their main positions. The presence of British armour on the inland flank, the apparent weakness of British artillery fire in the centre, and the pressure of time, all encouraged this decision.

At dawn on 7 February, thirty Italian M13s were launched against the British blockading force, now standing at fifteen cruisers and fifty-one light tanks. This final attack, in contrast to earlier ones, was supported by infantry and every available Italian artillery piece. The M13s advanced in the spreading light of dawn, concentrating on the British tanks and anti-tank guns. They pressed home their attacks with desperate courage, driving close to the British positions and firing point blank at their anti-tank guns. They suffered severe losses, but knocked out all but one of the British guns. The surviving M13s drove on into the British positions. The British infantry kept their heads down as the Italian tanks passed, but rose up to fire on the following Italian infantry. The British artillery fired on their own forward posts to prevent Italian infantry from breaking through. This combination of infantry and artillery prevented the Italian infantry from securing the penetration made by their tanks. The last few M13s were destroyed outside the British command post, one within 20 yards. The failure of this last effort, that had so nearly succeeded, and the arrival of 6 Australian Division in the Italian rear, brought the struggle to an end. The entire Italian force, including Generals Bergonzoli and Babini, surrendered to a British force that was much smaller than they had realized.

In view of the small armoured forces at their disposal, the Italian defeat in 1940 appears almost inevitable, the deployment of a largely immobile infantry army against mobile opponents inviting disaster. The conditions in the desert were more suited to mobile forces than to positional warfare, with open spaces and few impediments; these offered few readily defensible positions, and few possibilities for secure flanks. When the Italians lost their only front-line armoured unit in the very first British assault they were immediately thrown onto the defensive. Thereafter the only other organized Italian armoured unit under Babini briefly showed at Mechili what might have been achieved in more favourable circumstances. The poor situation facing the Italian forces generally effectively prevented it from playing a bigger role. Its part at Beda Fomm was noble but ultimately ineffective because its tanks were used in 'penny packets' rather than in a single mass in a co-ordinated attack. In fact it almost managed to break through the British blockade, even in this fragmented state. However, its demise seemed to herald the end for Italian armoured forces in Africa, and it appeared to be only a matter of time before the rest of Libya fell into British hands. This was not the case due to political decisions made in Italy, Britain and Germany.

In early 1941 the military reputation of the Italians was in tatters after the disastrous Greek campaign, the naval losses at Taranto, and the British victory in North Africa. The British naturally trumpeted their own successes, but others were probably more impressed by those of the Greeks. In consequence, the British became openly dismissive of Italian military abilities, regarding them as third-rate opponents worthy of little more than sympathy or contempt. This would be the basis for the subsequent British prejudice, which saw Italian units dismissed and their influence on events discounted. It was also one of the reasons behind some disastrous British political decisions about military priorities, which prevented them from completing the conquest of Libya. In early 1941, Britain decided to assist the Greeks, who stood in little need of help, and give priority to the conquest of Italian East Africa, which was already isolated and under siege. This prompted the diversion of significant military resources from North Africa, including one experienced motorized division to Eritrea and another to Greece. The withdrawal of the experienced 7 British Armoured Division to rest and re-equip exacerbated this situation. The loss of these units brought a reduction in British capacity to prosecute an advance on Tripoli. British forces therefore halted near Mersa Brega so that replacement units – consisting of new recruits with second-rate equipment – could be brought forward. It would prove to be a fatal mistake, and one that would extend the North African campaign by two years.

The Germans were also extremely critical of the poor military showing of their Axis partners. They had offered to assist their allies earlier by sending troops to Albania and North Africa, where the Italians had been conducting an independent 'parallel war', though with rather different objectives from those of Germany. But the Italians were concerned that their ally might use such assistance to secure control over the management of the Italian war effort, and had therefore resisted these overtures; and the Germans did not force the issue. However, the series of Italian disasters in Greece, at Taranto and in North Africa had fundamentally changed things, and the Germans were now concerned that their ally might suffer military and political collapse. On the Italian side, after a great deal of heart searching, Mussolini reluctantly accepted German military assistance – really because he was no longer in a position to refuse it. In the Balkans, the Germans prepared an invasion of Greece. In North Africa, their assistance took the form of a small expeditionary force under the leadership of General Erwin Rommel; this would become the *Deutsches Afrika Korps* (*DAK*). The Italians had already dispatched their own reinforcements to Libya, including a first armoured division, 132 *Ariete* Armoured Division under General Ettore Baldassare, a fifty-eight-year-old infantry officer. This formation arrived at Tripoli in January 1941, almost as the British appeared on the verge of final victory. It was sent in response to the tardy Italian realization that mobile units offered the best prospects for success in this theatre. It would create a very different reputation for the Italians in the next few years.

This combination of an increase in Axis resources and a reduction in British resources transformed the situation in North Africa. It is important, however, to clarify the purpose of this German assistance. In early 1941, Hitler was focused on the preparations for his forthcoming invasion of the Soviet Union in June. This would become the decisive theatre of war for Germany, while North Africa was never more than a side show; the purpose of German intervention there was simply to prevent Italian collapse and to keep the British occupied. It was not their intention to conquer Egypt or to drive the British from the Middle East. The initial commitment of a single panzer division and, subsequently, no more than two panzer and one motorized divisions, indicates the limited extent of their involvement. In an early reconnaissance, General Ritter von Thoma had recommended sending four panzer divisions, but these were never committed. Aside from an additional infantry division and some paratroopers sent in the summer of 1942, the number of German units was only increased significantly after the Allied landings in French North Africa in November 1942. Once again, this reinforcement was intended to keep Italy in the war rather than to defeat the Allies. This basic premise is sometimes ignored in British accounts, which view this campaign as of vital importance to the war. This is not surprising, since it was the one theatre where they directly engaged Axis ground forces for most of the war.

On 12 February 1941, a then almost unknown General Erwin Rommel arrived in Tripoli. He brought with him an ability to read a battlefield and to exploit any psychological weakness in his opponent. He had employed these skills to great effect in World War I against the Italians and Rumanians, and again in 1940 against the British and French. He was a *feldherr* or field commander, with no general staff training and little respect for those who had. It was an inferiority complex that would lead to many clashes with his staff-trained superiors, whether German or Italian. In such disputes he was quick to exploit his personal relationship with Hitler, developed while he commanded his military escort in Poland, to get his own way. This apparent trump card would, however, prove double-edged at Alamein in 1942. He also brought a common German prejudice against the Italians, who were widely believed to be weak, lazy, cowardly and militarily incompetent. In his own case such feelings had been reinforced by first-hand experience of the Italian collapse at Caporetto in 1917. This prejudice would find expression in frequent outbursts against his new allies, and he would often single them out for blame even on occasions when German troops had similarly failed to live up to his high expectations. This was the man who stepped onto African soil.

He arrived to find the *Ariete* Armoured Division, under General Ettore Baldassare, already there. It was still in an incomplete state with some eighty tanks, half of its intended complement, and very few anti-tank weapons. The new Italian commander in North Africa, General Italo Gariboldi, who had replaced the defeated and disgraced Graziani, ordered a stand to be made on the border of Tripolitania, and Baldassare was already under orders to move forward to Sirte. On 14 February Rommel ordered German reconnaissance units from his 5 Light Division to move forward, too. On 19 February, the first German forces accompanied a detachment of tanks from *Ariete* in an advance to Nofilia, where they made their first contact with British forces. On 7 March, Gariboldi approved Rommel's plans for an early counter-attack against the weakened British, and placed *Ariete* under his command at Nofilia. He probably little realized what would follow.

On 2 April, strong pressure from the Germans forced the British to withdraw from Mersa Brega. This withdrawal was followed up by the main Axis units, German 5 Light and Italian *Ariete* Armoured and 27 *Brescia* Infantry, together with a number of *ad hoc* mixed units of German and

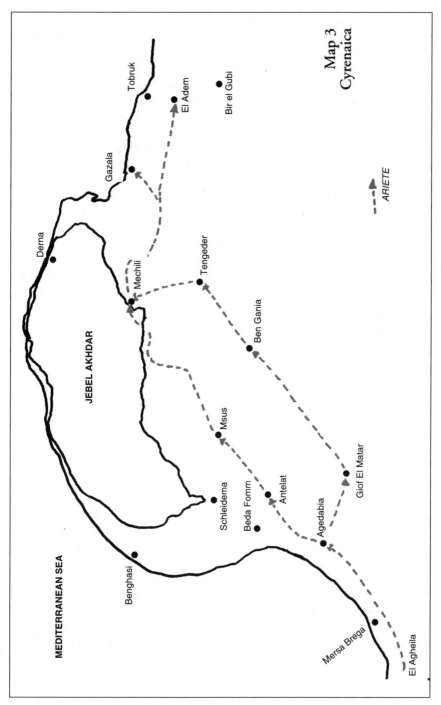

Map 3
Cyrenaica

Italian troops, who were sent forward to harass British forces at as many points as possible. This went against conventional military practice on the concentration of force, but proved highly effective in locating weak points for subsequent attack. On the next day, early in the afternoon, Rommel visited advanced units of *Ariete* east of Agedabia on the Trigh el Abd. He satisfied himself that this route was passable for vehicles, and ordered a mixed detachment called Group Schwerin to advance along it. This formation included a mixed motorized group from *Ariete* under Major Nicolini Santamaria, who had fought against Rommel during World War I. They were instructed to reconnoitre as far as Ben Gania before heading north along another track to Mechili.

The rapid advance and the division of forces alarmed Gariboldi, who feared that it would expose them to British counter-attack; he wanted to restrain Rommel, but was overruled – not for the last time – by orders direct from Hitler. This outside interference with the command decisions in North Africa was to become a common feature of the campaign, regularly exploited by Rommel to outflank his nominal superiors. On 4 April, freed from restraint, Rommel resumed his offensive plans by ordering *Colonna Fabris*, or Fabris Column – consisting of 3 *Bersaglieri* Battalion and some motorized artillery from *Ariete,* under Lieutenant Colonel Gino Fabris – to follow Group Schwerin. The rest of *Ariete* and 5 Panzer Regiment were sent towards Mechili along a track through Msus to the north, and 27 *Brescia* Infantry Division was sent along the coast road towards Derna. By evening Group Schwerin had reached Ben Gania with the various other Italian units scattered across the desert behind.

On 6 April, German forces invaded Greece and Yugoslavia in a major campaign that would destroy the British forces dispatched at such cost to their position in Africa. This Balkan campaign would effectively monopolize Axis resources and attention for two months, until the fall of Crete on 1 June. As a result, Rommel was left to carry out his improvised and comparatively minor offensive in North Africa with the limited resources already available. On that same morning, Rommel's forces were scattered across Cyrenaica with various components of *Ariete* strung out between Ben Gania, Tengeder and Msus, many having run out of fuel. Group Schwerin had reached Mechili to find it occupied by British forces, and needed support to deal with them. The day was spent trying to organize supplies for the scattered Axis forces to take them forward to this key point. Rommel himself pooled all available fuel supplies to enable the stranded units of Fabris Column to be brought forward. They reached Mechili ahead of 5 Panzer Regiment, the latter having been delayed by the remnants of 2 British Armoured Division at Msus. In spite of the exhaustion and disorganization amongst the small forces to hand, Rommel was anxious to exploit his success, and ordered them to attack Mechili the following day.

Mechili, April 1941

The first serious encounter between units from *Ariete* and British forces took place on 8 April at Mechili. It could be considered their baptism of fire, although it involved individual components rather than the whole division. The Axis plan was to seize Mechili, and capture or destroy the British garrison that was effectively surrounded. Group Schwerin was to the north and north-east; the Fabris Column, including 3 *Bersaglieri* Battalion and Major Santamaria's group, to the east; and 5 Panzer Regiment, which arrived too late to play a significant role, to the west. In the south, Colonel Ugo Montemurro, commander of 8 *Bersaglieri* Regiment, was just arriving from Msus with his *Colonna Montemurro*, or Montemurro Column, consisting of the rest of 8 *Bersaglieri*. The British garrison of Mechili consisted of 3 Indian Motor Brigade, under General Gambier-Parry of 2 Armoured Division, whose own force had already been overrun. He had already issued instructions for his forces to break out of the Axis encirclement. The resulting battle therefore quickly turned into an effort to contain this breakout, rather than to attack Mechili itself.

At dawn, Italian artillery laid down a heavy bombardment, whilst the Indians launched probes looking for weak points in the Axis encirclement. The probes to the north, east and west were all repulsed, but that to the south found a small gap between the Fabris Column and the newly arrived Montemurro Column. The Indians now attempted to escape through this gap under pressure from Axis forces to their rear. They were brought under fire by Fabris' 75mm field guns, and their flanks were harassed by the Fabris and Montemurro Columns. Montemurro then brought up his *Bersaglieri* to block their line of retreat, and brought them under fire from his artillery. The fight was brief but intense, until General Gambier-Parry surrendered to Colonel Montemurro just as 5 Panzer Regiment finally arrived on the scene. A total of 1,200 prisoners were taken by the Axis forces, although many others escaped in the confusion. The various units from *Ariete* had advanced 250 miles (400km) across difficult desert terrain. They had lost many vehicles to breakdowns, and others had run out of fuel and had to be abandoned. They had fought a short but sharp and successful battle at the end of this, and won a victory: it was a good start for the division. The very next day, an impatient Rommel arrived to order the Axis forces on towards Tobruk.

Tobruk, 1941

In spite of Italian knowledge of the strength of their own former defences in Tobruk, Rommel hoped to bounce the British into premature withdrawal by staging an immediate attack. The result was an improvised assault involving whatever forces were immediately to hand. This tactic had proved highly successful since the start of his offensive, and there seemed no reason to change it now. The Germans were also under the impression that a number of ships spotted in Tobruk harbour were there to evacuate the port. In fact they were bringing in reinforcements for the garrison, consisting of the tough 9 Australian Division and 3 British Armoured Brigade, which intended to make a stand behind the refurbished and reinforced Italian defences. A German attack on 10 April had already been defeated and its commander killed.

In the late afternoon of 11 April, a mixed force of seventy tanks attacked near Redoubt 33 on the Tobruk perimeter to the west of the El Adem road in three waves of twenty and one of ten. The tanks involved were twenty-five panzers from 5 Light Division, and a mixture of M13s and L3s from *Ariete*. They were engaged by Australian anti-tank rifles and light weapons, and returned fire. The Axis tanks were surprised by the ferocity of the defence, and sheered off to the east along the front of the Australian positions. As they did so, the Australians used two captured Italian 47mm anti-tank guns to knock out one M13 tank and hit several others. An Italian L3 light tank was disabled by small arms fire, and then knocked out by these guns and its crew captured. The Axis tanks then ran into a minefield and turned away. It was as they withdrew that British cruiser tanks arrived, and a half-hour skirmish ensued at long range between the latter and the last wave of ten Italian tanks. The result of these encounters was the loss of three L3s, one M13 and one panzer in exchange for two British cruisers. The Axis tanks withdrew until after nightfall when they probed the Australian defences, but retired when engaged by their patrols.

The failure of this hasty assault forced Rommel to reconsider his options, and on 13 April Tobruk was more formally invested. In this process *Ariete* was stationed between the El Adem road and a height called Ras el Medawar, with 5 Light Division on its right and the 102 *Trento* Motorized Infantry Division on its left. On 14 April *Ariete* was instructed to stand ready to exploit any penetration arising from a new attack by 5 Light Division. However, this entirely German assault suffered severe losses, breached the outer defences, but was driven back by British artillery and armour in some confusion. It was a clear sign that these hastily improvised attacks would not succeed against the well-prepared defences.

On 15 April Rommel refused to abandon the assault, and in the absence of any fit German units, opted to use the weak remnant of *Ariete*'s armour and some infantry drawn from 62 Infantry Regiment of *Trento*. This combination of forces from different units, which had not previously worked together, was not really a satisfactory basis for an assault force. It had been made necessary by the absence of most of *Ariete*'s own *Bersaglieri* under Colonel Montemurro, sent to guard the distant Egyptian frontier. They were ordered to attack Ras el Medawar, and penetrated between Redoubts 13 and 17. They encountered intense Australian artillery fire and suffered many casualties before falling back. According to Rommel, there was an immediate panic among the Italians, which only he was able to quell. The Australians, however, who captured some seventy-five Italians, failed to notice any sign of this general panic.

On 16 April Rommel personally directed a new Italian assault on Ras el Medawar. He launched a weak armoured battalion of *Ariete*, consisting of only six M13 and twelve L3 tanks, supported by 62 Infantry Regiment against a hill known as Point 187. The Italian tanks successfully penetrated the Australian positions and reached the summit. They then halted to await infantry support, which had been forced to go to ground back at the wire by the Australian artillery. They were then briskly counter-attacked by Australian infantry, which had taken cover while the Italian tanks passed, and now re-emerged, supported by some Bren carriers. The Italian infantry, without anti-tank guns or close tank support, showed little heart for a fight, and quickly surrendered. The Australians captured twenty-six officers and 777 men of *Trento* in this engagement. The loss of their infantry meant that the Italian tanks could not hold on to Point 187. They were heavily shelled by Australian artillery in their exposed location, and were forced to retreat before nightfall, when they would be at the mercy of close-quarter attack by enemy infantry.

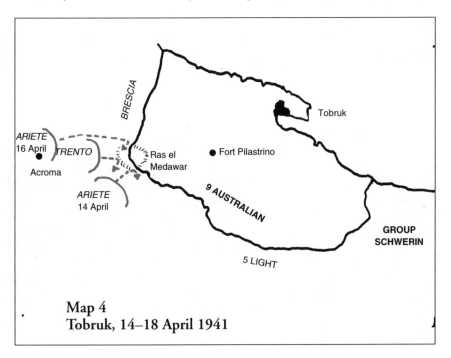

Map 4
Tobruk, 14–18 April 1941

This setback did not deter Rommel, however, who was completely obsessed with taking Tobruk, to the exclusion of all else. At 10:00hr the next morning, a mixed force of eight L3 and two M13 tanks and infantry returned to the attack. The tanks once again penetrated the enemy wire, this time near Redoubt 2, and rounding Ras el Medawar surprised an Australian anti-tank gun crew, who fled in a truck. The following infantry once again came under heavy artillery fire and were forced to go to ground. The tanks were again left unsupported and circled the old fort at Ras el Medawar, rather aimlessly, until they came under anti-tank fire. They did not retreat, however, but drove on into the Australian reserve positions. The British then sent seven cruiser tanks forward to engage the Italians; the latter, however, only fell back after losing a number of their tanks to a combination of anti-tank, artillery and tank fire. The Italians lost five tanks, including one M13, destroyed or captured, four were abandoned due to damage or breakdown, and only one M13 survived to reach safety. The Italian infantry meantime remained exposed on stony ground in front of the Australian wire under heavy artillery fire until nightfall.

On 18 April, Italian tanks from *Ariete* moved forward to cover the withdrawal of the remaining infantry from amongst the enemy wire. They opened fire on any Australian movements and prevented them interfering. The *Ariete* Division now had only ten tanks left from its original complement of eighty back in February. The Axis forces were too weak to attack Tobruk again, and required time to rest and re-equip before making another attempt. This series of attacks had failed because of hasty organization and the weakness of the Axis forces involved. The Tobruk perimeter now fell silent, apart from occasional artillery fire, while each side rested and reorganized.

It was not quiet for long, however, and early on 22 April the Australians launched a counter-attack, supported by five Bren carriers and three cruiser tanks, on forward positions held by 3 *Bersaglieri* Battalion under Fabris on the slopes of Ras el Medawar. The British armour quickly reached the far side of the hill, but then came under Italian artillery fire. They had lost contact with their infantry, which had also come under artillery fire and gone to ground. The British tanks nevertheless managed to reach their original positions before an Italian battery of 75mm field guns engaged and halted them. The Italian gunners were then surprised by Australian infantry and captured: the Australians had rounded up 368 *Bersaglieri* and captured four 20mm guns.

On 30 April Rommel issued orders for another German assault on Ras el Medawar, which the weak *Ariete* was to support. The plan was for the Italians to occupy any positions taken by the Germans, and they stood ready all day on 1 May. But the complete failure of the German attack meant that they were not called on, and the attack was cancelled next morning.

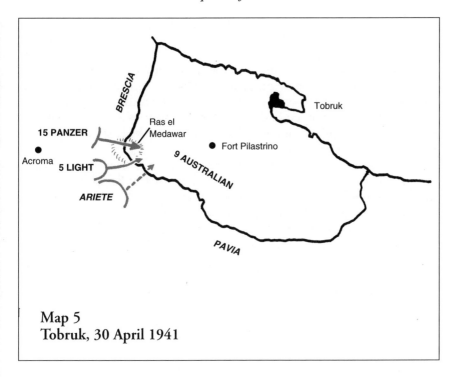

Map 5
Tobruk, 30 April 1941

On 4 May, the positions held by 5 Battalion of 8 *Bersaglieri* under Major Gaggetti around Redoubts 6, 7 and 8 were counter-attacked by the Australians. The Italians responded with strong defensive fire and launched a counter-attack supported by three L3 light tanks. The latter were quickly destroyed at close quarters, and the Australians captured Redoubt 7. The *Bersaglieri* counter-attacked almost immediately, supported by one M13 tank and three armoured cars, and forced them back. Major Gaggetti himself described the fighting:

> After more than three hours of a barrage of iron and fire there were bloody gaps opening up in the ranks of my *Bersaglieri*. I was gravely wounded in turn; conscious of the delicacy of the situation, with all the section commanders wounded or fallen, I remained among the survivors who were engaged in furious hand-to-hand fighting. The epic struggle of 5 Battalion was bitter, arduous, and to the death. It took place in a continuous stream of brilliant acts of valour. Redoubt R7, in which I found myself, was surrounded and the enemy was repeatedly attacking it because it was the mainstay of the position. They finally succeeded in penetrating it, but only for a moment, then a handful of survivors succeeded in repelling them once and for all.

The *Bersaglieri*, who had been fighting for a good seven hours, redoubled their steely efforts.

In this fierce fighting *Ariete* lost 150 men, but their robust defence caused the Australians to abandon plans for a series of similar counter-attacks. Thereafter the siege of Tobruk quickly settled into one of minor patrols and skirmishes. In May, the rest of 8 *Bersaglieri* Regiment of *Ariete* were brought back from the Egyptian frontier and stationed along the Fort Pilastrino to El Adem Road sector of the perimeter.

During the summer, a reorganized and reinforced *Ariete* was twice placed on standby to support their German allies in the face of British offensives at the Egyptian frontier. In mid-May they were posted to El Adem, south-west of Tobruk, in case the British broke through. In mid-June they were put on alert at Gazala to send armour to Ed Duda to support the Italian infantry investing Tobruk. On both occasions, however, the British were repulsed on the frontier, and there was no action. On 10 June, 8 *Bersaglieri* Regiment was finally relieved of garrison duties on the Tobruk perimeter by 17 *Pavia* Infantry Division.

Only a few days later, on 22 June 1941, the Germans launched their long-planned invasion of the Soviet Union. The war in North Africa, which might otherwise have become a focus of Axis operations after the close of the Balkan campaign, would be no more than a sideshow hereafter. It was in this context that all future Axis operations in North Africa would be conducted. On 26 June this revision of Axis priorities was endorsed by Italy, when Mussolini sent the first units of the *Corpo di Spedizione in Russia* (*CSIR*), or Russian Expeditionary Corps. This force would subsequently grow into an army of 230,000 men, a force larger than that deployed in North Africa. The 22,300 vehicles, 1,100 artillery pieces, including some of the most modern Italy possessed, fifty tanks and eighty-three aircraft sent to Russia with these troops, could have had a major impact in North Africa. This deployment was politically motivated in an attempt to maintain the illusion that Italy was a significant power. In fact this entire force had little impact on the wider Russian campaign, and failed to convince anyone that Italy was a major player in this German campaign. Thereafter, although the Axis forces in North Africa would receive reinforcements, these would be small in comparison to the forces invested in Russia.

In its first actions in North Africa the various components of *Ariete* Armoured Division under General Baldassare had experienced mixed fortunes. They had not fought together as a single unit as intended, but had instead been used as small *ad hoc* units in combination with other Italian or German units. They had been involved in a mad dash across the rough desert terrain, a series of minor skirmishes, and a few more prominent engagements at Mechili and Tobruk. They had encountered only scattered

British forces in their race to Mechili, but had been delayed by breakdowns and fuel shortages. They had been successful in close co-operation with the Germans in their first encounter with isolated British forces at Mechili. They had been less successful alongside their German allies in the attacks on prepared defences at Tobruk. The well-constructed defensive positions there had proved all too solid against the best that both the Germans and the Italians had been able to throw at them. The Italians had nevertheless pressed home their attacks with some determination, only to fail in the face of heavy defensive fire and fierce counter-attacks. This variation in performance reflected the fact that the real strength of armoured units lay in manoeuvre rather than direct assaults against prepared positions. In this respect it reflected the performance of their German partners, who had also succeeded in mobile operations against the British, but failed in the hasty and disorganized attacks against Tobruk. The Italians of *Ariete* had proved that they were capable of a good performance against reasonable odds, and had gone some way to restoring the tattered reputation of the Italian army. It remained to be seen how they would perform in fighting on a larger scale – but they would soon get their chance.

4
Trial by Combat

In the lull following the failure of the British summer offensives, the opportunity was taken to make a number of command changes. The Italian Commander in Chief, General Gariboldi, who had found it difficult to deal with the maverick Rommel, had been replaced by General Ettore Bastico. He was considered one of Italy's leading generals, with combat experience in Ethiopia and Spain, where he had commanded the *CTV* from April to October 1937, and was instrumental in restoring its reputation after the disaster at Guadalajara. It was hoped that he would do a similar job in North Africa, provide a better foil to Rommel, and prove better able to cope with the high-pressure demands of mobile warfare in this theatre. In practice Rommel, who was a brilliant tactician but had little appreciation for the practical problems of logistics, often ignored Bastico's sensible advice on this subject. Nevertheless, in spite of frequent tensions, Bastico retained his post as Italian Commander in Chief in North Africa until the end. Indeed General Westphal, Rommel's Chief of Staff, pays tribute to how he allowed Rommel 'wide freedom of action' while attempting to provide 'as much assistance ... as his resources allowed'. Bastico brought with him an almost inseparable companion, General Gastone Gambara, who would serve as his Chief of Staff as he had previously done in Ethiopia and Spain. In October 1938, Gambara had assumed command of the *CTV* during its final successful campaign in Catalonia and, more recently, had returned from the unsuccessful command of a corps in Albania. He was a better staff officer than field commander, and owed his position to his connections with Mussolini's son-in-law, Ciano, and with Bastico.

The Italian mobile forces in North Africa were also reinforced at this time. *Ariete* Armoured Division was provided with additional artillery, and its light tanks were finally replaced with M13/40 medium tanks. This major reinforcement had been accomplished by diverting M13 tanks intended for its sister division, *Littorio*. In November 1941, *Ariete* had 146 M13 tanks, sixteen 105mm guns, thirty-two 75mm guns, eight 47mm anti-tank guns and eight 20mm AA guns. It was therefore a more powerful formation than ever before. In the autumn of 1941 the Italians spent a lot of time training with this new equipment. As Lieutenant Enrico Serra, who joined *Ariete* in that period, recorded:

... we are profiting by the pause in activities to intensify the training of our units. We choose land that is variegated and irregular, and we prepare dummies made of the shells of abandoned vehicles. I explain the lessons over and over again. Our tanks must approach the enemy at a sustained speed ... they must pause for a moment to allow the tank commander to fire his gun, and then leave as quickly as possible ... I explain repeatedly that it is useless to fire while the tank is in motion, as the rolling motion makes it quite impossible to aim ...

The division was now under the command of General Mario Balotta, a fifty-five-year-old artillery officer, with General Ismaele Di Nisio, a fifty-three-year-old infantry officer, as his deputy. It had also been joined by the 101 *Trieste* Motorized Division under General Alessandro Piazzoni, which had arrived from Italy during August. In the spirit of the former Armoured Corps of the Army of the Po, these divisions had been formed into the *Corpo d'Armata di Manovra* (*CAM*), or Mobile Army Corps, with its own reconnaissance force, the *Raggruppamento Esplorante di Corpo d'Armata di Manovra* (*RECAM*).

The *CAM* was placed in a unique position in the Axis command structure in an attempt to maintain a certain amount of Italian independence. It was not subordinate to Rommel like the Italian infantry divisions, but was directly under the command of Bastico himself. It was commanded by Gambara, who continued to function as Bastico's Chief of Staff at the same time, and therefore could not possibly devote his full attention to it. In practice the burden of command would fall on General Balotta, *Ariete's* commander. This somewhat unusual arrangement would prove troublesome in practice, and Rommel was not long in seeking direct control of this unit.

In November 1941, as German forces in Russia fought their way towards Moscow, Rommel was preoccupied with preparations for a major assault of his own, designed to capture Tobruk. He was determined that this prize, which had eluded him in April, should be his at last. He had earmarked his strongest forces, the German *Deutsches Afrika Korps* (*DAK*), consisting of 15 and 21 Panzer Divisions, for this vital task and stationed it south-east of Tobruk. The Italian *CAM* had been assigned the subsidiary but important role of protecting his rear against any British diversionary attacks from Egypt, and was stationed south and east of Tobruk, with *Trieste* at Bir Hacheim and *Ariete* further forward at Bir el Gubi.

The British were meanwhile planning their own major offensive, which they hoped would defeat the Axis armoured forces and relieve the fortress of Tobruk. In the first phase it would involve three armoured brigades of 7 British Armoured Division driving north-west towards Tobruk on 18 November. It was envisaged that they would engage and destroy the Axis armour and clear the way for following infantry divisions to raise the siege of Tobruk. This plan would take the British armour right past the *Ariete* Division – but the British were not unduly concerned about this, although they were well aware of its presence. It clearly represented a potential threat to the left flank of their offensive, but they virtually ignored it: the British low opinion of Italian troops, derived from 1940, clearly still held sway in their minds. In practice, the presence of this powerful Italian unit would exercise a disruptive influence on British movements and help bring their offensive to an early crisis.

On the Axis side, the Italians were well aware of the impending offensive, from improved interceptions of British signals traffic. Indeed, General Bastico was anxious for Rommel to delay his own attack on Tobruk, either until the imminent British offensive had been dealt with, or until further reinforcements – principally the 133 *Littorio* Armoured Division, due in January 1942 – had reached the front. In contrast, Rommel discounted the British preparations as little more than attempts to distract him from his own attack, which he was anxious should proceed without delay.

On 18 November 1941, reconnaissance patrols of 22 British Armoured Brigade, on the left flank of 7 Armoured Division's advance, encountered a screen of Italian armoured cars from the *RECAM*, about 13 miles south of Taieb el Esem. A sharp skirmish ensued before the Italians withdrew northwards. In the evening, the main part of 22 Armoured Brigade leaguered about 10 miles south of Bir el Gubi. The British now issued orders for 22 Armoured and 7 Support Group to reconnoitre towards Bir el Gubi the next day, in anticipation that *Ariete* would withdraw. This was not an unreasonable assumption in that the Italians were isolated from German support and faced, in 7 Armoured Division, a superior Allied force. Thereafter Bir el Gubi would be occupied by 1 South African Division, allowing 22 Armoured to resume its advance to Sidi Rezegh with the rest of 7 Armoured. The British orders made clear, however, that Bir el Gubi itself was not a vital objective and should, if necessary, be ignored, the main objective being to secure Sidi Rezegh.

In spite of reports from Axis reconnaissance patrols, Rommel still refused to react to what he believed was no more than a British reconnaissance in strength. At 22:00hr he signalled to Gambara that he saw 'no reason for anxiety, but advisable for *Ariete* to maintain increased vigilance to east and south'. In fact Gambara, who was not under Rommel's command, chose to ignore this 'recommendation' and to listen to the intelligence reports. He realized that an attack on Bir el Gubi was almost certain, and towards midnight, issued orders to *Ariete* to prepare to repulse British armour the following day.

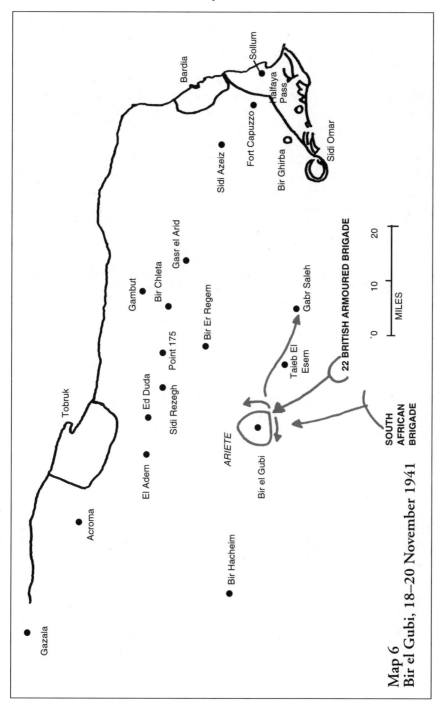

Map 6
Bir el Gubi, 18–20 November 1941

Bir el Gubi

In the morning of 19 November, General Balotta was in the process of completing his defensive dispositions at Bir el Gubi; these were known as 'The Lozenge' from their shape. He sent forward a company of sixteen M13 tanks to provide early warning of an enemy approach. He then deployed the three infantry battalions of 8 *Bersaglieri* Regiment in three strongpoints, supported by the divisional artillery and a battalion of 105mm guns from 4 Artillery Group of the *CAM* under Major Pasquali, and seven 102mm naval guns mounted on trucks under Captain Priore of the coastal artillery or *MILMART*. The latter were equipped with armour-piercing shells originally designed for use against naval armour plate, but which would now be pressed into the anti-tank role. They immediately began digging in, although all of their defences had not been completed, and the 146 M13 tanks of 132 Armoured Regiment were positioned to the rear of these strongpoints. It was in fact a fairly formidable position.

In the meantime, General Gott of 7 Armoured, whilst visiting 22 Armoured Brigade, ordered it to attack Bir el Gubi, in direct contradiction of their original orders simply to secure Sidi Rezegh. The reason for this change, which made a pitched battle with *Ariete* almost inevitable, remains unclear. It may be that Gott hoped to clear his left flank before the advance on Sidi Rezegh, or perhaps he wanted to blood this fresh territorial brigade against what he supposed was a 'weak' Italian opponent. Whatever the case, other British commanders remained ignorant of the change of orders for some time, and almost immediately afterwards British armoured cars reported the presence of Italian tanks at Bir el Gubi. The 22 Armoured, which consisted of three tank regiments equipped with a total of 158 of the brand-new Crusader tanks, one battery of 25pdr guns and one company of infantry, was brimming with confidence but completely untested.

The opposing forces were fairly evenly matched in armour, with 158 British Crusaders facing 146 Italian M13s; but the Italians had a clear advantage in infantry and artillery. At noon, 2 Royal Gloucestershire Hussars, the leading regiment of 22 Armoured, clashed with the forward company of sixteen M13s from *Ariete* just outside the Bir el Gubi defences. The 132 Armoured Regiment's Post-Action Report described this skirmish:

> At 07:00 hours, 19 November . . . 3 Company under Lieutenant Pracca left the 'Lozenge', accompanied by Captain Arturo Zanolla and reinforced with a 75/27 gun section. They were the last groups to move out on the alarm. At 08:00 hours enemy artillery opened fire on the Italian tanks from a fair distance. A duel followed, with attacks and counter attacks. At 11:00 hours a group of forty Cruiser Mark VI tanks approached from a position 4km to the north-east at

high speed. Our tanks turned round to face them, and though outnumbered, attacked head-on. A ten-minute-long fight followed, during which the enemy lost eight tanks before retiring. Three of our tanks were hit and their crews killed. Seven were hit by anti-tank fire, but returned to our positions. Three of these bore their dead commanders: Captain Zanolla, Lieutenant Umberto Sobrero and Second Lieutenant Fabbri Benito. A fourth, commanded by Lieutenant Pracca, barely reached our lines as it had been hit in the engine.

The greatly superior numbers of British tanks soon forced the Italian company to withdraw behind the Bir el Gubi defences.

In the true cavalry tradition of their regiment, the British made what was subsequently described by one observer as 'the nearest thing to a cavalry charge with tanks seen during this war'. The main thrust of their attack was successfully deflected by the Italian right-wing defences so that it collided with the Italian centre. It failed to make an impression there against well dug-in *Bersaglieri* equipped with 47mm anti-tank guns and supported by the 75mm field guns of 2 Group, 132 Artillery Regiment and the M13 tanks of Lieutenant Colli's platoon from 9 Armoured Battalion. This robust defence forced the British armour to swing further left into the Italian right wing, where 7 *Bersaglieri* Battalion had not had time to complete their defences. At 13:30hr, British tanks broke into this weaker position and the battalion was overwhelmed in very bitter fighting.

Initially, a large number of *Bersaglieri* surrendered to the British tanks, but they then discovered that no infantry had accompanied them to take them prisoner; whereupon many of them picked up their weapons and returned to the fray. The British tanks were then pinned down by fire from Italian 75mm guns and some well-dug-in 47mm anti-tank guns. The following British tanks, from 3 and 4 County of London Yeomanry, tried to work around the Italian flanks, but immediately ran into mines and concentrated artillery fire. At around 15:00hr, the British tanks 'bumped into [what] looked like a big bunch of lorries. But it turned out to be an extremely strong, cleverly camouflaged anti-tank position'. This appears to have been the truck-mounted 102mm naval guns of Captain Priore's *MILMART*, which wreaked havoc among the British Crusader tanks with their heavy armour-piercing shells.

This unexpectedly tough resistance quite effectively blunted the British attack, and threw them into considerable disorder. The final straw came when 3 County of London Yeomanry on the British left faced a heavy counter-attack mounted by the main body of 132 Armoured Regiment. The latter had earlier placed its 8 and 9 Armoured Battalions plus two companies from 7 Armoured Battalion in readiness for such a counter-attack. The attack is described in their Post-Action Report:

> . . . the enemy . . . attacked with one hundred AFVs. . . . The British tanks then ran into *Ariete*'s armour (about a hundred M13s). The 1 Company/7 Battalion was dispatched southwards to hook around the enemy assault on its front. The 2 Company/7 Battalion parried eastwards, and a violent fight followed. The 8 Battalion was committed then . . . The bulk of the enemy had already passed the Italian positions at Gobi, heading north at high speed ... The Italian batteries in the front line turned about and fired on the Crusaders that had passed already. . . . After an hour of fighting the enemy assault was defeated. . . . The Regiment ended the battle on the positions it was ordered to defend, at the cost of three tanks destroyed. Five officers were killed and five wounded, eleven *carristi* were killed and forty-five wounded. Sixty-five *carristi* were missing.

The Italian commander of 132 Artillery Regiment, Colonel Oderisio Piscicelli-Taeggi, described the bloody aftermath of this armoured battle in more poetic terms:

> At 5.00pm there was no more whistling of bullets, no more shell bursts. Here two tanks clashed with bows locked, they remained half suspended like rampant lions. Together they burned. One, two, three at a time, machine-gun rounds exploded with short sharp reports, like bits of wood cracking in the fireplace. A few feet away another tank had its turret thrown off and lying to one side, like the top of an orange sliced off with a knife, and smoke slowly emerging from the damaged hole. And with the coming of dusk, more fires became visible. All around fires were burning, and occasionally an explosion would occur with a flaming eruption.

At 16:30hr the severely battered 22 Armoured Brigade withdrew out of range and the action was broken off.

The British later admitted that only twenty-five Crusader tanks were lost and ten damaged, although this figure seems low. It is more likely to have been nearer the fifty suggested by Italian sources and accepted by some British ones. In response the British claimed to have destroyed forty-five Italian M13s, and to have captured twelve officers and 193 men. The Italians admitted thirty-four M13s lost and fifteen damaged but capable of repair, plus four 75mm guns and eight 47mm anti-tank guns lost, and fifteen men killed, eighty wounded and eighty-two missing. They themselves claimed fifty British Crusaders destroyed, and six officers and thirty-one men captured.

This was the first major engagement involving the whole of the *Ariete* Armoured Division. It had been a ferocious fight, but *Ariete* had emerged from it with credit. It highlighted the difference between the poorly trained and equipped Italian infantry divisions so easily defeated by the British in 1940, and a comparatively well trained and equipped armoured division making full use of its combined arms. The men of *Ariete* had absorbed the full impact and attention of a third of 7 Armoured Division at a crucial point in the opening phase of the British offensive; they stopped the British in their tracks, and held on to their original positions at the end of the day. The full consequences of their stout defence would only become apparent later. The pause they inflicted on 22 Armoured Brigade, combined with the diversion of 4 Armoured Brigade to face *DAK*, allowed only a single British armoured brigade to reach their original objective at Sidi Rezegh. The successful resistance of *Ariete* at Bir el Gubi effectively altered the subsequent course of the British offensive.

Ironically the stout Italian defence of Bir el Gubi went almost unnoticed by Rommel and the British alike at the time. Balotta expected further British armoured attacks, and stood to throughout the day. He was confident, based on their first successful action, that they could hold any more such assaults. In fact, however, nothing happened for the rest of the day, apart from a few exchanges of artillery fire. What was going on?

Throughout 19 November, the British appeared ignorant of the true situation around Bir el Gubi. They apparently assumed that *Ariete* had been decisively defeated, and at 16:00hr, ordered 1 South African Division to secure the area. They obviously believed that the latter had simply to occupy a position already abandoned by the defeated Italians. Within the space of an hour, however, they received contradictory information, indicating that Bir el Gubi was 'strongly held by enemy armoured and other units'. They accordingly notified the South Africans of this less-than-rosy prospect; the British commanders were clearly confused by this unanticipated Italian show of strength.

Ultimately, ingrained anti-Italian prejudice won out against wisdom, and at 20:45hr, the British concluded, in spite of all the evidence to the contrary, that a single infantry brigade, 1 South African, could handle the expulsion of *Ariete* from Bir el Gubi. They felt, presumably, that the Italians had been so badly mauled by 22 Armoured Brigade that any risk to the South Africans was minimal. An hour later they were again less sure, and instructed 22 Armoured Brigade to remain at Bir el Gubi to cover the arrival of 1 South African Brigade. In fact both 22 Armoured and 5 South African Brigade were both desperately needed to support an isolated 7 Armoured Brigade at Sidi Rezegh. This was a significant factor in the rather unorthodox final decision to leave a single infantry brigade to assault positions held by an enemy armoured division. It appears that no one considered that

Ariete presented a serious threat to British operations. Nevertheless, this confusion had postponed any action for the rest of the day.

On the Axis side meanwhile, as late as 21:00hr on 19 November, Rommel remained unconvinced that a serious Allied offensive was already under way. He requested that Gambara maintain his current positions in order to protect the southern flank of the attack on Tobruk that he was still planning to launch. In view of the fact that General Balotta and *Ariete* were comfortably installed behind their now well-tested defences, he was quite content to accept this particular request from Rommel.

On the morning of 20 November, 1 South African Brigade proposed to attack Bir el Gubi, while 22 Armoured provided a protective screen on their right flank. They moved forward at sunrise and came under attack from the air twice during their approach before they made contact with the British armour. The Italians were ready for them, and at 08:25hr their artillery batteries opened fire on the armoured cars leading the South African advance. Half an hour later the Italian 132 Artillery Regiment engaged the main South African motorized infantry columns with their 105mm and 75mm guns. At 10:00hr, before a serious clash occurred, the South Africans were ordered 'not to incur casualties unnecessarily'. In the face of the Italian barrage and their new orders, the South Africans halted and deployed to the south of the position occupied by *Ariete*. Thereafter little more than a series of intermittent artillery exchanges took place between these opponents.

This stalemate continued for the rest of the day. The Italians under Balotta, who had successfully repulsed a full armoured brigade, were unlikely to yield to infantry, and their instructions were in any case to stay put. The British were more concerned with sending 22 Armoured and 5 South African Brigades north to support the rest of their armour, as quickly as possible. At noon, therefore, 22 Armoured left for Gabr Saleh to support 4 Armoured Brigade against 21 Panzer Division. In the absence of armoured support, Brigadier Pienaar of 1 South African Brigade was reluctant to attack the Italians, and sought permission simply to 'mask' *Ariete* at Bir el Gubi. This would prove to be something of a tall order for his infantry, since the Italian armour proved able to exploit its mobility to move around the battlefield with little or no hindrance.

On 21 November, Rommel continued to recommend that Gambara 'hold the areas presently occupied by *Ariete* and *Trieste*'. This recommendation once again fitted Gambara's own intentions. He believed that *Ariete* was opposed by the whole of 1 South African Division to its south, and an unidentified but powerful enemy force, possibly 22 Armoured Brigade, to its north-east. Axis intelligence reports had mistaken 1 South African Brigade for the full division, and *Ariete*'s own reconnaissance forces appeared to confirm the presence of British armour. In these circumstances, Gambara must have felt that he had every justification for keeping *Ariete* in its present secure position. The Italians were content to monitor 1 South African Brigade during the day, locating infantry and artillery positions and observing large concentrations of motor transport. The South Africans attempted to work round the Italian flanks with armoured cars, but these moves were countered by Italian M13 tanks. Otherwise the Italians were content to exchange artillery fire with their opponents. This shelling continued intermittently for most of the day, with the strength of the Italian barrages appearing to increase as time wore on. This artillery fire, although sometimes intense, produced few casualties, since both sides were well dug in. There was a great deal of Italian motor transport movement between Bir el Gubi and Bir Hacheim, where *Trieste* was located. This was the main Italian supply route, along which supplies reached *Ariete* at Bir el Gubi without interference.

While holding his positions in the south, General Balotta undertook some reconnaissance to try to identify the more dangerous armoured force to his north-east. A company of twelve M13 tanks from *Ariete* was sent on a scouting patrol into that sector, demonstrating that *Ariete* was free to move its armour without interference from the South Africans. At 10:00hr, this company encountered armoured cars of 5 South African Brigade, that was making its way north towards Sidi Rezegh. The Italian M13 tanks had no infantry or artillery support and therefore had no intention of attacking. They were, however, engaged by South African artillery and anti-tank guns, and replied with intense fire from their turret-mounted 47mm guns and machine guns. They scored two hits on South African guns, but lost two of their own number in reply, which were later observed burning. This minor skirmish ended when the outnumbered Italians withdrew at around noon. The South Africans sent an infantry patrol in pursuit, which claimed seven damaged tanks destroyed and twenty-one prisoners captured. They then came under machine-gun fire from several more Italian M13s, and suffered four killed and thirteen wounded. After this, Italian M13 tanks continued to monitor and harass the movements of 5 South African Brigade.

At 15:30hr, an Italian force consisting of two companies of M13 tanks, thirty-two in all, supported by other vehicles, advanced in close formation towards 5 South African Brigade. The latter responded with artillery fire, and the Italians withdrew without casualties until only five tanks remained visible. A small number of British tanks arrived, possibly from 22 Armoured Brigade, and briefly engaged the few Italian tanks that could still be seen on the horizon. Thereafter an uneasy lull settled over the scene. A strong force of Italian M13 tanks manoeuvred to the south-west of the South Africans for the rest of the day.

It was on this day that the *Italian Official History* reported the capture by *Ariete* of 200 (more likely twenty) vehicles and 160 men from an unknown British unit: the latter had apparently blundered into their positions from

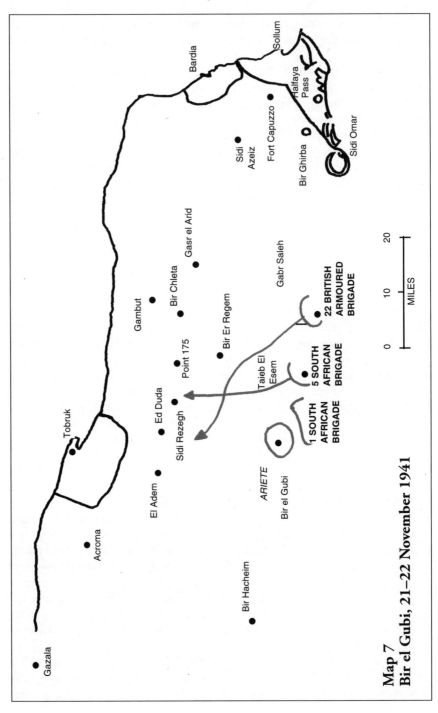

Map 7
Bir el Gubi, 21–22 November 1941

the north-east, believing them to be friendly. These trucks may have been from 22 Armoured Brigade or from supply units intended for 5 South African Brigade.

This relative inactivity by *Ariete* coincided with *DAK* reaping the benefits of the Italian intervention on the opening day of the offensive. On this same day, 21 November, they commenced the destruction of the isolated 7 Armoured Brigade at Sidi Rezegh to the north, a task completed by noon the following day. If *Ariete* had not delayed 22 Armoured on 19 November, the Germans might have found themselves facing tougher opposition from two armoured brigades rather than one. It is even possible that two British armoured brigades might have lifted the siege of Tobruk. However, this never happened because of *Ariete*.

On 22 November *Ariete* remained firmly installed at Bir el Gubi throughout the day, and reported the destruction of fifty-five British tanks since the start of the offensive. The artillery duel between *Ariete* and the South Africans resumed, with Italian fire particularly heavy during the morning. South African armoured cars reported sixty Italian M13 tanks at Bir el Gubi. In the evening Gambara reported the repulse of an attack by '1 South African Division (sic)' – although no such attack was launched. This could only have been South African probing attacks.

In the evening, Rommel issued orders for the following day. He proposed a concentric attack by *DAK* and *Ariete* on the British forces collecting at Sidi Rezegh. It required some vigorous negotiation with Bastico and Gambara, who was still not under Rommel's command, to secure their assent to the use of part of *Ariete* in this operation. The plan envisaged *Ariete*'s armour advancing north towards Gambut, while *DAK*'s panzers at Sidi Rezegh moved south to meet them. It was intended that the British forces would be crushed between the German hammer and the anvil of *Ariete*. In order to avoid friendly fire incidents, the orders included complex recognition signals, and also a reminder that *Ariete* was employing captured British vehicles. In the event, General Cruewell, commander of *DAK*, failed to receive Rommel's orders until the next morning and issued his own. They called for the panzers to head south and link up with *Ariete*. The combined Axis armour would then move north together to crush the British forces against the Axis positions around Tobruk. It was this second plan that went ahead the next day, probably because when Cruewell received Rommel's original orders it was simply too late to alter the plans again.

Sidi Rezegh

At noon on 23 November, the panzers travelling south made contact with elements of *Ariete* north-east of Bir el Gubi. The latter comprised about two-thirds of the whole division under the control of its deputy commander,

General Di Nisio. It consisted of four companies of tanks with eighty M13s, a battalion of 8 *Bersaglieri* Regiment, a battalion of 65mm guns mounted on trucks, and two batteries of artillery. On the way north its reconnaissance forces had briefly clashed with 7 Support Group south-west of Bir Reghem. Twelve light tanks and some M13s appeared and drove towards the British before being driven off by British 25pdrs. The rest of *Ariete* remained at Bir el Gubi under General Balotta to watch 1 South African Brigade.

The combined Axis armour now prepared to move north and push the British against the artillery and anti-tank guns of 21 Panzer Division that had remained behind at Sidi Rezegh. The advance started at 14:00hr with *Ariete* on the left, 15 Panzer in the centre and 21 Panzer on the right. The confusion over plans meant that 'no detailed co-ordination regarding objectives, boundary lines, mutual artillery support or signal services had been arranged'. This inevitably resulted in a lack of co-ordination in the subsequent attack. The Germans naturally blamed the Italians for this. Certainly, Gambara's continued independence from German authority did not help matters. The Italian lack of vehicle radios and vehicle compasses also hindered their operations. In the light of Rommel's earlier specific orders on these matters, the subsequent confusion should probably be attributed to Cruewell's late change in plans.

The Axis advance ran into 5 South African Brigade, and 15 Panzer came under fire from the left where *Ariete* should have been. The latter was 'hanging back noticeably', according to the Germans, so that the gap between them became wider and wider. In fact, *Ariete* was not only advancing into South African artillery fire, but also faced harassing attacks from 22 Armoured Brigade from their left flank. Lieutenant Enrico Serra describes the action:

> The battle has a stunning start. Indeed we lose no time in moving from the advance formation to attack formation. As soon as the enemy is sighted, we are upon them. Tanks take the lead, spearheaded by the battalion from Bir el Gobi, and artillery follow immediately behind them.
>
> Fire! Fire! Side by side, the two columns penetrate the enemy lines and steamroller inexorably through them. Grenades eat up the ground furiously, armour-piercing shells throw up plumes of smoke, outgoing and incoming fire mingle into one great pounding. Our tanks advance irresistibly, shooting with their usual precision. In front of them and on their left flank the enemy tanks vainly improvise an attack. Some of them are immediately set on fire, and others are forced to flee.
>
> From the top of his tank, with his top half sticking out, the colonel directs the manoeuvre, heedless as ever of the firestorm. The general,

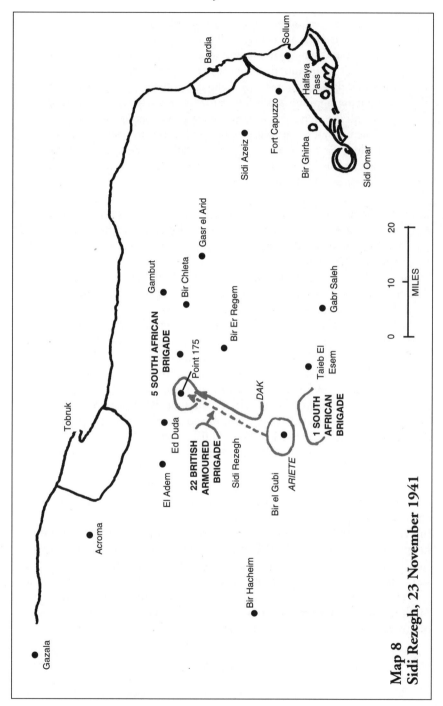

Map 8
Sidi Rezegh, 23 November 1941

too, is beside the leading tanks, calm and smiling in his car.

Our tanks keep advancing. Still shooting, they keep firing their cannons and machine guns remorselessly. Some of them have already run out of ammunition. We hear it from the first wounded tank crew, pale, but still more worried about that than their own fate. But without ammunition you still have to stay on the field: that is part of the standing orders for tank crews, one which is among the hardest of all. There is not a moment of indecision in this irresistible advance and when the first shadows of evening fall on the plain, the battle reaches its conclusion. The first white rockets go up from the Italian and German side. They say: 'Cease fire!'

5 South African Brigade was destroyed, and *Ariete*'s truck-mounted 65mm guns overran a battery of 25pdr guns. Colonel Piscicelli-Taeggi, of 132 Artillery Regiment, recalled having an opportunity to study these excellent enemy guns at first hand.

For much of this day, Rommel was unaware that his orders had been changed, and that the Axis armour was operating to a rather different plan. He did, however, achieve an important success of his own: he spent most of the day bombarding his superiors with complaints about the lack of co-operation between *DAK* and *CAM*. As a result, he finally received confirmation at nightfall that *CAM* would fall under his authority from the next day. This was a victory for common sense in that it placed all motorized forces in the field under one command – although Rommel viewed it more as a victory in his personal feud with Bastico, or 'Bombastico', as he dubbed him. The new arrangement was announced at midnight alongside news of the bloody victory over the British at Sidi Rezegh.

It was at this point that Rommel indulged in a huge tactical gamble, which might have won or lost him the battle. He believed that success at Sidi Rezegh secured him a crucial psychological advantage over the British: he felt that all he needed to do now was to push them and they would collapse into precipitate retreat as they had done back in March. He therefore ordered *DAK* and *Ariete* to stage a bold advance towards the Egyptian frontier 60 miles (100km) away. He hoped that this would scatter the British survivors of the recent fighting and their supply echelons, and start a panic that would sweep him on to Cairo in triumph. This radical idea might have succeeded, too, but for the British commander, General Auchinleck's steadfast refusal to panic, and his determination to continue his offensive in spite of Rommel's distractions.

Taieb el Esem

On 24 November the Axis armour set out on what became known later as the 'Dash to the Wire'. Naturally, *DAK* led the way, scattering isolated British supply echelons in its path. At the same time, *Ariete* moved down the Trigh el Abd on the German southern flank at their own more sedate pace, collecting *en route* those elements previously left behind at Bir el Gubi. The latter position was left with a small garrison from *RECAM* to safeguard the Italian supply dumps. The reconstituted *Ariete* meanwhile advanced south-eastwards until evening when they reported a 'large British formation' to their south. They halted their advance and engaged this unknown force with artillery fire. It turned out to be 1 South African Brigade who had fallen back from Bir el Gubi after the destruction of their sister brigade at Sidi Rezegh. The South Africans in turn reported a large 'probably German (sic)' force in their vicinity. An impressive display of flares put up by *Ariete* during the night persuaded the South Africans that they were virtually surrounded. The following day Rommel intended that *DAK* and *Ariete* together should attack British forces at the Egyptian frontier and crush them against the frontier positions of the Italian 55 *Savona* Infantry Division. He was unaware that *Ariete* had fallen behind and that *DAK* would have to attempt this alone. He ordered that *Ariete* 'move rapidly towards' the frontier – but since he had lost contact with his own signals unit, it is unlikely that this order ever reached Gambara or Balotta.

On 25 November, *Ariete* made full contact with the 'large British formation' located the previous day, which had occupied Taieb el Esem. The increasingly paranoid South Africans recorded the presence of 'a large force of tanks 2–3 miles east of their positions, fifteen tanks to the north and some enemy to the south'. In view of the recent fate of their comrades at the hands of Axis armour, it is perhaps not surprising that a nervous Pienaar decided to remain where he was until things became clearer. At 07:00hr, *Ariete*'s field artillery bombarded the South Africans who, not unnaturally, assumed that this presaged a major attack. They reported being in contact with a considerable force of tanks, and an hour later, followed this up with the dramatic news that they were being 'attacked by tanks'. The event that prompted this signal began with between forty and fifty M13s advancing towards the South Africans. This group halted 3 miles (5km) from the South Africans, and sent patrols out southwards (the bulk of *Ariete* remained further north, South African armoured cars reporting about a hundred motor vehicles). It was one of these Italian patrols, a company of twelve M13s, that had approached the South Africans; when they came under intense shellfire from the South African artillery, they turned back. In the fog of war, this probe was misinterpreted. At 09:15hr the nervous Pienaar requested armoured support since he was heavily engaged, and his divisional commander, General Brink, who had already lost one of his brigades, fully supported him. At 10:35hr the immediate crisis appeared over, when South African armoured cars reported that their artillery had

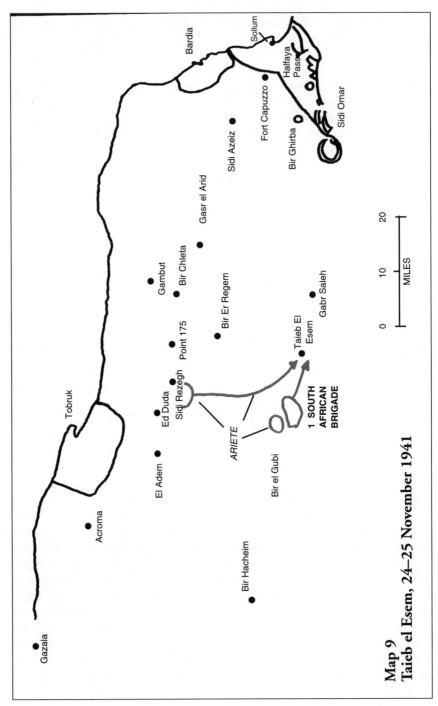

Map 9
Taieb el Esem, 24–25 November 1941

driven off the enemy. They also reported, however, that 'the Italian tanks are driven by Germans (sic) and have 50mm (sic) guns'. The South Africans appear to have assumed a German involvement, and this quickly produced the legend that they were holding off the entire *DAK*. In fact the latter were far away, and this clash can only have been with *Ariete*.

The Italians summarized the events of this day as '*Ariete* beat off enemy attacks', suggesting that they perceived their actions as essentially defensive. It seems that they were equally wary of their opponents, and had no intentions of initiating any major action against them; thus they spent the day countering intense enemy artillery fire and engaging in a series of minor armoured skirmishes. In spite of the tentative nature of these Italian probes, they clearly alarmed the South Africans, who interpreted them as a heavy attack lasting nearly an hour and involving tanks, motorized infantry with mortars, all supported by heavy artillery fire. They described how their artillery repulsed them with heavy loss to the enemy, but none to themselves. A case of exaggeration at the very least!

On the Italian side, General Balotta made preparations for a further probe of the South African positions. He was conscious of Rommel's original orders to proceed towards the frontier, and he therefore had no aggressive intentions towards the South Africans, but simply wanted to ensure that they would not endanger his passage eastwards. At 10:30hr he directed two companies of tanks, with twelve and thirteen M13s respectively, each supported by approximately one hundred truck-mounted *Bersaglieri*, to probe the flanks of the enemy positions. They were supported by the divisional artillery, including captured 25pdr guns. The South African artillery responded with heavy fire that caused the Italian tanks to sheer off within 1,000yd (900m) of their positions: the Italians were reluctant to expose their armour to such intense artillery fire, especially when they were urgently needed elsewhere. They therefore avoided coming within range, and the brief action ended after less than an hour. The encounter then subsided into an artillery duel with a great deal of Italian fire falling on the South Africans, but only three casualties reported.

Once again the South Africans overreacted, reporting an attack by 100 enemy tanks lasting an hour and a half, during which their positions were swept by tank and artillery fire. Indeed, so serious did things appear that it was imagined that they might be overwhelmed, and secret papers were destroyed to prevent their capture. They reported that no enemy tanks actually reached their perimeter only because of their intense artillery fire that destroyed an estimated twenty-five enemy tanks – though subsequently, none of these were found on the battlefield. They explained this embarrassing lack of corroboration by claiming the tanks had been salvaged. In fact the Italian M13s did not venture within range of the South African artillery.

In spite of their continued survival, the South Africans anticipated another major armoured assault at any moment. It was in this tense atmosphere that 4 British Armoured Brigade, equipped with American-built Stuart light tanks, finally arrived in response to their pleas for support at 11:30hr. They stationed themselves to the north of the South Africans, and remained there to discourage Italian attacks. The new arrivals almost ran into a defensive anti-tank screen on *Ariete's* flank, but turned aside just in time, withdrawing to about 1,200yd (1,100m). They encountered forty-two Italian M13s, but were unable to close with them because of heavy Italian artillery fire. At dusk, the British armour followed customary practice and withdrew to leaguer for the night a few miles south of 1 South African Brigade. This exposed the nervous South Africans, who feared that *Ariete* was preparing to launch a final assault, perhaps a night attack, involving their whole force.

In fact *Ariete* withdrew during the night, in response to urgent orders from Rommel to move to the Egyptian frontier. At 15:20hr, Balotta had acted on these orders by deploying forty-three Italian M13s towards the South Africans to prevent any interference with their withdrawal. The rest of the division, including another twenty-three M13s, *Bersaglieri* and artillery, abandoned its defensive positions behind this armoured screen and embussed for its advance to the frontier. It would seem that the South Africans mistook all this activity as preparations for a full-scale assault. It was an easy mistake to make amidst the dust and confusion caused by vehicle movements in poor light. The threat, however, was sufficient to cause them to withdraw southwards towards the British supply dumps, at dusk. In the end, of course, no attack came and the Italian tank screen itself withdrew. This exemplary withdrawal was completed during darkness, and *Ariete* headed slowly towards Fort Capuzzo on the frontier.

This series of apparently inconclusive actions between *Ariete* and 1 South African Brigade, and subsequently 4 Armoured Brigade, have usually been ignored in accounts of this period. Instead, attention has focused on the dramatic dash by *DAK* to the Egyptian frontier. In fact this German thrust failed in its prime objective of causing the British to panic and retreat, and the German panzers spent several days, isolated and out of fuel, on the frontier, far from the real focal point of the battle. This was at Sidi Rezegh where, in the absence of the Axis armour, 2 New Zealand Division secured key positions and linked up with the Tobruk garrison. In this context, *Ariete* arguably played a more important role in the battle than *DAK* by effectively preventing the South Africans from moving north to support the New Zealanders, and by distracting 4 Armoured Brigade for a time. If they had not done so, it is possible that this reinforcement of the British forces at Sidi Rezegh might have raised the siege of Tobruk and won the battle. The Italian actions at Taieb el Esem, which were dismissed as irrelevant, were probably more significant than the meanderings of their German allies.

M13/40 medium tanks in the desert –unidentified unit symbol on front hull. (Tank Museum)

LEFT: *Detail of M13/40 medium tank. (Tank Museum)*

BELOW: *An abandoned M14/41 medium tank. (TRH Pictures)*

ABOVE: *M13/40 medium tanks in open formation. (Imperial War Museum)*

Motorised infantry of 8 Bersaglieri Regiment, Ariete Armoured Division. (Imperial War Museum)

Tank crew repairing tr gear with an AB41 armoured car in the background. (TRH Pictures)

M14/41 tank captured by US forces in Tunisia. (Robert Hunt Library)

M14/41 tanks advance under fire in the desert. (Tank Museum)

Bersaglieri showing the distinctive black cockerel feathers in their hats. (Imperial War Museum)

Italian 20mm anti-aircraft units mounted on Spa Dovunque 35 trucks. (Tank Museum)

RIGHT: M13/40 medium tank crews receive orders – they wear early leather uniforms. (Robert Hunt Library)

BELOW: An abandoned M13/40 medium tank. (TRH Pictures)

Rommel with M13/40 tank in the background. (Tank Museum)

L3/35 light tanks in column. (Imperial War Museum)

Spa TL 37 truck with portee 75mm field gun. (Imperial War Museum)

Bersaglieri man a standard 47mm anti-tank gun. (Imperial War Museum)

ABOVE: L3/35 light tanks assault a trench system — possibly a training shot. (Robert Hunt Library)

A column of M13/40 tanks from Ariete Armoured Division. (Tank Museum)

Italian heavy 149mm artillery pieces in action against Tobruk. (Tank Museum)

M13/40 tanks advance into an artillery bombardment. (Tank Museum)

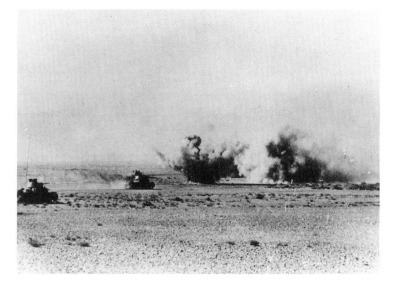

M13/40 tanks advance in column. (Tank Museum)

A Fiat 508C staff car hea a column of M13/40 tank from Ariete Armoured Division – note the divisional symbol on staff car door. (Imperial War Museum)

An Italian 20mm anti-aircraft unit in a Breda 51 truck. (Tank Museum)

A brand new Semovente da 75/18 the desert. (Tank Museum)

M14/41 tank in newly captured Tobruk, June 1942. (Tank Museum)

A Semovente da 75/18 is unloaded from its transport trailer – unit symbol on the rear hull indicates 5 Gruppo, Ariete Armoured Division. (Tank Museum)

M14/41 tanks and Semoventi in open formation – the tactical sign on the foreground vehicle indicates 1st tank 1st platoon. (Imperial War Museum)

M14/41 tanks in columns. (TRH Pictures)

M13/40 tanks advance with soft-skinned vehicles in the far distance – an unidentified unit symbol is on the front hull. (Tank Museum)

Italian-manned 88mm guns in their original anti-aircraft role. (Tank Museum)

M13/40 tanks advance under fire (Tank Museum)

Semovente da 75/18 – note the use of spare track links as additional protection. (Tank Museum)

114/41 tanks destroyed by heavy calibre shells at Alamein. (Tank Museum)

Fiat/Spa Camionetta Sahariana scout car during the retreat to Tunisia. (Tank Museum)

M14/41 tank abandoned in Tunisia. (TRH Pictures)

90mm anti-aircraft gun mounted on a Lancia 3RO truck from Centauro Armoured Division – divisional symbol on door. (Tank Museum)

emovente da 47/32s advance under fire in Tunisia. (Robert Hunt Library)

14/41 tanks advance under fire in Tunisia. (Robert Hunt Library)

Semovente da 47/32 in Tunisia. (Tank Museum)

Semovente da 47/32s advance with infantry in Tunisia. (Robert Hunt Library)

Bir Ghirba

Early on 26 November, in complete ignorance of *Ariete's* actions and their significance, General Cruewell signalled 'Where is *Ariete?*'. He was, perhaps naturally, narrowly focused on his own objectives, and unaware that the New Zealanders' occupation of Sidi Rezegh had made them completely irrelevant. In fact after a difficult night march from Taieb el Esem, *Ariete* had arrived some 10 miles west of Fort Capuzzo that morning. They spent most of the day thereafter engaged in preparations to attack a British position at Bir Ghirba, which later turned out to be empty. They probably also shelled in error the headquarters of the *Savona* Division, which were nearby. They were, quite naturally, also concerned about their own long supply lines, which stretched some 60 miles back to Bir Hacheim and were exposed to British attack. Fortunately the South Africans remained at the British supply dumps in the south, while 4 Armoured was rushed northwards and therefore interrupted Axis supplies only briefly.

On 27 November, General Cruewell came across *Ariete* at noon, while attempting to regain contact with *DAK* on the frontier. The Italians were still busily firing on phantom British positions at Bir Ghirba, and skirmishing with 7 British Support Group. On his own initiative Cruewell now ordered Balotta and *Ariete* back towards Tobruk. He was finally becoming concerned about the situation there, although he did not yet know how badly it had deteriorated. In the afternoon, therefore, *Ariete* turned around and headed towards an agreed concentration point west of Sidi Rezegh, where they would link up with *DAK,* who would also be sent back. This movement would evolve into a deliberate concentration of Axis armour against the New Zealanders at Sidi Rezegh. The withdrawal of *Ariete* caused 7 Support Group to congratulate itself on putting a whole armoured division to flight! They reported that *Ariete*, now north of Gabr Saleh, had been 'chivvied, harried and attacked by Support Group columns, and withdrew north'. In fact the Italians were still too powerful to be harmed by this minor force, and had they not been withdrawing north-west, they might have caused the cock-a-hoop British some difficulties.

On 28 November, *Ariete* attracted the attention of 22 Armoured Brigade as it came up on the southern flank of 15 Panzer Division near Bir Sciafsciuf. In the evening, Rommel and Cruewell once again proposed competing plans for tackling the New Zealanders at Sidi Rezegh. These were discussed at a conference at Bir Chrimeisa, which Generals Gambara of *CAM* and Navarrini of Italian XXI Corps also attended. The outcome was a plan to encircle the New Zealanders, involving *Ariete* advancing on an important piece of high ground at Point 175 to complete the encirclement with 15 and 21 Panzer Divisions.

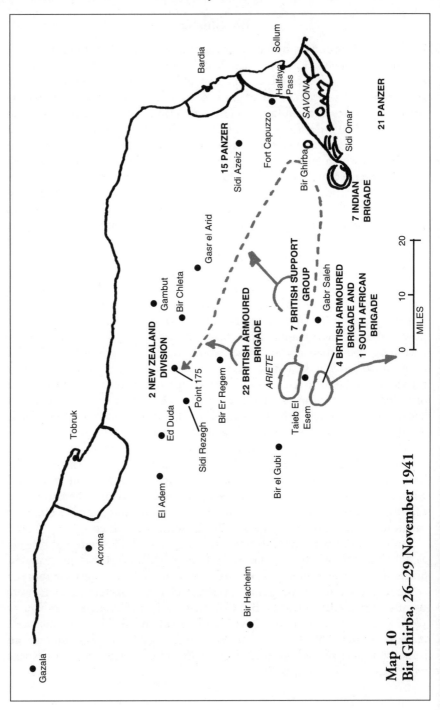

Map 10
Bir Ghirba, 26–29 November 1941

Sidi Muftah

The 29 November opened with *Ariete* and 21 Panzer Divisions facing 2 New Zealand Division, supported by 1 Army Tank Brigade, well dug in around Sidi Rezegh. In addition the still dangerous and slowly reviving remnants of 4 and 22 Armoured Brigades were now behind the Axis forces. At dawn, *Ariete* was approaching the New Zealanders from the south-east along the line of the Trigh Capuzzo. The presence of their armour made the British reluctant to send 1 South African Brigade north to join the New Zealanders. In the meantime, 4 and 22 Armoured Brigades moved cautiously northwards to Sidi Muftah, about six miles south of the New Zealanders. There, 4 Armoured had 'a brush with ... a column of 132 Armoured Regiment [of *Ariete*] moving west'. In spite of its exposed position between the New Zealanders and the British armour, *Ariete* was not immediately attacked. It did come under artillery fire, which caused Balotta to take the common-sense precaution of dispersing his vehicles, but did not otherwise hinder his operations. It was only after the British learned of 15 Panzer Division's attacks on the New Zealanders at Ed Duda that 4 and 22 Armoured Brigades were ordered to attack the Italians. The British had sixty Stuart tanks and twenty-four Crusader tanks respectively, and could call on powerful support from the artillery of 1 South African Brigade. The position looked distinctly ominous for *Ariete*.

At 14:00hr, 4 Armoured Brigade advanced north with 22 Armoured on its right. The latter kept a wary eye on twenty-five Italian M13 tanks from *Ariete* to the west at Sidi Muftah. The British armour had intended to engage enemy tanks reported at Sidi Rezegh, but it was now redirected to support 21 New Zealand Battalion on Point 175, which was threatened by 21 Panzer. An hour later, as 4 Armoured turned north-east, a force of forty enemy tanks, supported by 88mm and 105mm guns, appeared to their west and forced them to stand and fight where they stood. In spite of contemporary British uncertainty, this force was almost certainly not German and so must have been an Italian force from *Ariete*, although Italian sources have no record of attacks on 4 Armoured Brigade. It may have been the column of M13s that 4 Armoured had encountered that morning near Sidi Muftah. If so, their numbers had become exaggerated, and indeed armoured cars subsequently reported only twelve tanks. However, this rather confused skirmishing prompted 22 Armoured to release some tanks to assist their colleagues. The South African artillery was left to hold off the forty-seven Italian M13s from *Ariete* loitering menacingly to the east of 22 Armoured, which they did quite successfully. The confusion caused by this minor skirmish effectively prevented the British armour from concentrating against *Ariete* for the rest of the day. At dusk, the British armour withdrew south to leaguer for the night, leaving the field to the Italians. The feeble

British armoured attacks on *Ariete* had served only to delay its progress for a time, rather than to halt it, and an important chance to destroy the Italians had been lost. They did not prevent the major Axis success of the day, the seizure of a key New Zealand defensive position in a dramatic *coup de main*.

Point 175

The Italians were not distracted by the British armour from heading north towards their main objective at Point 175. The garrison of this objective, 21 New Zealand Battalion, had already beaten off two attacks by 21 Panzer. They were now expecting the imminent arrival of relief in the shape of 1 South African Brigade from the south: a South African liaison officer had already arrived to inform them that his brigade was actually advancing on Point 175. Shortly before 17:00hr, 21 Battalion was informed that a column was approaching from the south-east, and brigade headquarters confirmed that this was the South Africans. The strain of a very intense and difficult day of confused fighting and a large portion of wishful thinking now combined to produce one of the most confused episodes of the entire North African campaign.

The New Zealanders later reported that a column of soft-skinned vehicles approached at a steady 6mph (10kmph) from the east, led by a few high-turreted vehicles that appeared to be South African Marmon-Harrington armoured cars. The column was approaching in open order, the hatches of the armoured vehicles were open, and the khaki-clad crews were waving what appeared to be tank-crew black berets at them. A large number of New Zealanders thereupon abandoned their dug-outs to return this friendly greeting. Too late, they noticed that the lead vehicles were in fact Italian tanks, which suddenly opened fire on them, closely followed by truck-mounted *Bersaglieri*. The neighbouring battalion received a desperate call from the commander of 21 Battalion: 'They are into my lines with three tanks and are taking prisoners. Artillery support at once, for God's sake!' This was followed by: 'Everyone has left, what shall I do? They are right on top of me...!' The Italian *Bersaglieri* quickly dismounted from their lorries and rounded up and disarmed the surprised New Zealanders as night fell. The latter had little alternative but to surrender, although a few individuals slipped away in the confusion.

It seems most likely from this description that what happened was the result of a double misunderstanding. The New Zealanders clearly thought the approaching force was their long-anticipated relief, and emerged from their foxholes to welcome them. On their part, the Italians apparently assumed that 21 Panzer were already in possession of the position, which they had already attacked twice earlier in the day, and that they were approaching a friendly force and had no need to take any precautions such as closing hatches or deploying for action. This is apparent from the descriptions of their approach – at slow speed, in open formation, and with no defensive measures adopted. This complex situation was ripe for confusion. What *is* important, however, is that the Italians were the first to realize the true position, and that they recovered more quickly than their opponents. It was this that won the day for them.

As a result of quicker reflexes, *Ariete* found themselves in possession of a vital position at no cost. They had achieved this dramatic success despite the fact that most of their tanks were preoccupied with the attentions of British armour on their left flank. The *Italian Official History* rather understates this success by recording that at 'dusk on 29 November, *Ariete* was also in contact with 2 NZ Division, from which it collected 200 prisoners'. The whole incident was witnessed by Brigadier Kippenberger:

> About 5:30pm a damned Italian motorised (sic) division (*Ariete*) turned up. They passed with five tanks leading, twenty following, and a huge column of transport and guns, and rolled straight over our infantry on Point 175. About 200 of the 21st came past us as prisoners. Fighting went on in the moonlight until 11.00pm.

Ariete was now short of ammunition and supplies, but it was still full of fight. They had inflicted a severe defeat on the New Zealanders at almost no cost – indeed the latter still appear to be somewhat embarrassed by this incident. The *Official History* of the 21 Battalion recounts the entire episode in considerable detail, but completely fails to name the enemy formation involved, or even to acknowledge that it was Italian. It seems that the constant deluge of British propaganda about Italian military incompetence both during the war and ever since made the New Zealanders, even in 1953, reluctant to admit that the 'incompetent' Italians were responsible for inflicting one of their most embarrassing defeats.

Meanwhile, what had happened to the missing South Africans? In the afternoon of 29 November, they had been ordered to advance north to the relief of 21 New Zealand Battalion on Point 175. However, they were almost immediately delayed by reports of a large formation of tanks from *Ariete* to the north-east (those spotted earlier by 22 Armoured). They therefore demanded protection from 22 Armoured before moving; but because the latter had just sent tanks to support 4 Armoured, it was unable to comply. At 16:50hr the British confirmed the presence of forty-seven Italian tanks and six guns south of Point 175, and suggested that the South Africans move forward using the British armour as a shield. At 18:30hr, they were about to follow this advice, when news arrived that Point 175 had fallen to *Ariete*. They quickly cancelled their plans, and the Italians were left to consolidate their hold on Point 175 unmolested.

In the early morning of 30 November, Rommel issued orders to his armour to complete the encirclement and destruction of 2 New Zealand Division. In this process *Ariete* was specifically tasked with seizing Sidi Rezegh in co-operation with an *ad hoc* German force called Group Mickl. In response, *Ariete* opened proceedings by engaging New Zealand artillery from Point 175. In reply, a concentrated New Zealand barrage managed to scatter *Ariete*'s motor transport, which had foolishly been left visible on the high ground. The soft-skinned vehicles were quickly withdrawn behind the crest, but *Ariete*'s tanks held on unchallenged and her artillery observers were still able to direct fire on the New Zealand positions. At 10:00hr, some Italian M13s began to move west in the direction of Bir Chrimeisa, until this movement was discouraged by intense artillery fire. The Italian tanks remained a threat throughout the day, even though they were in urgent need of fuel and ammunition, and distracted by contacts with the British armour to their south.

The now merged 4/22 Armoured Brigade reported the 'aggressive attitude' displayed by *Ariete* during the day. At 08:50hr, they reported an estimated nineteen armoured cars and 150 motor vehicles advancing against their night leaguer. This was probably *Ariete*'s motor transport seeking refuge from artillery fire, or attempting to open up a supply route: they were shelled by British artillery and turned west. At 09:25hr, two companies of M13 tanks, twenty-four in all, attacked the right wing of the 4/22 Armoured Brigade to protect their vulnerable transports, but retired an hour later with the loss of a single tank. There were further armoured clashes between M13s of *Ariete* and British Stuarts as the British counter-attacked from the south. The British struck the Italian flank and claimed sixteen M13s destroyed with no loss to themselves. The Italians reported resisting 'continuous pressure from an enemy armoured unit which had the support of numerous guns'. This action continued into the afternoon, with British Stuarts advancing north to engage Italian M13s south of Point 175, with more visible to the south-east. At 15:45hr the British claimed to have attacked an enemy motor transport column and scattered it, although this incident is not recorded by the Italians, and may therefore have been no more than units manoeuvring. At 17:00hr, British tanks demonstrated against some Italian M13s to the south-east, which withdrew towards the edge of the escarpment. The day's fighting ended when the British armour withdrew into night leaguer. They reported the loss of five Stuart tanks, presumably to *Ariete*.

In spite of an apparent British superiority in these clashes, suggested by Italian tank losses, the former failed to exploit their success. In contrast, the Italians demonstrated considerable tenacity, and secured a tactical success by containing the British armour. The Italians record with some satisfaction that the 'enemy tanks were successfully driven back to the south'. Although

Ariete had failed in its original mission to link up with Group Mickl at Sidi Rezegh, it had prevented 4/22 Armoured Brigade from opening up a route to Point 175 for the South Africans. This allowed *DAK* to destroy the New Zealanders without interference, and with some assistance from *Ariete*. At 17:00hr, 25 New Zealand Battalion was preparing to withdraw from the encirclement when *Ariete's* tanks attacked from behind Point 175. The New Zealanders engaged the four leading M13 tanks with their 2pdr anti-tank guns, setting two on fire, damaging a third, and causing the fourth to withdraw. The Italians succeeded nevertheless in forcing the New Zealanders to abandon this breakout attempt.

In these difficult days of confused action around Sidi Rezegh, *Ariete* had once again proved its worth. It had returned from the Egyptian frontier and secured the vital position at Point 175; this allowed Axis observation of most of the ground held by the New Zealanders, and provided a useful point from which to launch attacks against them. In addition to this, however, *Ariete* also held off the British armour to the south, and prevented them intervening to protect the New Zealanders or securing a passage for the waiting South Africans. This allowed *DAK* the freedom to destroy 2 New Zealand Division without hindrance, and restore for the moment the Axis siege of Tobruk.

During the night of 30 November/1 December, *Ariete* was in action assisting German reconnaissance forces against 1 South African Brigade. A company of Italian M13s was sent to approach the South Africans from the north, and pressed home their attack to very close range in the darkness. They then came under heavy anti-tank fire and lost four M13s before withdrawing. In spite of this success the South Africans once again chose to withdraw south until dawn in the face of this Italian armoured threat. The M13 company from *Ariete* spent the following day repulsing renewed attacks by the South Africans from hull-down positions with the support of their artillery on Point 175.

Early on 1 December, the 4/22 Armoured Brigade with about 115 tanks, mainly Stuarts, finally managed to slip through between Italian forces on Points 175 and 178 and reach Sidi Rezegh. They came under heavy artillery fire from both *Ariete* on Point 175 and *Trieste* Motorized Division under General Piazzoni, now on Point 178, and lost several tanks. This British advance was intended to cover the withdrawal of the surviving New Zealanders, but it soon came to grief, largely as a result of pressure from the M13s of *Ariete* at Point 175. A foolhardy attempt by the New Zealanders to escape right under the noses of the Italians on Point 175 was thwarted by their artillery and tanks. In addition, 4/22 Armoured Brigade reported Italian tanks on its flank, which stayed out of range, but presented a threat sufficient to persuade them to break contact with the New Zealanders. Rommel urged Balotta to strike at the reluctant British armour, but with

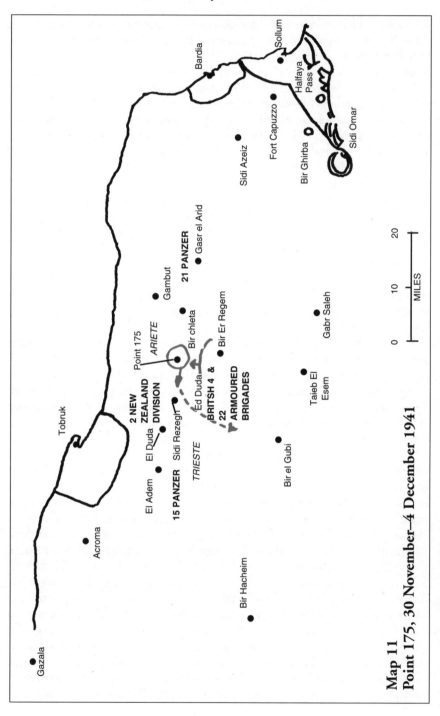

Map 11
Point 175, 30 November–4 December 1941

admitted losses of twenty M13s in the last two days, he was not prepared to do so. In the end, he effectively prevented the southward withdrawal of the New Zealanders, and they actually escaped north-east through a gap left by 21 Panzer Division.

At the close of 1 December, Rommel believed that the destruction of the New Zealanders meant that the British were beaten. In fact they were just pausing for breath, and were bringing up reinforcements before resuming the offensive. In ignorance of this, and anticipating imminent victory, Rommel was anxious to relieve the isolated and increasingly desperate Axis garrisons on the Egyptian frontier. The heavy losses suffered by *DAK* meant that *CAM,* including *Ariete* and *Trieste,* now represented his strongest mobile force. He therefore issued orders for Gambara to proceed eastwards the next day with *Ariete* and *Trieste* towards Sollum. It took *Ariete* some time to disengage from its secure positions around Point 175, and Balotta did not therefore begin the eastward journey until 3 December. He managed to reach Gasr el Arid, while *Trieste* halted at Bir el Chleta, and this unexpected thrust alarmed the British sufficiently to send a restored 4 Armoured Brigade in pursuit. This exposed 11 Indian Brigade advancing on Bir el Gubi to seize the Italian supply depots still garrisoned by *RECAM.*

On 4 December, 11 Indian Brigade, which had moved quietly up from the frontier while the Axis armour was preoccupied at Sidi Rezegh, was preparing for a dawn attack on the supply dumps at Bir el Gubi, still being guarded by *RECAM.* The plan was to approach from the west and surprise the Italians, whom British intelligence predicted 'would not put up much fight'. But the Indians were in for a nasty surprise, since *RECAM* included two *Giovani Fascisti,* or Young Fascist volunteer battalions recruited from fanatical Fascist students who had also been well trained and equipped. They differed sharply in almost every respect with the weak and flabby Blackshirt units of 1940. They had been ready for an attack since the previous evening, when Gambara reported 'my intelligence ... anticipates an attack tomorrow'. The stubbornness of their two-day defence against superior forces came as a complete surprise to the British, and would become one of the epics of the campaign. It ended with the destruction of 11 Indian Brigade, with some help from *DAK.* This encounter is not detailed here since it is not part of the story of the Italian armoured divisions. It does, however, demonstrate what might have happened had Italian forces been as well motivated as their German or Japanese allies. It is doubtful if the Allies would have won the war as quickly had all Italians been similarly motivated, but the shortcomings of the Italian leadership negated this possibility.

On 4 December, the threat to Bir el Gubi prompted Rommel to recall *CAM* from its futile drive towards the frontier. The next day, *Ariete* commenced its withdrawal towards El Adem, under constant harassment from 7 Support Group. It was also bombed by German Stukas, which caused some casualties and a great deal of irritation. The *Italian Official History* also admitted that *Ariete* 'suffered considerable losses from intense shelling', while the British claimed two tanks and two artillery batteries destroyed, and 200 prisoners taken. These attacks were little more than a nuisance, however, and *Ariete* continued towards El Adem unchecked. On 6 December, 7 Support Group shelled a large column of infantry and armour, from *Ariete*, which was moving westwards. At 08:00hr, 4 Armoured Brigade clashed with thirty enemy tanks, which quickly withdrew and were not pursued: they were probably M13s from *Ariete* that had reached this area and was moving south from El Adem towards Bir el Gubi. It was now that Rommel finally accepted that the battle had been lost, since Axis supplies of fuel and ammunition were at critical levels and tank numbers at a very low ebb. The news that fresh supplies were unlikely to arrive before January clinched matters. He ordered *DAK* to await the arrival of *CAM* at Bir el Gubi; they would then hold these positions to cover the withdrawal of the Axis infantry to Gazala. On the afternoon of 7 December, *Ariete* finally linked up with 15 Panzer Division and eased the pressure on the German flank, although not before their artillery had briefly engaged the Germans by mistake.

As Rommel reluctantly conceded defeat to superior numbers in North Africa, events elsewhere reduced even further his already slim chances of receiving substantial reinforcements. On 6 December, the Soviets launched their great winter counter offensive against the badly overstretched Germans outside Moscow. This counter-attack using fresh reserves, many transferred from the Far East, shattered the exhausted German armies and sent them reeling backwards in what was almost a rout. It would continue well into the spring and cause significant and irreplaceable losses for the Germans. The Germans had failed in their attempt to defeat the Soviets in a short campaign, and now faced a long war of attrition that would absorb increasing numbers of German troops and leave very few for Rommel. Only a day later, on 7 December, the Japanese attacked Pearl Harbor, bringing the United States into the war. This might not have been immediately significant for Rommel, except that Germany and Italy declared war on the United States on 11 December. This formidable combination of enemies – Britain, the Soviet Union and the United States – was far too much for Italy to cope with, and would soon prove beyond the capabilities of the Germans and Japanese, too. In the long term it meant that Axis prospects were now likely to be increasingly grim; but in the short term it meant that North Africa was likely to receive even fewer Axis resources, as priority went to new and more important theatres of war: the Eastern Front, the U-Boat Campaign and the defence of Europe. It was a dark prospect for a retreating army to face.

Alam Hamza

On 13 December, *CAM* was installed in positions at Alam Hamza near Gazala with the infantry of Italian X Corps to their north, and *DAK* to their south. *Ariete* had been reduced to a shadow of its former self, with only thirty M13 tanks, eighteen field guns, ten anti-tank guns and around 700 *Bersaglieri*. It was here, at around noon, that 5 Indian Brigade attacked the severely depleted *Ariete* and seized some high ground called Point 204. A company of ten to twelve M13s from *Ariete* counter-attacked but were driven off by the Indians with the support of nine heavily armoured Valentine tanks and a troop of 25pdr guns. They claimed three tanks destroyed, but mistakenly identified them as German. In the afternoon a larger force of sixteen M13s renewed the counter-attack and succeeded in overrunning the 25pdr guns; but it failed to recover Point 204. The next day, *Ariete* launched another assault, which was also repulsed until *DAK* arrived in support and the position finally fell. This minor success at Alam Hamza boosted Italian morale and made them reluctant to withdraw any further. It was only the threat that Rommel would abandon them that forced them to retreat all the way back to El Agheila.

This winter campaign had seen the *Ariete* Armoured Division fight as a single complete entity for the first time, and had demonstrated that it could be a formidable force in the right circumstances. It had stopped 22 Armoured Brigade in its tracks from defensive positions at Bir el Gubi, and had inflicted heavy losses on the British in the process. It had kept 1 South African Brigade out of the fight for extended periods simply by the threat offered by its presence, and it held its own in the face of considerable harassment from various British armoured formations throughout the fighting. It captured a vital position from tough New Zealand troops almost without firing a shot, and helped its German allies to destroy the rest of 2 New Zealand Division. In the final withdrawal it fought back against its British pursuers at Gazala in spite of its much weakened state, and only withdrew at German insistence. Its performance had been impressive at many levels, and it is arguable that it made a more positive contribution to Axis success than its German allies at a number of points during the fighting. This was a significant change from the Italian army of 1940, and it hints at what might have been achieved had properly equipped armoured divisions been deployed to North Africa at that time.

5

The Cauldron of Battle

In late December 1941, although the balance of the wider war appeared to be swinging against the Axis, the conflict in North Africa was about to take a turn in their favour. An entire German Air Fleet, withdrawn from the severity of winter on the Eastern front, arrived in Sicily to bombard Malta into submission. It proved highly successful in this task, and by 10 May 1942 the Germans declared Malta subdued. On 18 December Italian frogmen steered three *maiale* human torpedoes into Alexandria harbour and sank two British battleships. On the same day the British naval squadron based at Malta was effectively destroyed by Italian mines. This combination of events restored Axis dominance of the central Mediterranean and allowed fresh supplies of fuel and reinforcements to reach North Africa unhindered. This injection of additional strength would permit the retreating Axis forces to strike back at their pursuers.

On 21 January 1942, only sixteen days after the last of the Axis rearguards had reached El Agheila, Rommel suddenly turned the tables and resumed the offensive. The arrival of fifty-five new panzers inspired him to strike against the overstretched British forces facing him – although he omitted to inform his own superiors or his Italian allies; nevertheless, he achieved complete surprise against his opponents, who were thrown completely off balance and sought refuge in retreat. The successor to *CAM* under Gambara, the Italian XX Motorized Corps, commanded by General Francesco Zingales, a fifty-eight-year old infantry officer, played a largely supporting role in this offensive. On 27 January they were advancing on Benghasi from the south when the appearance of German forces under Rommel's command to the north of Benghasi cut off the retreat of 7 Indian Infantry Brigade. The Indians decided to attempt to break out of this encirclement to the south through Schleidema, before heading east towards Mechili. They took a risk by cutting directly across the front of the Italians, but appalling weather and a great deal of luck allowed them to slip through the scattered Italian units. The few Italians that did encounter them were too surprised to do more than fire a few shots at them. The Indians successfully escaped to Mechili, although they had to abandon all their heavy weapons. The Axis forces did not follow up the British retreat but remained in the area of Benghasi, partly due to fuel shortages but also to take their pick of the immense spoils abandoned by the British in the town. This short campaign had not involved the Italian armour in a significant way, but had provided a useful proving ground for the new *Semovente da 75/18*, an improvization that proved very effective in practice. The M13/40 medium tank was increasingly obsolescent, but had to remain in production in the absence of the appearance of the planned P40 heavy tank with its 75mm gun. The essential problem was how to mount a heavier gun on a medium-tank chassis in the short term. In the light of German experience with self-propelled guns, where a 75mm gun was mounted on a Panzer III chassis, Colonel Berlese of the artillery constructed a number of prototypes. He utilized the basic medium-tank chassis, and tried mounting various artillery pieces on it. The best of these pairings was the *Semovente da 75/18*, where a standard Italian 75/18mm howitzer was mounted in an armoured box on the medium-tank chassis.

This improvised vehicle proved excellent and very flexible, and was much admired by its crews. It not only supplied additional mobility to the artillery as originally intended, but also provided a welcome addition to anti-tank capability. Although its 75mm gun was not the highest velocity weapon available, it could penetrate 50mm of armour plate at 1,000m (3,280ft), and this allowed the Italians to tackle increasingly heavily armoured Allied tanks such as the Grant or Sherman, which proved largely immune to the 47mm guns of their medium tanks. It was an important Italian innovation that appeared almost nine months before the nearest Allied equivalent, the M7 or Priest or Bishop self-propelled guns, which did not appear until Alamein in October 1942.

In January 1942, two groups of *Semovente da 75/18*s arrived in North Africa, each consisting of eight *Semoventi* and four command vehicles. They were assigned to reinforce the 132 Artillery Regiment of *Ariete* Armoured Division, but were temporarily attached to German forces during the offensive, and provided welcome additional punch. Captain Traniello, reporting on their performance, wrote in March 1942:

> They have proved themselves excellent, and everyone is enthusiastic about them. They have been employed both as support artillery and as anti-tank vehicles. In the latter role their armament combined with their low silhouette, which aided concealment, and made them a valuable weapon, admired equally by the enemy in his own official reports.

Over the winter, the Italians also restructured their armoured divisions as a result of their experiences during 1941. They had recognized the relative weakness of the current division in terms of anti-tank and other artillery, and now sought to increase their striking power in numbers of guns while reducing their total establishment. The intention was to produce a leaner and stronger division with fewer useless mouths to feed and, almost as important, to transport. Thus in spite of a reduction in manpower, the new 1942 North African Armoured Division would be stronger than its predecessor since it had more powerful artillery support. The new division had a smaller complement of 6,500 officers and men, but it had additional firepower: twelve more 105mm artillery pieces, eight brand new 90mm AA guns – the Italian equivalent of the German 88mm and just as deadly in an anti-tank role – six more 47mm anti-tank guns, twenty-six more 20mm AA guns, and twenty-four new *Semoventi*. This represented a significant increase in strength for the armoured division.

In May 1942, newly promoted General Ettore Baldassare, the former commander of the *Ariete*, assumed command of the new XX Motorized Corps. It consisted of *Ariete* Armoured Division, now under General Giuseppe De Stefanis, a fifty-seven-year-old artillery officer, with General Francesco Arena as his deputy; and *Trieste* Motorized Division, now under General Arnaldo Azzi. Its constituent divisions had been significantly restructured and reinforced, following the losses suffered during the winter battles, and they were now better equipped and more effective than ever before. In addition, a second armoured division, 133 *Littorio* Armoured Division, under General Bitossi, had arrived in January and was currently acclimatizing to the new theatre. There were a total of 228 tanks, almost all the marginally improved M14/41 model, with the two Italian armoured divisions in Africa. The *Ariete* had 138 M14 tanks and twenty-four *Semoventi*, and *Littorio*, with only two rather than three armoured battalions, had ninety M14s.

The Axis forces now faced an entirely new challenge at Gazala, a fixed enemy defence line protected by barbed wire and extensive minefields similar to those of World War I. It was manned by infantry brigades, supported by artillery and some infantry support tanks, arranged in a series of fortified 'boxes'. This line was to be supported by armoured forces concentrated behind it to prevent Axis armour from encircling the individual boxes. It was a formidable defensive position that sought to deprive Rommel of his freedom of action and force him into a battle of attrition against superior British forces. Unfortunately, it had some weaknesses that Rommel could exploit. It was open to outflanking in the south, and although armour had been positioned to cover this, any failure in its co-ordination or concentration would provide opportunities to the Axis armour. In addition, many of the infantry 'boxes' were isolated and unable to support each other, particularly in the central and southern sectors of the line. This meant that they could be isolated and destroyed individually, especially if the supporting armour was either distracted or eliminated. Indeed, this feature of the British 'boxes' calls to mind Graziani's disastrous

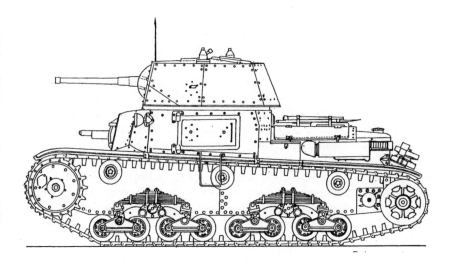

M14/41 medium tank. (Ian W. Walker)

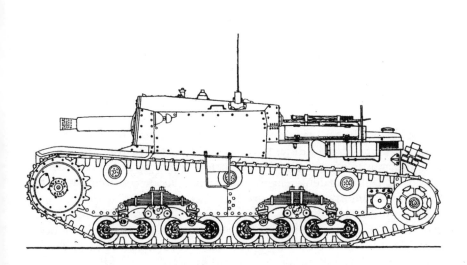

Semovente da 75/18. (Ian W. Walker)

camps around Sidi Barrani in 1940.

It was, indeed, Rommel's intention to exploit the open southern flank of the Gazala line in the confident assumption that his superior manoeuvrability would enable him first to defeat the British armour, and then to isolate and destroy their infantry piecemeal. He planned to launch a feint attack in the north with his infantry, powerfully supported by artillery, to distract the British and draw their armour northwards. In order to reinforce the impression that this was his main thrust, he borrowed tanks from the Axis armoured divisions, including an armoured battalion from *Ariete*. They would advance in the north, creating as much dust as possible, before turning back after dark to rejoin their divisions at Rotunda Segnali for the main assault in the south.

On 26 May, the Axis deception operation in the north commenced, with small numbers of tanks from *Ariete* and *DAK* moving forwards in support of the Axis infantry. The armoured forces were accompanied by aero engines mounted on lorries, which stirred up enough dust to simulate the movement of large numbers of vehicles. The main objective of these forces was to be as visible as possible in order to persuade the British that this was the main offensive. Although carried out with considerable dash, this elaborate deception failed completely to distract the British, who already knew from Ultra that the main attack would occur in the south.

In the south the real plan was for *DAK*, including 15 and 21 Panzer, XX Motorized Corps, including *Ariete* and *Trieste*, and 90 Light Division to set off from their forming-up area at Rotunda Segnali, and make a wide wheel around the southern end of the Gazala line. They would then turn north behind the British positions and advance to the coast, effectively isolating the British infantry in their fortified 'boxes' from their armoured support and their supplies in Tobruk. In the final hours before the attack, Axis intelligence detected a previously unidentified 'box' at Bir Hacheim and some British armour immediately behind the southern end of the Gazala line. This new information about enemy forces, directly in the path of the planned Axis advance, caused a last-minute adjustment to their plans: the Germans were ordered further south to deal with the British armour, while XX Corps was to capture Bir Hacheim before following *DAK* northwards to the coast. Unfortunately, reliable intelligence about the strength of this position was almost completely absent.

Early on 26 May, the Axis mobile forces set out from Rotunda Segnali under cover of a fierce sandstorm, and almost immediately their plans began to go awry in the fog of war. *Trieste* had not received notice of the late change in plans, and proceeded according to the original until it ran headlong into minefields to the north of Bir Hacheim. It then spent most of the day slowly clearing a narrow passage through these under close observation and artillery fire from 150 British Infantry Brigade in their 'box'

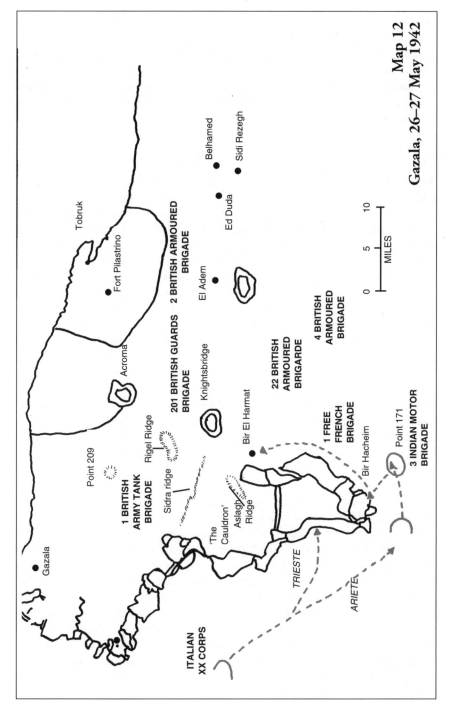

Map 12
Gazala, 26–27 May 1942

to the north. In the meantime *Ariete*, which had no idea where *Trieste* had gone, continued southwards in line with *DAK* and the revised plan. At 20:00hr, British patrols to the south of Bir Hacheim reported the approach of enemy columns, and these were closely shadowed as they turned around the southern end of the Gazala line. This was the full armoured might of the Axis, consisting of *Ariete*, *DAK* and 90 Light Division, estimated to contain 10,000 vehicles of all kinds.

Point 171

At 06:00hr on 27 May, M14s of *Ariete* under De Stefanis were the first Axis forces into action. They were deployed with 8 Armoured Battalion under Colonel Enrico Maretti on the right, and 9 Armoured Battalion under Colonel Pasquale Prestisimone on the left in the vanguard. They were followed by 10 Armoured Battalion under Major Luigi Pinna in reserve with 8 *Bersaglieri* Regiment. The leading armoured battalions reported running into 'a big enemy stronghold', which they assumed to be their intended objective of Bir Hacheim. In fact it was another position that Axis intelligence had failed to spot, held by 3 Indian Motor Brigade to the south of Bir Hacheim. The Indians had only recently occupied this area around a rise, known as Point 171, and were not yet fully dug in. They were well equipped with artillery, but had only thirty of their full complement of sixty-four 2pdr anti-tank guns. They were capable nevertheless of disrupting the Italian advance. At 06:30hr, a large concentration of soft-skinned vehicles from *Ariete* was fired on by the Indian artillery and rapidly dispersed. The Italian M14s were quickly deployed for an attack, and an alarmed Brigadier Filose of 3 Indian Motor Brigade nervously reported that he was facing 'a whole bloody German (sic) armoured division', and called for armoured support.

At 07:30hr, De Stefanis ordered 132 Armoured Regiment to mount an immediate assault on this position, which he assumed was Bir Hacheim. In spite of heavy enemy artillery fire, an assault force of sixty M14s was drawn up, supported by *Ariete*'s available artillery and its excellent 90mm anti-tank guns. The advancing Italian M14s encountered a force of Bren carriers emerging from Point 171, which were swiftly destroyed. The Italians then drove straight through the hurriedly constructed positions of the 18 Indian Cavalry Battalion before emerging on the other side. A second wave of M14s, estimated by the nervous Indians at '200 (sic) tanks', overran the neighbouring positions of 2 Royal Lancers shortly afterwards, although these were, once again, wrongly identified as Germans. The leading 8 and 9 Armoured Battalions then resumed their interrupted advance by turning northwards. They left the mopping up to 10 Armoured Battalion and supporting *Bersaglieri*, although a short delay in their arrival allowed Filose and some of his men to escape.

The ferocious action was described by Lieutenant Coglitore of 12 *Bersaglieri* Battalion:

> We of 12 Battalion are all on the ground not far from our truck. Suddenly a large number of armoured cars and *Semoventi* advance from our position and decisively attack the enemy stronghold, starting a furious battle. Dust, smoke, clanking, track noise and grenade explosions fill the air. Some tanks are already on fire, while others are advancing further and further. This is the scene that meets our eyes in the early hours of the morning. Our M13 tanks are by this time quite far from our waiting area, but we notice that several have already reached and broken through the enemy defences. We are surprised and wonder why we *Bersaglieri* are still staying put.
>
> The enemy reacts strongly with all its firepower, hitting and immobilizing other tanks, but the remaining tanks keep advancing and overcome all obstacles. . . From the combat zone, however, some M13s are turning back, still managing to move slowly even under enemy fire. They have dead and wounded aboard, some of them seriously hurt. They stop a short distance from us, where other wounded and fallen soldiers have been collected from the battlefield by vehicles from the tank regiment. They are unforgettable sights of how much the human body can be mutilated. The wounded are entrusted to the ambulances, while the dead are to be buried on the spot, and quickly because at any moment the division is sure to recommence the advance. All this is happening while the fighting is going on.
>
> Suddenly an order is shouted: '*Bersaglieri* forward! Quickly! Move out!' In a lash we all jump aboard the lorries that already have their engines running, and speed off quickly in open formation. Having crossed the battlefield, strewn with the carcasses of our tanks, some of them pouring with thick columns of black smoke, we jump out and run at the enemy with weapons at the ready. They come out of their holes and put their hands up in a sign of surrender.

In a little over half an hour it was all over, with the Indians acknowledging forty-one officers and 453 men killed, and 600 prisoners taken.

The *War Diary* of *Ariete* reported these events rather more prosaically:

> . . . at 07:10 [we] overcame with a rush the very strong enemy reaction, the *Ariete* tanks penetrating deeply into the enemy position. The garrison, composed of coloured and Congolese (sic) troops, surrendered for the most part [including] about 1,000 men and one general and three colonels.

In fact the general referred to here was seventy-two-year-old Admiral Sir Walter Cowan, a famous hero of World War I, who somewhat reluctantly surrendered to Major Pinna of 10 Armoured Battalion. *Ariete* itself admitted to having lost thirty dead, six missing and forty wounded in this short but sharp encounter. It was reported the next day that twenty-five Italian M14 tanks were found abandoned on the field, twenty-three completely burnt out. In spite of these losses, this early success by the Italian armour boosted Italian morale enormously.

Bir Hacheim

The Italians now learned from their captives that the post they had stormed was not in fact Bir Hacheim, so they immediately turned north towards their original objective in high spirits, expecting to deal with it just as successfully. However, it would prove a much more formidable obstacle, a well prepared and well camouflaged position, built for all-round defence. It was garrisoned by 1 Free French Brigade under General Koenig, with 3,600 men and thirty-six Bren carriers, supported by twenty-four French 75mm guns, a couple of British 25pdr guns and forty-four mortars; these were all ensconced behind more than 50,000 carefully planted mines. They also had a formidable array of anti-tank guns, including forty-six anti-tank rifles, eighteen Hotchkiss 25mm, seven captured Italian 47mm, and eighteen 40mm Bofors AA guns. They would not present such an easy target as 3 Indian Motor Brigade.

During the approach, the Italian 9 Armoured Battalion, under its Sicilian commander Colonel Prestisimone, veered to the left and became separated from the rest of *Ariete* for reasons that remain unclear. Prestisimone had lost his own command tank, with its reliable vehicle compass and radio, in the encounter with 3 Indian Motor Brigade, and may simply have strayed off course. Whatever the reason, at 08:15hr, 9 Battalion found themselves immediately in front of the barbed wire of the French positions at Bir Hacheim. The latter had been stood to since the early hours and were fully aware of numerous vehicle movements to the south. They initially believed that these were British, but realized their mistake when they saw them adopt assault formation. They then quickly recognized them as Italian M14s of *Ariete*, and were therefore fully prepared for the imminent attack.

At 09:00hr, Colonel Prestisimone's battalion of fifty M14 tanks charged directly at the French position, completely unaware that it was protected by dense minefields, unlike that of the Indian Brigade that had been breached so easily only hours before. This first attack struck the French defences soon afterwards with considerable panache and penetrated their minefield and barbed wire. In the process, a large number of M14s were lost to mines and French anti-tank guns, including Prestisimone's second mount of the day. In spite of these losses, six M14s managed to run the gauntlet and break into the main French positions. They bore down on a French company command post and one put a shell into it from only 15yd away. A French officer burnt the company standard to prevent its imminent capture, but some French 75mm guns engaged the tanks at close range and destroyed all but one. This last survivor was immediately attacked by French legionnaires, who leapt onto its hull and killed the crew by firing revolvers through the observation slits.

Undaunted, the Italians mounted a second attack almost immediately, with thirty M14s again under Prestisimone in his third tank of the morning. This assault met with even less success, coming to grief on the minefields and failing to breach the French positions. In the process Prestisimone lost his third and last tank and was wounded before falling into French hands. In the face of such unexpectedly strong resistance from well entrenched and well armed troops, and because of the loss of their commander, 9 Battalion finally withdrew shortly after 10:00hr. They had lost a total of thirty-one M14 tanks and a single *Semovente* in these attacks, seven of these being claimed by a single French 75mm gun. The Italians suffered 124 casualties, including sixty prisoners, one of them the bold but rash Prestisimone. Ironically, one wounded Italian was captured by three foreign legionnaires who turned out to be fellow Venetians! In return only a single Frenchman had been wounded. This attack, although pressed with great determination, had been decisively repulsed as a result of poor intelligence about the strength of the French positions. There were no further attacks on that day, as the Italians withdrew to regroup and reassess their options.

In the two major engagements of this hectic first day of the offensive, *Ariete* had lost nearly half of its original tank strength, a total of fifty-five M14 tanks. It had also been significantly delayed and was now urgently needed to the north, where *DAK* and 90 Light had advanced north towards the coast and clashed heavily with British armour. But they found themselves isolated in the rear of the Gazala line, badly in need of support and supplies, and under attack by strong British armoured forces. They were also cut off from their supply echelons that lay at Bir el Harmat to their south. As a result, De Stefanis abandoned plans for further, better planned assaults on Bir Hacheim and ordered *Ariete* north to link up with *DAK*. They reached Bir el Harmat at nightfall and provided welcome support for the vulnerable German supply units.

This first day of the Axis offensive had been one of mixed fortunes for *Ariete*. They had scored a swift early success over 3 Indian Motor Brigade, but had then received a damaging rebuff at the hands of the French in Bir Hacheim. The latter had been due to poor intelligence and poor preparation, rather than any Italian ineffectiveness. Indeed, this strong French position proved largely invulnerable to almost everything thrown against it. It would only fall two weeks later on 11 June, after it had been evacuated by its garrison. Although *Ariete* had suffered almost 50 per cent losses in tanks during these encounters, it remained in action and would still play a vital role in the Gazala battles.

Bir el Harmat

On the following day, 28 May, Rommel arrived at Baldassare's headquarters, set up at Bir el Harmat. He wanted *Ariete* to hasten northwards to complete the concentration of his scattered armour in preparation for anticipated British counter strokes. Immediately after breakfast, *Ariete* moved north to link up with *DAK* and 90 Light around Rigel Ridge. In the process, they escorted German supply echelons through a dangerous area under attack by British armour. In the late morning, 1 British Army Tank Brigade mounted a number of unco-ordinated attacks with Valentine tanks against Axis forces from the 'box' held by 150 Brigade to the west, some of which fell on the left flank of *Ariete*, inflicting some losses. They were, however, fairly easily repulsed by Italian artillery, and failed to prevent their movement northwards.

The British attacks might have been more effective if they had been properly co-ordinated with those of 2 British Armoured Brigade from the east. A mixed force of Grant and Crusader tanks from the latter attacked *Ariete*'s right flank during the early afternoon. In spite of the inferiority of their own M14 tanks and their reduced tank strength, the Italians fought back tenaciously and inflicted a number of losses on the British with their still potent artillery and 90mm guns. In the midst of this fighting, Rommel arrived with a German supply column and found himself under 'wild fire', which forced him to beat a hasty retreat until after dark. In the evening, British tanks managed to reach Bir el Harmat, but failed to deliver a fatal blow to *Ariete*, which had already moved north to join its German allies. The British subsequently withdrew to leaguer at nightfall, leaving Bir el Harmat to be reoccupied by 90 Light Division during the night.

In spite of an overall superiority in numbers and the superiority of their individual tanks, the British armour proved little more than a nuisance. They claimed that the engagements of this day had gone 'slightly in favour of the British'. This was an illusion, reinforced no doubt by the apparent withdrawal of the Axis armour before their attacks. They were unaware that this withdrawal was in line with Axis orders, rather than one forced on them by the British. The latter had failed not only to destroy the Axis armour, but also to prevent it concentrating behind the Gazala line. They had found it difficult enough to deal with individual Axis armoured units, and it could only be more difficult to cope with it in a single concentration. It needed co-ordinated action to prevent the concentration of Axis armour at Rigel Ridge – but this opportunity was lost.

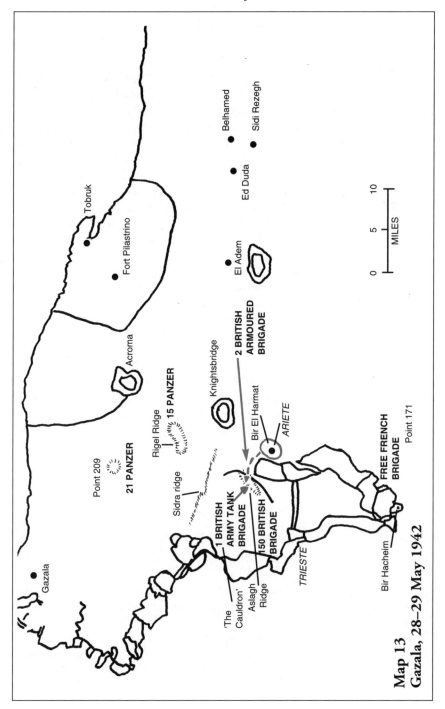

Map 13
Gazala, 28–29 May 1942

Tobruk

Fort Pilastrino

Acroma

Point 209

21 PANZER

Rigel Ridge

15 PANZER

Sidra ridge

Knightsbridge

1 BRITISH
ARMY TANK
BRIGADE

150 BRITISH
BRIGADE

'The
Cauldron'

Aslagh
Ridge

TRIESTE

Gazala

Bir El Harmat

2 BRITISH
ARMOURED
BRIGADE

ARIETE

El Adem

Ed Duda

Belhamed

Sidi Rezegh

FREE FRENCH
BRIGADE

Point 171

Bir Hacheim

0   5   10

MILES

Aslagh Ridge

On 29 May Rommel ordered the Axis armour to concentrate, and *Ariete* was directed to plug the gap between *DAK* on Rigel Ridge to the north and 90 Light Division at Bir el Harmat to the south. The Italians set off north at 08:00hr towards Aslagh Ridge, a small rise that would become all too familiar to them over the next week. At 11:00hr they found 2 Armoured Brigade in front of them, apparently in a last attempt to prevent them linking up with *DAK*. There was a brisk exchange of fire, but the British were already engaged with 15 Panzer to their north, and could not focus on the Italians. At midday, 2 Armoured found itself under attack from three sides, from 15 and 21 Panzer Divisions on Rigel Ridge to the north, and from *Ariete* pushing north towards Aslagh Ridge against its south-west flank. In spite of the arrival of 22 Armoured Brigade in support, the British were unable to prevent the Axis armour from meeting up. The action was ended by a violent sandstorm, and 2 Armoured Brigade, with only thirty tanks left, had no option but to withdraw.

The newly combined and re-supplied Axis armoured units were now concentrated in an area that would become known as 'The Cauldron'. It was a low-lying area immediately behind the Gazala line, boundeed by Rigel Ridge, Aslagh Ridge, Birel Harmat and a fortified 'box' held by 150 British Infantry Brigade. This had escaped Axis reconnaissance and now prevented Axis supply convoys breaching the British minefields to the west. By the evening of 29 May, Italian infantry from *Trieste* and *Brescia* Divisions had managed to clear a few narrow lanes through the minefields, one north and one south of 150 Brigade. Unfortunately, these lanes were subject to interdiction by British artillery fire and offered no more than a tenuous route for Axis supplies. It was vital that a secure supply route was opened up as soon as possible, but this could only be done if the Axis armour was left free from attack.

The encircled Axis armour fully expected to be attacked by strong British armour and infantry forces the next day. *Ariete* was now stationed along Aslagh Ridge facing east, the most likely direction from which an attack might originate, and De Stefanis made careful preparations to meet these anticipated assaults. He stationed 5 and 12 Battalions of 8 *Bersaglieri* Regiment with their 47mm anti-tank guns along the ridge itself. He constructed a strong anti-tank screen behind them with his 88mm, 90mm AA guns and some old 76mm Skoda guns. He kept 132 Armoured Regiment with its remaining M14s, from north to south 8, 9 and 10 Armoured Battalions, out of sight behind the ridge ready to counter-attack any breakthrough. In turn, the field guns of 132 Artillery Regiment were behind the tanks and could call on additional support from the combined artillery of XX Corps, *DAK* and 90 Light, if necessary. This strong position stood a good chance of opposing the full-scale British armoured counter-attack that appeared imminent.

On 30 May there were indeed some attacks from 2 Armoured Brigade on the positions occupied by *Ariete* on Aslagh Ridge. They commenced at 07:30hr, when without artillery preparation, enemy 'tanks came suddenly attacking ... firing with all guns', according to Lieutenant Calabresi, commander of 14 Artillery Battery. The Italian anti-tank screen proved highly effective, although it suffered heavy losses in the process. Its 31 Artillery Group lost forty-nine men and five 88mm guns, having fired no fewer than 1,748 rounds. At one point a British Crusader tank advanced to within 200yd of an Italian 88mm gun that was fast running out of ammunition. In spite of this desperate situation the crew continued to fire, and finally managed to stop the British tank in the nick of time. Calabresi was wounded in the leg during this action, and shortly thereafter was awarded the Iron Cross First Class by Rommel himself in the field hospital. The British armoured attacks were successfully repulsed.

Unexpectedly, there followed five crucial days during which *Ariete* was left unmolested while the Allied armour undertook little more than patrol activity. On 31 May, for example, 2 Armoured Brigade spent the day watching their 25pdr guns shelling a line of Italian M14 tanks that appeared on the skyline of Aslagh Ridge. Otherwise they devoted themselves to reorganizing and replenishing their disorganized units. It seemed that De Stefanis' resolute defence on 30 May had given the British pause for thought. A severe sandstorm on 2 June cloaked much of the battlefield, although it did not prevent artillery exchanges. The British frittered away valuable time in complete inaction while the Axis forces set about improving their own position in a methodical fashion.

In this same period, *DAK* crushed 150 Brigade and secured Axis supply lines from the west behind the effective shield provided by *Ariete*. In the south, *Trieste* and 90 Light Divisions completed the investment of the isolated French at Bir Hacheim. The success of these well-targeted actions transformed the shape of the battle. It was no longer a contest apparently destined to end in Axis failure and destruction, but one that was at least evenly balanced if not tipping slightly in favour of the Axis. In this process *Ariete* performed a vital, if largely unacknowledged role by securing the German rear while they dealt with 150 Brigade.

'The Cauldron'

It was not until 5 June that the British were finally able to organize a major counter stroke against the Axis armour in 'The Cauldron'. The plan called for 9 and 10 Indian Brigades to attack the positions held by *Ariete* under cover of darkness with heavy artillery support. They would open a path through which 22 Armoured Brigade could penetrate the Italian anti-tank screen and destroy the isolated Axis armoured forces. It was a sound plan, but it was simply too late, since *DAK* had already completed the destruction of 150 Brigade and opened up a supply route. They were also completely free to support *Ariete*. In addition, the proposed command arrangements for this attack were nothing short of chaotic, with command of 9 and 10 Indian and 22 Armoured Brigades split between two divisions. The corps commander was the only person in a position to issue instructions to both infantry and armour and co-ordinate their actions. This was in sharp contrast to the Axis situation, where *Ariete*, for example, included all arms, and close co-operation between them under the authority of De Stefanis was straightforward.

The British assault commenced at 02:50hr with a heavy artillery bombardment; this, however, fell on some abandoned forward posts well short of *Ariete*'s main defences – indeed, De Stefanis signalled at this point that he could discern no signs of an enemy attack. Ten minutes later 10 Indian Brigade advanced and occupied its objectives without opposition – the same abandoned forward posts. It was not until 2 Highland Light Infantry of 10 Indian Brigade advanced to the area of Bir et Tamar that they were pinned down by heavy artillery, mortar and machine-gun fire from *Ariete*'s real positions. In spite of this, the Scots managed to push 8 *Bersaglieri* Regiment off part of Aslagh Ridge after a fierce struggle. However, 2 West Yorkshires from 9 Indian Brigade, who were supposed to exploit this breach, were stopped by intense artillery fire only 1,200yd (1,000m) further on. As dawn broke there was no sign of 22 Armoured Brigade, and *Ariete* continued to shell the British lodgement for the rest of the day. At 07:30hr the West Yorkshires found themselves facing a 'German' counter-attack involving forty tanks and seventeen armoured cars. This menacing development caused the Allies to call off their offensive soon afterwards, and attempt to consolidate their increasingly precarious hold on Bir et Tamar. In mid-morning Italian M14 tanks from *Ariete* overran one company of the West Yorkshires, and the rest were ordered to withdraw at nightfall to prevent the same happening to them.

In the meantime 22 Armoured Brigade, with a mixture of 156 Grant, Stuart and Crusader tanks, had set out at dawn and penetrated a few miles into the Axis positions further north. Here, however, they encountered 15 Panzer Division and came under heavy German artillery fire from Sidra Ridge; during this encounter they lost sixty tanks. They fell back behind 2 Highland Light Infantry, still holding on near Bir et Tamar, and were then ordered to hold their ground. In the early afternoon, *Ariete* and 21 Panzer Divisions mounted a series of counter-attacks against Bir et Tamar, and these gradually increased in strength. They eventually forced the remnants of 10 Indian, which had suffered heavy casualties, to withdraw from Aslagh

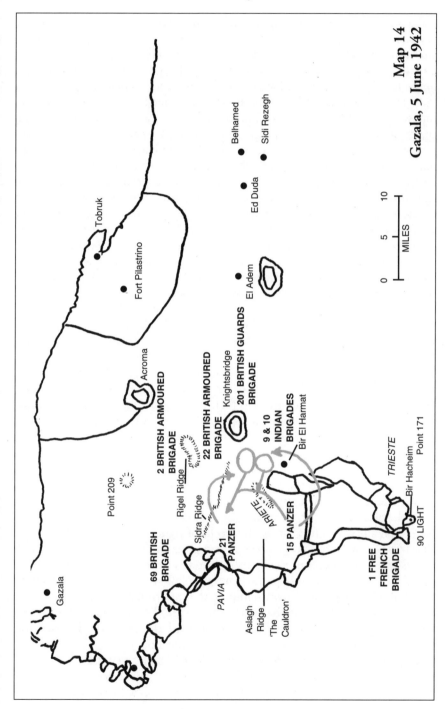

Map 14
Gazala, 5 June 1942

Ridge. These received no support from the nearby 22 Armoured, which appeared to interpret the order to 'hold its ground' quite literally. In mid-afternoon the remnants of 10 Indian and 22 Armoured Brigades were strung out along the extreme eastern edge of Aslagh Ridge, desperately holding on in the face of Axis armoured attacks and continuous artillery fire.

In the late afternoon Rommel prepared a general counter-attack for the following day. This would involve *Ariete* and 21 Panzer striking eastwards against the British still on Aslagh Ridge, while 15 Panzer Division passed through a gap in the minefields south of Bir el Harmat and then turned north to attack their southern flank. As luck would have it, this plan would be facilitated by some fatal errors in British dispositions. At dusk, 22 Armoured Brigade pulled its surviving tanks back 7 miles (11km) to leaguer for the night, which effectively abandoned the infantry still clinging on to Aslagh Ridge to their own devices. The minefield gap which 15 Panzer intended to use to pass into the British rear was virtually undefended, being covered by a single infantry battalion without artillery or anti-tank guns. Thus at nightfall, Aslagh Ridge was held by little more than the weak remnants of 10 Indian Brigade. They were doomed.

At dawn on 6 June, the powerful Axis counter stroke fell on the depleted British forces, and they were almost completely destroyed. Nevertheless, they gave a good account of themselves and went down fighting. Major Count Marco Folchi-Vici, an artillery officer attached to *Ariete*, described how a troop of 25pdr guns held out until only a single gunner remained, who continued to fire the four surviving guns in succession. The Axis tank crews surrounding him briefly held their fire to allow him to surrender with honour, but when he continued to fire they concentrated on his position and overran it. The body of this unknown hero and those of his comrades were later buried with full military honours. The British armour once again played little part in the action: 22 Armoured Brigade observed some Italian M14 tanks to their south, which were shelled and dispersed; but otherwise they made no effort to assist their infantry.

In the aftermath of this crucial action, Rommel recorded a rare tribute to his Italian allies, noting that 'in the weeks of fighting round Knightsbridge, the *Ariete* – covered, it is true, by German guns and tanks – had fought well against every onslaught of the British, although their casualties had not been light.' This rather grudging praise is nevertheless an important indication of the vital role played by *Ariete* in holding the eastern face of 'The Cauldron'. They prevented any British interference with the vital German actions against 150 Brigade, which effectively secured the Axis supply lines and punched a hole through the centre of the Gazala line.

On 8 June, *Ariete* reported seventy M14 tanks on strength, having been reinforced after its early losses on 27 May. It now spent over a week in its positions on Aslagh Ridge, while the other Axis mobile forces destroyed the rest of the Gazala line. On 11 June, *Trieste* and 90 Light Divisions at last occupied Bir Hacheim, which had finally been evacuated by the French, after an intense and prolonged struggle. This completed the destruction of the southern half of the Gazala line and secured the Axis supply routes. At long last Rommel could turn his attention to a resumption of his original offensive plans. On 13 June he initiated a series of operations designed to reach the coast and cut off the British forces still holding the northern half of the Gazala line, and to isolate Tobruk. The following day, 21 Panzer drove northwards to the coast, and 90 Light and *Trieste* were sent towards El Adem to outflank Tobruk. Meanwhile *Ariete* remained stationed on Aslagh Ridge to protect the Axis supply lines against the remnants of the British armour. But the Axis advance to the coast came too late to encircle the British forces in the Gazala line, which extricated themselves in the nick of time, leaving the Axis trap almost completely empty.

In mid-June, between the end of the fighting around the Gazala line and the encirclement of Tobruk, British long-range reconnaissance forces reported sighting tank reinforcements moving up from Tripoli on the coastal highway. This was 133 *Littorio* Armoured Division which had been undertaking training and acclimatization in Tripolitania since January; it was under the command of a pioneer of the Italian armoured units, General Gervasio Bitossi, with General Emilio Becuzzi as his deputy, and was finally moving up to the front and into action at Rommel's urgent request. On 16 June, *Ariete* was brought forward from Aslagh Ridge to protect the rear of 90 Light while it attacked 29 Indian Brigade at El Adem. Accordingly, *Ariete* advanced south-eastwards to support the screening German reconnaissance forces that were under severe pressure from 7 British Motor Brigade, attempting to relieve the Indians. Thereafter *Ariete* continued to move east, pushing 7 Motor Brigade back as far as Sidi Rezegh. It was then recalled on 18 June as part of the Axis preparations for the climactic assault on Tobruk.

Tobruk 1942

On 18 June, *Trieste* effectively completed the isolation of Tobruk by cutting the coast road to the east of the port. It was also on this day that Rommel issued orders for the attack on this fortress, which had eluded him throughout 1941. He planned to rectify previous errors and send the full weight of the available Axis armour against a narrow sector of the south-east perimeter held by 11 Indian Brigade. The assault would be supported by heavy artillery and air bombardment, and once a breach was secured it would be exploited towards Fort Pilastrino and the harbour. The plan called for the Italian XX Corps under Baldassare, its two component divisions reunited at last, to break through a sector of the perimeter between Redoubts 49 and 57. In the six months since December 1941, the defences

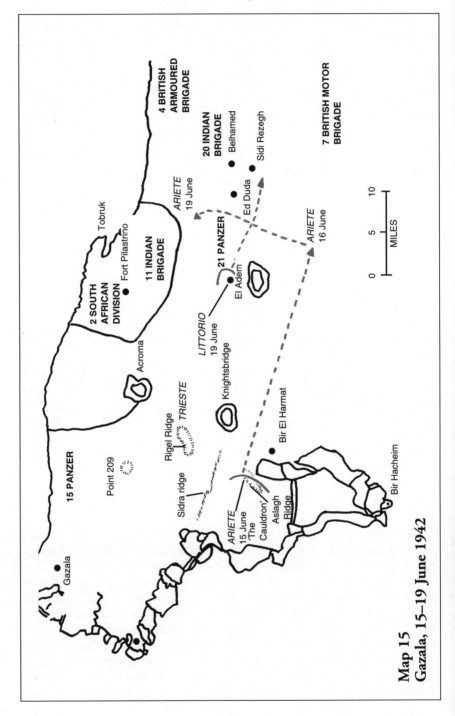

**Map 15
Gazala, 15–19 June 1942**

of Tobruk had lost much of their effectiveness, through the removal of its barbed wire and mines for use in the Gazala line. The desert winds had covered up many trenches and dugouts, and several sections of anti-tank ditch had silted up. It was no longer the tough nut that had defied all Rommel's efforts the year before – indeed, almost until the last minute the British had not intended to hold it at all: it was political interference that forced them to hold it against their better judgement.

The new *Littorio* under Bitossi had now arrived at the front and would be stationed south-east of Tobruk near El Adem, where its role would be limited by its weak state. It was somewhat understrength, consisting of 133 Armoured Regiment, with only two armoured battalions, 12 and 51, rather than three; 12 *Bersaglieri* Regiment under Colonel Amoroso with only two motorized battalions; and 133 Artillery Regiment with only a residue of its normal establishment of artillery pieces. It had surrendered a fair proportion of its tanks and artillery to replace losses in *Ariete* and *Trieste*, and had donated most of its motor transport to the central pool used to transport the non-motorized Italian infantry. On arrival at the front, *Littorio* was deficient in artillery and armour, and had no integral engineer units or supply echelon. It was only because Rommel insisted that its presence was essential that the Italians reluctantly sent it forward at all. Its task would be to protect the rear of the Axis assault forces from any interference.

On 19 June the Axis forces moved into their starting positions for the assault on Tobruk. *Ariete* Division was returning from Sidi Rezegh after driving off 7 Motor Brigade. The assault was planned for early the following morning, but to preserve the element of surprise the Axis forces would only move into their final positions shortly before dawn. It was reported that *Ariete* had eighty M14 tanks available for this attack – about half of its full establishment. This followed a very busy period for the Italian repair and recovery teams on the recent battlefields. Its infantry and artillery had also suffered losses in the recent battles. The sector of the defences facing *Ariete*, between Redoubts 49 to 57, was held by 2 Cameron Highlanders, with 800 men and six 6pdr anti-tank guns, supported by four batteries of artillery.

At dawn on 20 June *Ariete* reached its start positions on the Axis left next to *DAK*, and exactly on cue, at 05:20hr, the Axis air and artillery bombardments commenced. *Ariete* began its own assault at 07:45hr, and initially this proceeded according to plan. In a little over an hour they penetrated the minefields and outer defences as far as the anti-tank ditch, which was fully 6ft (2m) deep at this point and represented a serious obstacle to armoured vehicles. At 09:00hr *Ariete*'s advanced engineer teams reported having crossed the ditch and reached the wire in front of Redoubt 53. They then came under heavy defensive fire, and many of the attacking *Bersaglieri* were caught and killed in the open. Count Folchi-Vici reported that the British 6pdr anti-tank guns were highly effective against the Italian

M14s. It seems that the Scots had escaped the worst of the Axis preparatory bombardments, which mainly fell on the Indian troops in front of *DAK* on the right.

In spite of some isolated advances, *Ariete* was unable to make much more significant progress, and an hour later 15 Panzer on their immediate right were complaining that the Italians were still at the anti-tank ditch. The resistance was patchy but ferocious, and Count Folchi-Vici considered that there were too few defenders to cover the ground adequately; thus the pockets of fierce resistance had each to be enveloped and eliminated in turn. At noon *Ariete* reported that it had suffered heavy casualties, but that it would renew the assault after further artillery preparation. In the early afternoon, 15 Panzer again complained about Italian lack of progress, but conceded that *Ariete* had captured Redoubt 54 from 'the English (sic)'. The pressure exerted by *Ariete* had nevertheless been sufficient to cause the Scots to request armoured support; but this was denied as a result of a German breakthrough further east.

While *Ariete* struggled, *DAK* had successfully penetrated the Tobruk defences, but was meeting increasingly stiff resistance, particularly from British artillery at Fort Pilastrino. The capture of Pilastrino had originally been allocated to *Ariete*, but its delayed appearance meant that 15 Panzer

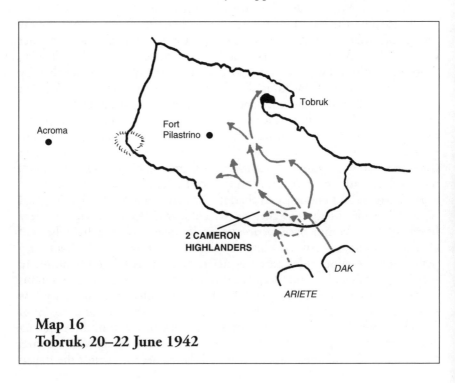

Map 16
Tobruk, 20–22 June 1942

was allocated this as an additional objective. This does much to explain the frequent German complaints about the slow progress of their Italian ally! They were so anxious for *Ariete* to assist them that at 15:15hr, De Stefanis ordered *Ariete* to move to the right in order to pass around the still defiant Scots and enter the fortress through the breach already secured by its German allies. A number of South African prisoners recalled seeing Italian tanks entering the fortress as they were led out into captivity. By late afternoon *Ariete* was finally inside the perimeter and turning westwards behind the Scots. The stubborn defence by the Camerons not only kept *Ariete* at bay, but severely disrupted Rommel's plan.

As Tobruk fell into Axis hands at last, *Littorio* was deployed in a fan-shaped formation to the south-east and was playing an important role in blocking any British relief attempts. At 18:45hr, Bitossi reported moderately heavy artillery fire from 7 Motor Brigade directed against *Littorio's* artillery emplacements. The Italians returned this fire while their M14 tanks staged demonstrations to hint at counter-attacks, although they were too weak to risk any actual confrontations. Fortunately this artillery exchange proved to be the maximum extent of the British relief effort, and *Littorio* suffered no inconvenience from this. The performance of *Littorio* in this limited mission must have been impressive, since 7 Motor Brigade reported that it had been 'held off by considerable enemy forces'. This flattering report would certainly have pleased Bitossi, had he known of it.

On the following day, 21 June, General Klopper, commander of Tobruk, surrendered to *DAK*. In spite of this, some units continued to fight on, and *Ariete* was preoccupied with mopping-up operations. It was now inside the perimeter and still engaged with the stubborn Camerons, who refused to accept the orders to surrender as genuine. Instead, they had formed all-round defensive positions in expectation of an attack from within the fortress. At 08:00hr *Ariete* sent three M14s forward from the direction of Tobruk to approach the hastily organized Scots' positions. They were within a couple of hundred yards when a single, well concealed 6pdr anti-tank gun knocked out all of them, and the infantry picked off their crews as they bailed out. The Italians subsequently lost another three M14s in the same way. A seventh M14 appeared with an officer in the open turret, who vainly searched for the concealed gun through binoculars until he was shot dead and his tank blown up. At 13:00hr *Ariete* reported that its armour was meeting 'strong enemy resistance', including anti-tank, machine-gun and mortar fire. It therefore called for concentric artillery fire on the enemy positions from both inside and outside the fortress. In spite of this the Camerons held out for a second day and only surrendered next morning, 22 June, when threatened with bombardment by the entire Axis artillery.

The dramatic fall of Tobruk left the road into Egypt open to the Axis forces for the first time. It also brought with it some 30,000 prisoners, but more importantly an immense haul of booty. It is estimated that they captured half a million gallons of fuel, three million rations, 7,000 tons of water, 130,000 rounds of artillery shells and 2,000 motor transport vehicles. This was enough to meet Axis requirements in these key areas for the immediate future at least. This double bonus made it possible for Rommel to contemplate an immediate invasion of Egypt, and it was a golden opportunity that he was only too eager to exploit. He found the siren call of the Nile and the Suez Canal impossible to resist, and would soon launch the Axis army on its final quest for glory.

In the fighting around the Gazala line *Ariete* had largely confirmed its reputation as a tough fighting force. On the opening day of the new offensive it had suffered a significant success, but then a notable, if understandable, reverse at Bir Hacheim. Nevertheless it went on to play a key role in the battles around 'The Cauldron' that broke the Gazala line. It played an important, if less distinguished, role in the fall of Tobruk. But throughout this fighting its strength slowly ebbed away, and it was about to face its greatest challenge in its weakest condition.

6
The Mirage of the Nile

During the planning of the Gazala offensive, Rommel had accepted that, if Tobruk fell, Axis resources would be switched to an invasion of Malta. This would lead to the permanent elimination of that island's potential to interfere with supply convoys to North Africa. On 22 June 1942, Tobruk fell – but Rommel was reluctant to abandon his own plans in favour of a Malta invasion. He had tasted victory and was eager to press his advantage and capture Alexandria and Cairo while the British were off balance. Axis resources in the Mediterranean would not stretch to supporting two major offensives simultaneously, and a choice had to be made. There had never been any real enthusiasm about the Malta invasion, especially amongst the Germans. It was widely believed – quite justifiably in view of British access to Ultra intelligence – that it would be at least as costly as the invasion of Crete in 1941. There was also a strong feeling that air bombardment had already neutralized Malta by 10 May, and that an invasion was no longer necessary. In the end, this crucial decision proved easy to take.

But this decision has been criticized as ultimately fatal to Axis prospects in Egypt and beyond. This criticism is unfair, however, since Rommel had only a slim chance of reaching Cairo, and almost none of getting further. This slim chance, he realized, lay in chasing the British into Egypt and attempting to rush their defences before they had a chance to catch their breath. If instead he had halted for two or three months until Malta fell, as it probably would have done at however great a cost, he would have found himself facing heavily reinforced British forces firmly entrenched at Alamein. He would have been faced with fighting an Alam Halfa rather than a First Alamein. He certainly would have had a chance to restore his own forces from their weakened state, but only to the level allowed by the capacity of the Libyan ports and the long road to Egypt. In contrast, the British would have won any contest of reinforcement and supply, and massively expanded their own forces. In these circumstances any Axis invasion of Egypt in September 1942 would have failed. The securing of Axis supply lines around Malta might have postponed a British breakthrough at Alamein, but it could not have prevented it. The overwhelming superiority of the Allies would have triumphed regardless of any additional supplies reaching Rommel, since the priority of the Eastern

Front meant that it would never be more than a trickle. In the best possible case, Rommel would have held on at Alamein only until the Allied landings in French North Africa in November 1942 forced him to retreat to protect his rear.

On 23 June, the plans for a Malta invasion were scrapped and Rommel was given a free hand, and he immediately ordered an advance into Egypt. But it was a tired and depleted Axis force that drove into Egypt in the scorching summer heat of 1942; it was also unlikely to be substantially re-equipped or reinforced in the near future. It had, however, been boosted by recent victories over superior British forces, and was running on the adrenalin of success as well as captured fuel supplies. In what condition were the Italian armoured divisions, *Ariete* and *Littorio*, at this point? They had been operating for almost a month without interruption, and their numbers had been severely reduced by losses from breakdown and enemy action. They had no more than 1,000 men each from an original establishment of 6,500 and 189 tanks. *Ariete* had thirty-four M14 tanks, fifty field guns, twenty armoured cars and 100 lorries, while the relatively fresh *Littorio* was slightly better off with sixty M14 tanks. They had also lost their pristine peacetime appearance due to their recent experiences.

They had attempted to improve their situation by introducing a high proportion of captured vehicles and equipment into their establishments. The rate of breakdowns and losses in recent operations had proved significantly higher than the rate of repair and re-supply. In these circumstances they had been forced to utilize every stopgap available, and the recent victory at Tobruk had made a great deal of abandoned British equipment available to them. The Italian armoured divisions were therefore not only largely equipped with captured motor transport, but they were also making use of several highly prized 25pdr guns. The large stocks of uniforms captured in Tobruk, and the condition of their own, caused many to adopt various bits and pieces. It was therefore a rag-tag force that swept into Egypt in June 1942.

On 23 June, XX Corps, *Ariete*, *Littorio* and *Trieste*, under General Baldassare and fresh from the conquest of Tobruk, enveloped the British defences at the Egyptian frontier. It was a bold strategy for a force now reduced to about 3,600 infantry and ninety tanks – but the defences were empty, the British having already withdrawn to Mersa Matruh. The Axis forces faced increasing air attacks from Allied aircraft based in Egypt. XX Corps, advancing north of the railway, reported uninterrupted bombing attacks from mid-morning onwards, and was also bombed during the night. In the desert to the south, *Littorio* was forced to halt under intense air attack such as they had never previously experienced. The impact of constant strafing and bombing would be a major factor in the forthcoming fighting. A round-the-clock cycle of air attacks against the advancing Axis columns meant that the exhausted Axis forces would get little rest even at night.

On 25 June, Baldassare led XX Corps past Sidi Barrani and the previous high point of Axis conquest. They passed close to Nibeiwa where their predecessors had been annihilated in the open without even a chance to man their tanks. But there was no time now for memories as the relentless advance continued towards Mersa Matruh. It was a chaotic period of mad dashes to the east, interspersed with periods of waiting around as fuel ran out and the advance stopped until fresh supplies were brought forward. *Littorio* was immobilized by lack of fuel for most of 25 June. The skies were filled with Allied planes strafing and bombing any visible targets, stationary or not. The Axis forces frequently crossed paths with retreating British forces, at times without realizing it. The consequences were sometimes violent and the opponents clashed, but at other times they were so exhausted that there was a mutual understanding that they ignore each other until they were able to disentangle themselves.

Mersa Matruh

On 26 June Rommel issued orders for an immediate assault on the British forces at Mersa Matruh. The Italian XX Corps, with *Ariete* and *Trieste*, was ordered to support *DAK*, which would strike at the centre of the Allied position on either side of Minqar Qaim, while 90 Light would encircle Matruh itself. *Littorio* was placed in reserve ready to exploit any Axis breakthrough. At this point XX Corps reported its tank strength at only forty-four M14s as a result of breakdowns and losses to air attack. It was during the preliminaries for this attack that the Italians suffered a heavy blow. At 10:30hr, General Ettore Baldassare, commander of the XX Corps, was as usual well forward with his leading elements, urging them onwards. He was with a forward column from *Trieste* near Bir el Kanayis, travelling in two staff cars with General Guido Piacenza, his artillery commander, and Colonel Vittorio Raffaelli, his engineer commander. There had been reports that 7 British Armoured Division was in the area, and he intended to organize XX Corps to locate and attack them.

Only forty minutes later, a small formation of Allied fighter bombers appeared overhead, just like those that had been harassing Axis forces ever since they crossed the frontier. They quickly spotted the two staff cars and swung around to attack them. The Italian drivers took evasive action but the aircraft managed to straddle the cars with bombs and they were blown into the air. Piacenza was killed outright, and Raffaelli and Baldassare were mortally wounded, Raffaelli dying at the scene. Baldassare remained conscious and was transferred to the field hospital of the *Ariete*, his old command, which was nearby; but even with the best available medical attention, he was beyond help. Yet in spite of his condition, the fate of his

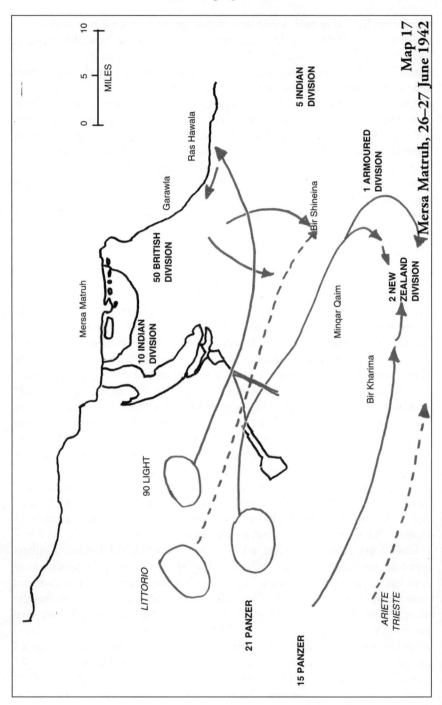

Map 17
Mersa Matruh, 26–27 June 1942

troops was his main concern. He summoned General Giuseppe De Stefanis, commander of *Ariete*, and surrendered XX Corps to him. He died at 14:00hr on 26 June 1942. The loss of these three important officers was a major blow to the Italians, particularly that of Baldassare, who had led them successfully through the battles of May and June.

There was little time for mourning, but Baldassare's death and the consequent reorganization of commands significantly delayed the progress of XX Corps. De Stefanis took over XX Corps and was replaced at *Ariete* by his deputy, General Francesco Arena. The Italians were late in arriving for Rommel's assault on Mersa Matruh, but they were not alone in this. The delays were caused by lack of fuel and air attacks, and *DAK* and XX Corps also clashed briefly with a concentration of British tanks from 4 British Armoured Brigade near Kanayis and together destroyed eighteen British tanks. At 17:00hr XX Corps was still west of Kanayis behind the right of 15 Panzer. The whole Axis advance did not actually begin until late evening.

The Axis attack on Matruh finally commenced at dawn on 27 June, with *Littorio* supporting 21 Panzer and 90 Light in the north, and XX Corps supporting 15 Panzer in the south. The southern prong was quickly blunted when 15 Panzer ran into 4 Armoured and 7 Motor Brigades on the Siwa track. XX Corps came up in support, and together they drove the British back to Bir Khalda in the afternoon. In the north meanwhile, 21 Panzer, with only twenty-one panzers, managed to get behind 5 New Zealand Brigade at Minqar Qaim, while 90 Light advanced round Mersa Matruh to cut the coast road beyond it, and *Littorio* reached Bir Shineina in support. The end of the day found Axis forces deep inside the British defences, but badly overstretched and isolated from one another. In the north, 90 Light was on the coast road, with *Littorio* more than 10 miles (16km) to the west and 21 Panzer another 5 miles (8km) to the south. In the south, 15 Panzer and XX Corps were another 5 miles (8km) to the west near Bir Khalda. The British appeared unaware of the desperate weakness of the Axis position and ordered their forces to withdraw to avoid encirclement. They did so that night, successfully reaching Fuka the next morning, except for the British X Corps in Matruh itself, which failed to receive the order and was left behind.

On 28 June, Rommel ordered his armour to pursue the retreating enemy without regard for the enemy forces in Matruh. They therefore set off to the east, leaving the overstretched Axis forces around Matruh even weaker. In the evening the British X Corps broke out of Mersa Matruh and straight through the weak encirclement presented by the widely dispersed Axis forces. This breakout was witnessed by Rommel, who was at Bir Shineina with *Littorio*. The 69 British Infantry Brigade burst through this area during the night in chaotic circumstances. Rommel described the scene:

A wild mêlée ensued, in which my own headquarters, which lay south of the fortress, became involved. Kampstaffel Kiehl and units of the *Littorio* joined in the fighting. The firing between my forces and the New Zealanders (sic) grew to an extraordinary pitch of violence, and my headquarters was soon ringed by burning vehicles, making it the target for continuous enemy fire. I soon had enough of this and ordered the headquarters and staff to withdraw to the south-east. One can scarcely conceive the confusion that reigned that night.

In the evening, 12 *Bersaglieri* Regiment of *Littorio* arrived to collect water from some wells near Wadi Nagannish. They were surprised to find ten armoured cars from 7 Armoured Division waiting in ambush, and were quickly surrounded and captured. But the rest of *Littorio* was short of water, and Bitossi ordered Lieutenant Umberto Musolino, commander of a section of *Carabinieri* or military police, to take a company of tanks and clear the wells. He succeeded in his task, driving off the British armoured cars and releasing the *Bersaglieri* from captivity.

On 29 June, Rommel sent 90 Light straight along the coast road to Fuka and El Daba with *Littorio* in close pursuit, and *DAK* and XX Corps through the desert to the south of the road. The Italian armoured divisions were now in a very poor state: *Ariete* had only ten M14s, fifteen artillery pieces and 600 *Bersaglieri*, while *Littorio* had a slightly better thirty M14s, eleven artillery pieces and 1,000 *Bersaglieri*. At one point during the day, Rommel found himself under machine-gun fire and fell back on to 90 Light – only to discover that *Littorio* was responsible. They had mistaken his captured vehicles for those of the retreating enemy, the sort of incident common during this period. After nightfall, *Littorio* headed south into the desert from the area around Fuka. It advanced in two columns: Bitossi with 51 Armoured Battalion of 133 Tank Regiment under Lieutenant Colonel Zappala was near the coast; and Becuzzi, his deputy, with 12 *Bersaglieri* Regiment under Colonel Amoroso, was further inland. The going was reasonably good, and the night was lit up at regular intervals by flares dropped by Allied aircraft looking for targets. There was no chance of avoiding observation as the race for Egypt continued apace.

First light on 30 June revealed that the desert between El Daba on the coast and the Qattara Depression in the south was scattered with Allied and Axis units. They were in no particular order, and knew little about their own location, and even less about where their opponents were. The confusion was immense, and the scope for unforeseen clashes enormous. In the early morning, XX Corps was thrown into complete confusion by an attack on its rear by 7 Motor Brigade, which had been hastening towards safety only to find their way blocked by the Italians. They hit out vigorously to break through, and then blocked the progress of XX corps, which described them as a fresh enemy 'against which attack was hopeless'. In normal circumstances this brigade should not have presented a challenge to a motorized corps, but the current circumstances were far from normal, with XX Corps reduced to fourteen tanks, thirty-eight artillery pieces, and fewer than 2,100 men. An exhausted, tense and increasingly desperate Rommel had little sympathy, and signalled De Stefanis: 'I demand that your Corps should carry out the attack, destroy the enemy and reach its objective. The enemy is under orders to withdraw.' He followed this up an hour later with the even more abrupt, 'Trust your Corps will now find itself able to cope with so contemptible an enemy.' This was an unnecessary and uncalled-for rebuke, and XX Corps managed to push 7 Motor Brigade aside later in the morning and continue east.

On the same morning, Bitossi's *Littorio* was south-west of El Daba, heading east in its two columns, when they clashed with 4 Armoured Brigade and suffered a worse disaster: at dawn, Zappala's 51 Armoured Battalion came under accurate and heavy artillery fire, during which he was mortally wounded, although he continued to command his men until he died. A large number of M14s were knocked out, including a number that burst into flames. *Carabinieri* Lieutenant Musolino knew the threat that enemy armour presented to *Littorio*'s vulnerable southern column, which had no armour of its own. He leapt onto the nearest M14 and deliberately placed himself between the British armour and the southern column. He succeeded in decoying the British away, but his M14 was hit and burst into flames. He escaped from the inferno and evaded the British for over an hour before being captured.

It was fortunate for Axis forces that their opponents were intent on reaching El Alamein to avoid being cut off, otherwise they might have destroyed them. The British armour simply crashed straight through 51 Armoured Battalion, firing madly and inflicting as much damage as possible in passing. Nevertheless, in this short sharp action, 4 Armoured claimed thirteen M14s knocked out, but lost some of their own tanks. In fact *Littorio* reported that all thirty of its runners had been hit, and twenty put out of action, and that 100 men had been lost. In addition, 133 Artillery Regiment had been reduced to only six guns, and ammunition supplies were nearing exhaustion.

El Alamein, July 1942

In the afternoon of 30 June, Rommel set out his highly risky plan to break through at El Alamein using the same tactics as at Mersa Matruh. He would push through the British centre with *DAK* and 90 Light while the Italian mobile forces supported his southern flank. He gambled that the British would once again retreat to avoid encirclement. It was an ambitious plan in

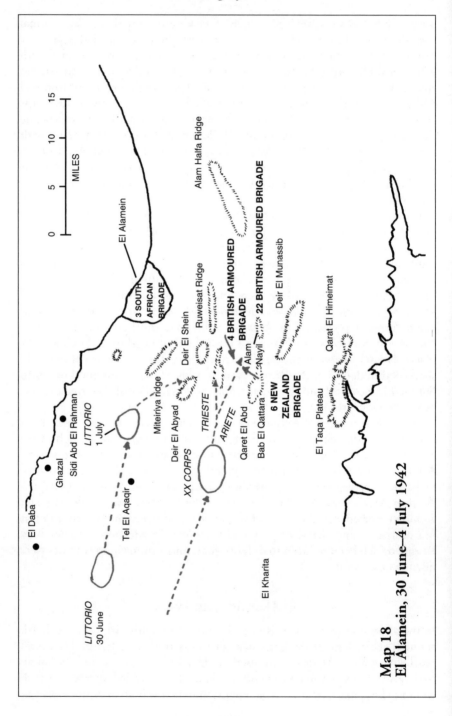

Map 18
El Alamein, 30 June–4 July 1942

view of Axis weakness and a lack of accurate information on British strength and dispositions. *Littorio*, its meagre artillery temporarily reinforced with two batteries of 88mm guns, was expected to oppose a reinforced 1 British Armoured Division, believed to be south of Qaret el Abd. The Italian XX Corps was expected to attack the 2 New Zealand Division, thought to be at Qaret el Abd itself. This highly optimistic plan would prove entirely unworkable for a number of reasons: it was based on faulty intelligence of Allied dispositions; it assumed that the Allies just needed a shove to induce their retreat; it assumed that the Axis forces would be in a position to attack after a 35-mile (56km) night march over unknown terrain; and it expected miracles from a force that, as a result of breakdowns and casualties, was little more than a shadow of its former self. The strength of the Italian XX Corps and *Littorio* combined now stood at a pathetic thirty M14 tanks, forty-five field guns, and fewer than 3,000 infantry.

In spite of this, Rommel was anxious to exploit any confusion resulting from the hurried British withdrawal, and the attack duly went ahead as planned. On 1 July the Axis forces advanced, amazingly without intervention from British armour, since 1 Armoured Division was still reorganizing following its clashes with *Littorio* and *DAK* the previous day. At noon Rommel remained optimistic, in spite of long delays in the approach march and unexpected obstacles. He was convinced that he would begin the pursuit phase during the early afternoon and XX Corps and *Littorio* were told that this would begin in a couple of hours. They were directed to pass through El Hamman and sever the road between Alexandria and Cairo at El Amiriya. In the current circumstances this was all fantasy, possibly inspired by nervous exhaustion or the dazzling prospect of the Nile. A pencil note scribbled on the original signal by Colonel Nuncenelli of *Littorio* suggests that the Italians at least still retained a grasp on reality: it ran, '*Littorio* has fuel for only 20km. To Alexandria is 150km!'

Rommel was quickly forced to review this over-optimistic scenario as a result of the complete exhaustion and increasingly shaky morale of his German units. In the centre, *DAK* had managed to capture Deir el Shein late in the day after a tough battle with 18 Indian Brigade, but they were unable to do more. In the north, 90 Light completely failed to encircle El Alamein in the face of ferocious British artillery fire, and a panicky rout was only just prevented. The clear signs of strain amongst his German troops should have warned Rommel of the potential for disaster. Instead, he remained hopeful that one last push would be enough to force a British withdrawal, no doubt influenced by reports of panic in Cairo and the withdrawal of the British fleet from Alexandria. He ignored contradictory intelligence about the presence of fresh Allied divisions. He was riding his luck, as he had done so often before – but it was about to run out.

On 2 July, Rommel resolved to gamble all his forces, however weak and worn out, on one desperate throw. While *DAK* and 90 Light attacked the British centre, the Italians were to protect their southern flank; De Stefanis was ordered to advance against Alam Nayil, held by the entire 2 New Zealand Division. But in the face of intense Allied air attacks and fearsome artillery fire, none of the Axis forces made much progress. On the southern flank, an advance by three M14s and three armoured cars from *Ariete* was driven back by artillery fire and no fewer than twenty Grant tanks of 4 Armoured Brigade. In the north, 90 Light advanced less than half a mile before stopping dead under intense artillery fire and refusing to move further. Their war diary noted despondently that 'The last hope that remains is the Italian divisions, which have seen but little action so far (sic) and are therefore more fit. However, from such comrades there is little to be hoped.' This note was no doubt influenced as much by pessimism following their own complete failure, as by the usual German contempt for their ally.

On 3 July, the Germans once again made no progress whilst incessantly complaining of lack of air and artillery support. At 09:00hr, XX Corps attempted to fulfil their ambitious orders to seize Alam Nayil, with *Ariete* moving tentatively south-east. The few M14s of 132 Armoured Regiment (it had reported only fifteen runners on 30 June) were engaged by 4 Armoured Brigade from the left, which inflicted casualties on the weaker Italians. The rest of *Ariete* deployed in support of their armour facing north-east against 4 Armoured. *Trieste*, which should have protected *Ariete*'s exposed right flank, was pinned down in the rear by 'incessant aerial bombing', and *Ariete* was badly exposed towards the south-east. They offered a superb target for the artillery of 2 New Zealand Division, located on Alam Nayil, which observed the Italian deployment and brought them under fire. The Italians hastily redeployed their few field guns to return fire, but came off worst in the unequal contest.

The New Zealanders then sent in the 800 men of 19 Battalion of 4 New Zealand Brigade from Deir el Munnassib in their Bren carriers. They advanced unseen under cover of their artillery, and their carriers scattered the few Italian reconnaissance vehicles present. The New Zealanders then debussed and overran the Italian outposts before being pinned down by artillery, mortar and machine-gun fire from the 600 *Bersaglieri* of *Ariete*. The New Zealand artillery responded with a heavy bombardment that silenced 132 Artillery Regiment. A trio of M14s that appeared to challenge the New Zealand infantry were quickly engaged by anti-tank guns and withdrew. 19 Battalion charged the Italian positions with fixed bayonets and overran the Italian guns, which continued to fire until they ran out of ammunition. The New Zealanders captured 350 men and forty-four assorted guns, virtually all of *Ariete*'s remaining artillery, including twelve 105mm, eleven 88mm, sixteen 75mm, five captured 25pdr guns, some 20mm infantry guns and mortars, and 100 assorted motor vehicles. At least two M14s were also found damaged and abandoned on the field. It was all over in an hour, and 19 Battalion suffered only two killed and twenty wounded. The captured Italians were described as 'a dirty, greasy, unkempt mob, without fighting spirit' – which is hardly surprising given their involvement in two months of continuous action since 26 May.

The remnants of *Ariete* that escaped this débâcle, mainly from 8 *Bersaglieri* Regiment, withdrew westwards. A few M14s of 132 Armoured Regiment that had escaped destruction at the hands of 4 Armoured were driven back against 15 Panzer. At midday General Arena of *Ariete* despondently reported that he had only five M14s and two field guns left. This was a double disaster. It spelled the end of *Ariete* as an effective fighting force for some time to come. It also effectively ended Rommel's attempts to rush the El Alamein position. He was forced to abandon his unrealistic plans and assume the defensive all along the front. He was only too ready to blame his allies, complaining that *Ariete* had lost 350 men 'without offering resistance worthy of the name'. In a more rational frame of mind, he subsequently admitted that the Italians 'were no longer equal to the very great demands being made of them'. He had simply demanded too much.

On the same day, 12 Armoured Battalion of *Littorio*, with twenty M14s, was advancing towards British positions on Ruweisat Ridge, but they ran into 1 British Armoured Division, as related by Lieutenant Armando Luciano:

> We're lined up facing east, with the sun blinding us and making our tank armour shine. In the distance in front of us, I can make out the silhouettes of the enemy tanks backed up against a large mound of earth. This is it – the moment of our first combat has come, the moment for which we've been training since August of last year with so much mental and physical preparation.
>
> Major dell'Uva gives the last orders, the battalion advances to get in range, then the exchange of fire starts and tank platoons start moving. At the same time we are bombarded with enemy artillery fire, which gets more and more frequent and well aimed.
>
> In the distance in front of me I make out an enemy tank flying a pennant from its radio antenna; it must be a command tank . . . 'Halt!' I cry to Ramazzotti, 'Aim 600, fire!' Following the trail of the tracer, I see the shell hit the enemy armour, but I wait in vain for the usual black smoke of burning fuel to pour out of the tank, or to see the crew throw themselves out of the vehicle. Our armour-piercing shell must have misfired – it is probably an American Grant tank, a beast with too thick a skin.
>
> I try again with another armour-piercing shell, but almost simultaneously I feel a blow on our right flank and hear the screams

of the radio operator who seems to be going mad and whom Visentini, the gunner, is trying to calm down.

The tank has taken a hit, fortunately not a direct hit, but on its right side, on the track, which is now hanging uselessly while the exchange of fire is getting more intense and other tanks are being destroyed. Captain Giupponi is killed, and Lieutenant Marotta seriously wounded. It seems that they are firing on the 12 Battalion from all around.

This attack also failed, and Rommel was now forced to deploy 21 Panzer and *Littorio* to fill the gap left by *Ariete*, and to order all his units onto the defensive. He could not consider further offensive action until his mobile forces had been replaced with infantry and he had established a mobile reserve once again.

Mungar Wahla

On 6 July, *Littorio*, which had moved into the area exposed by *Ariete's* collapse, was installed in the depression at Mungar Wahla. But unnoticed during the previous night, 4 New Zealand Brigade had penetrated to within 700yd (640m) of them. As dawn broke the New Zealanders found *Littorio* spread out below them, 'completely oblivious to our (NZ) presence, and it was very interesting to watch [his] troops getting up, folding blankets and preparing breakfast at their slit trenches.' The New Zealanders opened fire on this peaceful scene and the Italians, including a troop of four 75mm guns and a machine-gun platoon, went to ground and returned fire. A number of tanks and lorries visible in the distance were also engaged by the New Zealand artillery. By 08:00hr, 12 *Bersaglieri* Regiment were returning fire with mortars and small arms and making preparations for a counter-attack. On several occasions New Zealand artillery fire dispersed Italian concentrations, but they were not discouraged. The Italian 133 Artillery Regiment became engaged, and small arms and artillery exchanges continued until noon, when a heat haze reduced visibility and the conflict subsided. In the course of the afternoon *Littorio* was able to mount its counter-attack and push the 4 New Zealand Brigade back.

On 7 July the Italians reported that they had sixty M14 tanks in their two armoured divisions. This increase in numbers from the nadir on 3 July reflects the tireless work of the vehicle recovery and repair units, and the efforts of Italian coastal forces to bring them forward. The latter were using motorized lighters to supplement road transport and bring urgent heavy supplies, including M14 tanks, forward to Mersa Matruh. On 8 July, as non-motorized Italian infantry divisions gradually entered the front line, so Axis mobile units were withdrawn into the reserve. The official strength of

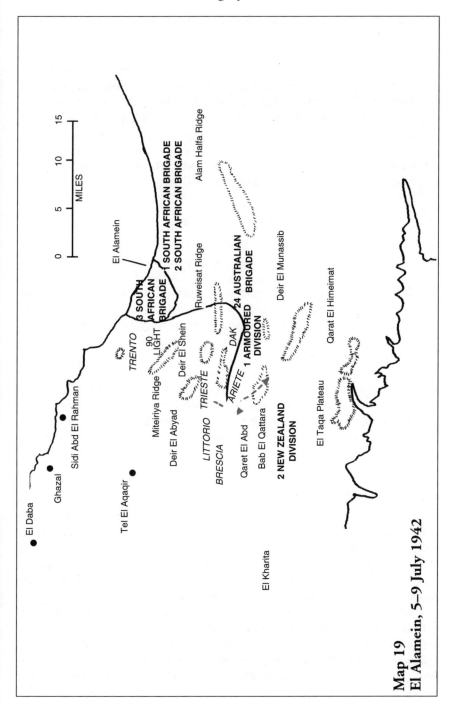

Map 19
El Alamein, 5–9 July 1942

the Italian XX Corps, under De Stefanis and now including *Ariete, Littorio* and *Trieste,* stood at fifty-four tanks and eight motorized battalions with 1,600 men, forty anti-tank guns and six light gun batteries. They should have had 430 tanks and 120 anti-tank guns. It remained Rommel's intention to use the Axis mobile units, free from front-line duty, to penetrate the British front, but the British were themselves preparing to counter-attack the weak Italian infantry divisions that had just arrived at the front. The plan was to destroy these Italians piecemeal and compel the Axis mobile forces to support them. This would prevent them being employed offensively and would inflict heavy losses on them, by forcing them into action against British armour in prepared positions.

Bab el Qattara

In the absence of any alternative, Rommel's hopes were still invested in an offensive that would somehow break the British will to resist. It was clearly an increasingly desperate strategy, but it did at least offer the chance to retain the initiative, which would otherwise fall to the enemy. On 8 July he once again proposed to break through the British centre, and 21 Panzer, 90 Light and *Littorio* were ordered to capture Alam Nayil before striking north for the coast. The next day, following an artillery barrage, 21 Panzer and *Littorio* mounted a full-scale assault on the former New Zealand positions at Bab el Qattara. This attack was led by a squadron of 3 Group Novara Lancers equipped with L6/40 light tanks under Captain Dardi. The fragile light tanks formed up in the open and moved forwards at top speed. Dardi was having difficulty directing the attack through the narrow observation slits in his turret. He therefore decided to open the hatch and command from a better vantage point, clear of the smoke and dust caused by vehicle movement and enemy artillery fire. He guided his squadron to its objectives but was killed by shrapnel fragments from enemy artillery. Unfortunately, the whole *Littorio* attack fell on an empty stretch of desert and encountered only artillery fire. The New Zealanders had evacuated this position the day before and were able to watch appreciatively, from a safe distance, as the tanks, guns and lorries of *Littorio* advanced in battle order into their abandoned position. The position was then garrisoned by *Littorio,* while the rest of XX Corps was moved to cover the Axis front south of Ruweisat Ridge, which was considered to be relatively quiet.

The Axis focus on the centre had drawn their armoured forces away from the north. There, two fresh British infantry divisions, heralded by the most intense artillery bombardment since World War I, struck the newly arrived Italian *Sabratha* Infantry Division. *Sabratha* quickly buckled under the pressure and collapsed. This forced Rommel to dispatch German mobile forces to prevent a British breakthrough and restore the front line. This

British attack had inflicted severe damage on Rommel by capturing his radio intercept unit, that had been stationed behind the front at this point. This disaster deprived the Axis of their main source of signals intelligence on Allied strengths, dispositions and intentions. They had already lost access to the reports of Colonel Fellers at the end of June when Ultra revealed this leak. Hereafter Rommel would increasingly be fighting in the dark, while his opponents had an almost complete knowledge of his own strengths, dispositions and intentions through Ultra. This made the fight increasingly one-sided and the ultimate defeat of the Axis forces inevitable. It was now a matter of time.

Ruweisat Ridge

On 14 July, elements of 90 Light and *Littorio* were ordered to advance north from Bab el Qattara on a spoiling attack towards Alam Nayil. They formed Group Baade, under General Baade from 90 Light, with *Raggruppamenti Rochetti*, a company of eleven M14s from *Littorio*. They found their route blocked by 22 Armoured Brigade near Alam Nayil, which chased them back to Bab el Qattara. This minor Axis expedition was not entirely futile, however, since it distracted the attention of 22 Armoured at a crucial time. On the same day, 2 New Zealand Division had launched a major attack against the Italian *Brescia* and *Pavia* Infantry Divisions on Ruweisat Ridge. This attack made significant progress against the weak Italians before meeting a counter-attack by *DAK*. As a result of the actions of Group Baade, the British armour was unable to assist 4 New Zealand Brigade on Ruweisat Ridge, where it was destroyed by 15 Panzer. The British counter-attacks were undermining the Italian infantry and keeping the Axis armour busy, but they were also proving increasingly costly to the British. The battle was slowly heading towards stalemate.

On 15 July, General Carlo Ceriana-Mayneri, commander of 2 *Celere* Division based in the Balkans, received orders to fly to North Africa to assume command of the *Littorio* Division. He arrived in North Africa shortly before 22 July to take over from General Bitossi. The new commander was a fifty-five-year-old royalist cavalry officer with little time for Fascism. He had only limited experience of armoured warfare, although 2 *Celere* had been involved in initial planning for conversion into a fourth armoured division. He had no experience of North Africa, which was something of a shock, as he noted:

> The heat saps your energy: a non-stop Turkish bath, 43°C in the shade. Newcomers cannot get acclimatized. The water is bad; never any fruit or vegetables, only tinned foods and biscuit. The diet gives rise to continual stomach disorders among young and old.

He also noted the high morale of the men, and the sense of comradeship forged by the common desert experience: 'Here amid the sandstorms and the mirages, a special race of men is being formed, speaking the same language regardless of rank . . . they go into action together, they share the life of the dug-out . . .'. He would soon be leading these men into battle.

Deir um Khawabir

On 18 July, 24 New Zealand Battalion launched a raid against positions held by 8 *Bersaglieri* Regiment of *Ariete* at Deir um Khawabir in the southern sector of the front. This was intended as preparatory reconnaissance for a major attack on Deir el Mreir to the north. A New Zealand patrol, consisting of thirty men in Bren carriers supported by a troop of 6pdr anti-tank guns, set off at 20:30hr under cover of supporting artillery fire. They penetrated the minefield and captured some well-constructed *Bersaglieri* posts, using grenades. They then came under infantry, machine-gun and anti-tank fire from more *Bersaglieri* to their left. The Bren carriers, which had followed their infantry, engaged the Italians, silencing one 88mm and two smaller anti-tank guns. But Italian resistance quickly stiffened as they called up M14 tanks in support, and one Bren carrier was destroyed by a 47mm anti-tank gun. Italian M14 tanks approached, fired on the New Zealanders and destroyed two Bren carriers. 24 Battalion quickly withdrew, but claimed forty-two *Bersaglieri* captured for the loss of only two killed, two wounded and one missing. The Italian prisoners were apparently disillusioned and ready to talk. They reported that their companies had been reduced to an average strength of 100 men, three 47mm anti-tank guns, three heavy and three light machine guns. One individual reported that he had seen six M14 tanks and four *Semoventi* at headquarters, which he believed represented the entire divisional armoured strength. In fact this was not far off the mark, since an official return of 17 July from *Ariete* reported only fifteen M14 tanks. This figure would slowly increase as reinforcements gradually arrived at the front.

Bab el Qattara

On 21 July, the Allies were preparing another major assault on Italian forces at Ruweisat Ridge, involving 5 Indian, 2 New Zealand and 1 Armoured Divisions. As part of this, 18 New Zealand Battalion was to protect the flank of 6 New Zealand Brigade while it attacked Deir el Mreir, with the support of the New Zealand Cavalry and 22 Armoured Brigades. At 19:00hr, as 18 Battalion assembled, it almost immediately came under intense artillery fire from *Ariete*, which had observed its arrival. This bombardment, which lasted for more than an hour and only ceased as darkness fell, significantly delayed their assembly. It was not until some two hours after 6 New Zealand Brigade had already set off towards Deir el Mreir that the battalion was finally ready.

At 21:00hr, 18 Battalion commenced its advance under another artillery barrage from *Ariete*. In spite of this, one company penetrated the dense Axis minefield and turned west across rising ground in bright moonlight. The *Bersaglieri* sent up flares and laid down a blanket of machine-gun fire. The New Zealanders replied with machine guns and grenades, and charged with fixed bayonets. The *Bersaglieri* brought the foremost troops under crossfire from well-sited positions, and killed and wounded many. The real surprise, however, awaited them just beyond the brow of the ridge: a line of Italian M14s in hull-down position. The New Zealanders had neither the numbers nor the firepower to face enemy armour, however weak it might be. Then a second New Zealand company encountered a trip-wire that set off a series of mines and caused many casualties. The *Bersaglieri* immediately laid down heavy machine-gun and small-arms fire on the exposed enemy, who then charged with the bayonet. But they quickly suffered further casualties, and were forced to withdraw without making direct contact. The company commander was killed, and the company reduced to only seven men. As they withdrew, two M14 tanks moved forward to surround the survivors, and forced them to flee. A third company of reinforcements came under fire from M14s at 200yd (180m) range, and quickly went to ground. The entire New Zealand battalion withdrew just before midnight.

At dawn the next day, 22 July, the shaken New Zealanders found themselves exposed on rocky ground where they could not dig in. A patrol of three Bren carriers sent to assist them came under heavy fire from *Ariete*'s tanks and had to run for cover. The New Zealand artillery opened fire on the Italian M14s that had formed up for a counter-attack, and forced them to take cover behind the ridge. There were no further attacks, and the opponents spent the rest of the day cautiously observing one another. The Italians maintained a desultory shelling of the New Zealanders throughout the day and were supported by some Axis bombers during the afternoon. The British 22 Armoured Brigade finally arrived to support the New Zealanders, but made no serious attempt to attack the well-entrenched Italians. The Italians hit several British tanks, which then withdrew, leaving the infantry to fend for themselves. At 20:45hr, the latter were finally withdrawn as a result of the disastrous defeats suffered by British forces on Ruweisat Ridge to the north.

On the night of 26–27 July, 2 New Zealand Division launched a feint attack on Bab el Qattara to distract the attention of *DAK* from the northern sector of the front. It failed in this purpose, since the only reaction was that *Littorio* stood to for several hours. The British attack on Miteirya Ridge in the north was initially successful against the Italian 102 *Trento* Infantry

Division, but quickly came to grief when British armoured support failed to arrive quickly enough to oppose the Axis armoured counter-attacks. This action appeared to signify the mental and physical exhaustion of both sides. The entire front now settled down to static defence punctuated only by patrol activity.

The brief midsummer dream of an Axis invasion of Egypt had quickly faded under the blazing sun of July. On 28 July, the German summer offensive on the Eastern Front commenced, involving forces on a scale that Rommel could only dream of. It would ultimately take the Germans all the way to Stalingrad on the Volga. It concentrated German attention and resources on Russia, including the aircraft that had so effectively subdued Malta in the spring. This eased pressure on the island and allowed the British to revive their attacks on Axis supply convoys during the autumn. The Eastern offensive also diminished further Rommel's already bleak prospects of securing additional reinforcements and supplies for his overstretched forces. He was generously permitted to draw on the forces earmarked for the invasion of Malta, including some élite parachute units. They were excellent troops, but they had no transport and were therefore of limited use in the desert. The essential requirement there was mobile formations, but none would be forthcoming until after the British offensive in October.

On 31 July 1942 Captain Giacomo Guiglia of the Italian radio intercept unit reviewed the condition of the Italian forces. He noted that the Italians had 240 M14 tanks on 26 May, but reached Alamein on 1 July with only sixteen. By the 8 July, however, they had managed to increase this to fifty-four through the work of the repair shops, in spite of continued losses. On 31 July, however, the Italians had only forty tanks again, which was far short of their full establishment. The physical condition of the Italian units, while clearly not good, was certainly not as bad as it had been at the beginning of the month. The psychological condition of the Italian armoured units at this point was healthier. It might have been expected that the shattering of any hope of taking Egypt would have left their morale at a very low ebb, but this was far from the case, as many observers noted – and in this they appear to contrast with their German allies. Ceriana-Mayneri, the new commander of *Littorio*, recorded that his troops, ill armed and poorly equipped as they were, remained in high spirits, and that he was completely satisfied with their *esprit de corps*. On 25 July, Major Pellegrini sought permission for 3 Mobile Artillery Regiment, *Duca d'Aosta*, which had been attached to the dissolved *Sabratha*, to join XX Corps. He declared that its survivors 'earnestly desire to continue the regimental name and honour in future actions', although they had only three captured 25pdr guns and five 20mm guns; but they were able to boast that they were 100 per cent motorized with captured vehicles. The request was granted.

In contrast, one sign of the strain affecting the Germans was noticed by De Stefanis, commander of XX Corps. He was visiting Rommel's command post at Ghazal when yet another Allied air attack began and anti-aircraft artillery responded. The astonished Italian watched a nervous Rommel leap up and urge him to shelter in a nearby dug-out amongst the sand dunes. In the event the air attack was not serious and passed without incident. De Stefanis was surprised because Rommel had previously shown no fear in far more dangerous circumstances. The Axis forces were also becoming accustomed to incessant air attacks and they usually took cover only when directly targeted. He attributed Rommel's unusual behaviour to the strain of exhaustion and defeat, and an increasing sense of helplessness in the face of superior Allied air power. It was a new experience for the Germans, although the Italians had already been on the receiving end of enemy air superiority in 1940.

It was not until 16 August that Rommel finally completed the withdrawal of all his mobile formations from the front, where they were replaced by infantry. The release of these forces permitted Rommel to consider the possibility of staging an offensive. It was typical that Rommel, when faced with a choice between attack and defence, preferred the former even in adverse circumstances. In order to attack, however, he needed to reorganize and rebuild these badly weakened formations into something approaching their original strength. This was a relatively slow process involving few replacement vehicles from Europe due to Allied action against supply convoys. The Axis forces relied instead on the recovery and repair of vehicles damaged in the earlier fighting. At the end of August 1942 the Italians had a total of around 33,000 men and 281 tanks, mainly M14s, in North Africa. The Italian tanks were of poor quality, being refurbished vehicles salvaged from the battlefields and therefore susceptible to breakdowns. In spite of this, these increased numbers encouraged Rommel to take the offensive.

Alam Halfa

The new offensive proposed to make full use of all available Axis mobile forces, since nothing less than this could possibly succeed in penetrating the powerfully reinforced British positions. The assault would strike the southern end of the Alamein line, which Rommel believed was its weakest point, and turn north behind the fixed defences, exactly as at Gazala. The Italian XX Corps, incorporating *Ariete* and *Littorio* Armoured and *Trieste* Motorized Divisions, was deployed at El Kharita on the northern flank of the Axis thrust, with 90 Light to their north and *DAK* to their south. The southern flank would be protected by the Qattara Depression and by German and Italian reconnaissance units. The Italian corps was still not at full strength, with perhaps less than half of its establishment of 16,000 men

– though it is difficult to be certain since it left part of its non-motorized infantry and artillery elements behind to protect the flank of 90 Light. It did have about 250 M14 tanks, however, which was the bulk of the available Italian armour.

The task facing the Axis forces was immense. They had not been fully restored to their former condition and remained weak, especially in air support. They had collected enough fuel for a quick and successful offensive, but there was none to spare for any unforeseen problems. The recent loss of Axis signals intelligence meant that they had only a sketchy knowledge of British strength and dispositions. In contrast the British had been heavily reinforced, had no shortages, and enjoyed almost complete air superiority. They also had complete foreknowledge of the Axis plans from Ultra, and had made detailed preparations to defeat them. They had simply to wait in their prepared positions and blast the Axis forces as they came towards them. In short, it was, had the Axis forces known it, a suicide mission. The Italian units involved, which had to rely on the use of movement to compensate for their weak armour, had little chance of making an impact in such a one-sided battle. In addition they had to advance some 20 miles (30km) in five hours over largely uncharted terrain during darkness, simply to reach their dawn objectives. The Italians were then scheduled to drive north-eastwards in broad daylight under direct observation and fire from British positions on Alam Halfa Ridge. The latter was strongly held by 44 Infantry and 10 Armoured Divisions, with 7 Armoured Division on their left flank. In the highly unlikely event that they managed to capture the ridge, the Italians were then to drive eastwards, using fuel supplies captured from the British, and cut the road between Alexandria and Cairo!

In the early evening of 30 August, the Axis forces formed up on the plain at El Kharita for the offensive, and already their plans began to unravel. The assembling vehicles were spotted by Allied aircraft and heavily bombed. The Italian XX Corps eventually moved off late, quickly strayed off course to the north, and then encountered a deep enemy minefield, consisting of three main belts of mines. They were halted by the mines and by heavy enemy artillery fire from the north. They also found themselves blocking the advance of 90 Light. They attempted to turn east to make way for the Germans but found themselves moving obliquely through the enemy minefield rather than crossing it. All the time Allied aircraft mounted round-the-clock bombing missions on anything that moved, including the dust clouds thrown up by moving vehicles. As a result, the Axis forces made slow progress and lost many of their men and vehicles to mines and artillery fire. The only Axis forces to reach their intended objectives by dawn were *RECAM* and 185 *Folgore* Parachute Division on the extreme southern flank.

The experience of *Littorio*, under Ceriana-Mayneri, was fairly typical.

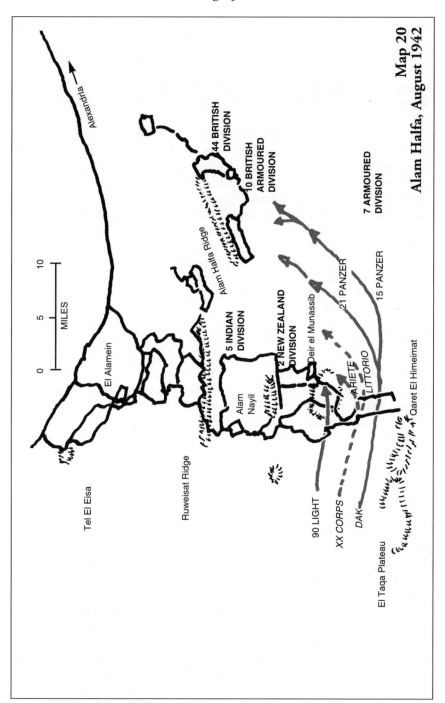

Map 20
Alam Halfa, August 1942

They found the minefield gaps, made by their engineers during the night, poorly marked and many vehicles struck mines, including Ceriana-Mayneri's own command tank. He was wounded, but simply changed mounts, cavalry style, by climbing into another M14. *Littorio* continued through the darkness under the intermittent glare of flares and constant Allied bombing and artillery fire. In the early hours of the morning they reached Point 115, and Ceriana-Mayneri switched vehicles once again to a staff car to facilitate observation of the battle. This was risky in the circumstances, and he subsequently lost his driver and radio operator to enemy fire, although he escaped unscathed. He had lost contact with *Ariete* on his left and 21 Panzer on his right, and now found himself faced with an area described in reconnaissance reports as 'good terrain', but which consisted of fine sand dunes scattered with mines. It was also under British observation and artillery fire from Alam Halfa. It was not a promising prospect – but at least *Littorio* managed to reach its jumping-off area roughly on schedule. The rest of XX Corps were still stuck in the minefields, and failed to arrive.

At 09:00hr on 31 August, although *Littorio's* M14s were ready to advance, their rear echelons were still threading their way through minefields. The late arrival of the Axis assault forces, and the fact that British forces were already fully alert, forced Rommel to adjust his plans. At 14:00hr he ordered the Axis forces to turn north and capture Alam Halfa Ridge, to flush out and destroy the British armour. In this revised scheme, XX Corps was to head for Point 102, a small rise on the right behind 2 New Zealand Division. Unfortunately *Littorio*, desperately trying to make up for lost time under intense bombing and in a sandstorm, trespassed into 21 Panzer's assembly area. A full hour of chaos ensued as the two divisions tried desperately to disentangle their units, and it was not until 15:00hr that *Littorio* was ready to advance and the rest of XX Corps finally escaped from the minefields. In the evening, the New Zealanders stationed at Deir el Muhafid observed a long column of Italian tanks passing to their south. In view of the severe delays in Axis deployment, Rommel postponed the proposed advance until the next day; besides, the Axis formations were all desperately short of fuel, and exhausted by the strain of constant bombing. The Italians were glad to abandon this largely unproductive advance.

On 1 September, the Axis forces awoke tired after another restless night of continuous bombing. In the early morning, 2 New Zealand Division located M14 tanks of *Littorio* on the southern rim of Deir el Muhafid, and hastily withdrew. The Italians exchanged fire with the New Zealanders, but otherwise maintained defensive positions for the present. In mid-afternoon the advance resumed, with *Littorio* moving up to protect the exposed left flank of 21 Panzer and to link up with 90 Light. A number of M14s were disabled, but many of these were victims of breakdown or bomb damage and were later repaired and brought back into action. A large force of tanks and lorried infantry from 90 Light and XX Corps drove east across Deir el Muhafid. The New Zealand artillery opened fire on this tempting target below them, claiming numerous hits. By dusk, a few tanks and infantry from this force had advanced to within a mile of the New Zealand positions. The latter feared that this might portend an assault, but it was only part of a series of unrelated Axis movements. The advance continued for another terrible day, but once again made little progress. It was not until late on 2 September that Rommel finally admitted defeat and ordered his spent forces to withdraw in stages. *Littorio* was ordered to hold its present position while *DAK* fell back first. Thereafter *Littorio, Trieste* and 90 Light would fall back in sequence. Once again, Axis units were subjected to a non-stop pounding by Allied bombers during that night; they got little sleep and suffered heavy losses, especially amongst their soft-skinned vehicles and guns.

On 3 September, the Axis withdrawal began behind a screen of anti-tank guns. On the southern flank M14 tanks of *Ariete*, which had been switched to this flank the previous day, repulsed probes by 4 Light Armoured Brigade towards Himeimat. At noon, on the northern flank, *Littorio* was ordered to move back into reserve while *Trieste* to their west moved into Deir el Muhafid to relieve 90 Light. In an exposed location under heavy bombardment, *Littorio* responded so smartly to this welcome withdrawal order that they triggered the move of *Trieste* ahead of schedule and left 21 Panzer exposed. As night fell, 90 Light, *Littorio* and *Trieste* all converged on a single narrow desert track. The resultant massive traffic jam attracted the attention of the New Zealand artillery, which inflicted further casualties on the Axis forces.

On the night of 3–4 September, 26 Maori Battalion was preparing to counter-attack the flank of the Axis penetration. *Ariete* and *Littorio* had been tasked with holding the front behind the retreating Germans, and became involved in skirmishes with the pursuing Allies. They detected the Maori offensive preparations, and laid down a barrage of artillery and mortar fire to disrupt them. In spite of this, the Maoris reached their objectives, which had already been abandoned, without encountering serious opposition. At dawn the Italians brought them under artillery fire, and at 08:00hr an Italian patrol captured Brigadier Clifton of 6 New Zealand Brigade, who had been forward on reconnaissance. The Italians spent the rest of the morning preparing a counter-attack involving a combination of *Bersaglieri* and tanks. They sent out patrols to probe the Maori positions, that were also engaged by the Italian artillery. The Italian concentrations were fired on and forced to disperse, which prevented the planned counter-attack.

In the confusion, the Italians had, however, surrounded an isolated Maori company that had advanced beyond its objectives. They prevented relief forces from reaching them, and by midday their supplies of ammunition were running low and they were unable to contact their battalion. They were in a desperate position, but held out all day in the hope of news or relief; but none arrived. In the late afternoon, Italian artillery ranged on their positions and, shortly afterwards, laid down heavy and sustained concentrations of fire as the prelude to a major assault. This barrage kept the Maoris' heads down and prevented any withdrawal. Immediately afterwards, *Bersaglieri* attacked in force and, despite tough resistance, overwhelmed the Maoris, capturing Captain Hall and twenty-one men.

The lack of progress and the loss of one of their companies caused the New Zealanders to order a withdrawal at dusk. 22 New Zealand Battalion moved up to cover the withdrawal of the Maoris, but were too late to save them all. They faced heavy fire from 'small shells', probably from the 47mm guns of Italian M14s, as well as '88s'. The Maoris had passed through 22 Battalion when the latter noted clear signs that the Italians were preparing an attack with increased shelling, mortaring and machine-gun fire. The New Zealanders replied with an intense barrage, and the front went quiet.

At noon on 5 September, the Italians launched fifty *Bersaglieri* and a few tanks towards an isolated enemy position. The Italians managed to get very close before the New Zealanders were able to call up supporting artillery fire – and in spite of the latter, the Italian attack continued undaunted, one Italian officer standing in the turret of his stationary M14 to take a relaxed look around. The Italians succeeded in forcing two enemy platoons to seek shelter behind a ridge, and were only stopped by mortar fire and 6pdr anti-tank guns, which knocked out three M14s. The New Zealanders reoccupied their forward positions, but fell back once more as an Italian second wave arrived. The Italians pressed this attack for three hours, and only gave up in the face of increasingly intense artillery fire. On 8 September, the skirmishes that closed the Alam Halfa fighting came to an end. *Ariete* and *Littorio* had completed the task of securing the front after the withdrawal. The new Axis front line ran from Deir el Munassib to Himeimat in the south in the sole success of the Alam Halfa offensive. It was a poor return for their losses. The Italian casualties were 1,051 men killed, and twenty-two guns, eleven tanks and ninety-seven assorted vehicles destroyed.

In reality there had been no possibility of the Axis forces breaking through to the Nile: it was a mirage that evaporated at Alamein in the heat of July. They had been beaten by a combination of determined resistance by superior British forces, and the complete exhaustion of Axis resources, both human and material. The British were ready for them and their overall superiority in aircraft, tanks, guns and men ensured their success. Even if the Axis forces had broken through in July, it is unlikely that this would have made a significant difference to the wider war. They were so overextended that they would have faced enormous difficulties in advancing to the Nile. They would have been faced with larger British forces on all sides, including to their rear, while they themselves were desperately short of fuel and ammunition. They would have needed to capture British fuel supplies to reach Alexandria, never mind Cairo. They had too few men to garrison the Egyptian towns and cities. They had no boats or engineering equipment to cross the Nile. The imminent start of the summer offensive on the Eastern Front meant that they had little prospect of receiving significant reinforcements. Even the capture of Alexandria might not have eased their supply problems, since it would probably have been sabotaged and would need to be restored to operation. Ignoring all of these difficulties, a successful Axis invasion of Egypt would in any case have faltered with the Allied invasion of French North Africa in November 1942. In a wider context, the Japanese defeat at Midway in June, and Soviet resistance at Stalingrad, meant that there was no prospect of relief or assistance from those quarters. The grandiose vision of converging Axis thrusts into the Middle East from Egypt, Russia and India was no more than fantasy, and in September the disastrous Alam Halfa battle showed that the writing was on the wall: the Axis forces were doomed to adopt a defensive posture, while slowly recovering their feeble strength to a level where they had at least a slim chance of resisting the inevitable Allied counter offensive.

In the summer of 1942, Axis success in North Africa was at its height, but Axis strength was at its lowest ebb. In these circumstances the performance of the two Italian armoured divisions was as good as might have been expected. They fought against the odds in every encounter, and inevitably suffered a number of setbacks. The disastrous reverse suffered by *Ariete* on 3 July at Alamein is highlighted in almost every account, and used to confirm existing prejudices about the poor performance of the Italians. If, however, the condition of the division is taken into account, the situation appears very different. In fact, at this point this armoured 'division' better resembled a battalion with its 600 men, forty-four assorted guns of all calibres, and fifteen or so M14 tanks. Also, after more than two months of continuous action, heavy losses and almost no sleep for more than a week, it was at the end of its tether. In this context its performance on 3 July can be readily understood. What is important is that the Italian armour remained constantly in action in circumstances that should have seen them withdrawn and replaced.

7

Iron Coffins

In October 1942 the end of the long, see-saw Axis campaign in North Africa was finally in sight. There would be no more spectacular Axis offensives against the odds. Instead, the campaign had become exactly the kind of holding action that had originally been intended back in February 1941. The role of the Axis forces was now to delay the inevitable victory of the Allies for as long as possible. They therefore constructed a series of complex defensive positions, screened by dense minefields and supported by artillery and armour. The Axis forces were slowly rebuilt after their failed offensive at Alam Halfa, although they remained puny in comparison with their opponents. Indeed, the quantitative and qualitative strength of the Allies increased with every day that passed. They received a regular influx of new divisions, and new and more powerful weapons, including Sherman tanks and 6pdr anti-tank guns. It could not be long before the full weight of this military power was turned against the Axis forces; the latter knew that a major Allied offensive was inevitable, and on 20 October, thinned out their forward positions in anticipation.

In late October the tank strength of the Italian XX Corps, commanded by General Giuseppe De Stefanis, stood at 278 M14 tanks, distributed as follows:

132 *Ariete* Armoured Division	129 M14 tanks
133 *Littorio* Armoured Division	115 M14 tanks and 20 L6 light tanks
101 *Trieste* Motorized Division	34 M14 tanks

This potentially powerful armoured corps was not in a concentrated body, however, but rather was dispersed behind the forward positions held by the Axis infantry. This unusual deployment had been largely dictated by two key factors: Axis fuel shortages, and Allied air superiority. The ideal arrangement was for the armoured forces to be concentrated ready to move to any threatened sectors; however, there was not enough fuel to permit this flexibility, and the Allied air threat meant all movement on the ground would be costly. *Trieste* under General Azzi was stationed on the coast with 90 Light Division. *Littorio*, now back under General Bitossi, was positioned behind the northern sector of the line with 15 Panzer Division, in three combined Italo-German battle groups, consisting of a mix of armour, infantry and artillery. *Littorio's* battalions were allocated as follows: 4 Armoured Battalion to the northern group, 51 Armoured and 23 *Bersaglieri* Battalions to the central group, and 12 Armoured and 36 *Bersaglieri* Battalions to the southern group. *Ariete* under General Arena was positioned behind the southern sector with 21 Panzer Division, also in three battle groups. The furthest south of these consisted of 10 Armoured and 12 *Bersaglieri* Battalions. The individual headquarters of each of these groups were located close to each other to facilitate communications and enhance command and control.

This close pairing of German and Italian units, known as 'corseting', also applied to the infantry deployed in the front line. It involved small mixed battle groups of Italians and Germans operating closely together. It was not new, since Rommel's first offensive in April 1941 had employed similar mixed Italo-German units, but it was the first time that the entire Axis army had been deployed in this way. It was intended to provide stiffening for the Italians, but not, as is generally assumed, to prevent the 'cowardly' Italians from surrendering. The real purpose was to provide physical support from German heavy weapons for poorly equipped Italian units. The Italians were vulnerable to the superior numbers and quality of Allied weapons, and they stood a much better chance with the support of German heavy weaponry. In 'The Cauldron' in June 1942, *Ariete* had repulsed British attacks with such support, and it was hoped that the entire Italian army could benefit in the same way.

The central and southern groups from *Littorio* and 15 Panzer Divisions had been deployed immediately behind where the main Allied offensive would fall. They had constructed a screen of anti-tank guns and hull-down tanks, running due south from the Trigh Sidi abd el Rahman, with their artillery posted behind. They had dispersed their mixed armour and infantry groups close behind the front ready to counter-attack against any breakthroughs, and were ideally positioned to support the forward infantry if any Allied forces managed to penetrate their positions. They would quickly cause the Allies major problems when the long-awaited offensive finally began. The arrangements were therefore in place, but Rommel was not there to lead the defence: he had been sent to Europe to convalesce from a combination of mental and physical exhaustion. He was replaced temporarily by General George Stumme, a panzer officer from the Eastern Front.

The Allied offensive commenced on the night of 23 October 1942 with a massive artillery bombardment of World War I proportions. This made it obvious that the offensive had begun, but it also severely disrupted Axis communications with the front line. The Allies also commenced shuttle bombing of the Axis rear to disrupt their movements. It was therefore difficult to know exactly what was happening on the ground, and Stumme went to find out for himself. He immediately went missing, and only later was it learnt that he had died of heart failure. The Axis forces were paralysed without a leader, and confused about the location of the main Allied thrust, and no instructions for concentration or counter-attack were issued. The Axis armour therefore remained in its positions, dispersed behind the front. It was only in the afternoon, with the fortuitous arrival of General von Thoma at headquarters, that a decision was taken to organize counter-attacks against what appeared to be the more serious Allied penetration in the north.

In the morning of 24 October, Allied infantry had successfully penetrated the Axis infantry positions in the north as far as Miteiriya Ridge, and called their armour forward to complete the breakthrough. The latter were severely delayed by mines and made slow progress. On the Axis side, in the absence of orders from above, 15 Panzer and *Littorio* took it upon themselves to act. They launched a number of local armoured counter-attacks against the largest Allied penetration in the north during the day. The southern battle group sent 12 Armoured Battalion and parts of 15 Panzer against 2 New Zealand and 51 Highland Divisions, and the central battle group directed 51 Armoured Battalion and parts of 15 Panzer against 51 Highland and 9 Australian Divisions. On the southern flank of the main Allied penetration, some M14s from 12 Armoured Battalion and thirty panzers with *Bersaglieri* and German infantry in support, struck 5 New Zealand Brigade from the south-west. They made some progress, but failed to drive the New Zealanders back. The early counter-attacks proved costly in tanks lost to Allied anti-tank screens, but were at least temporarily successful in preventing any further penetration. The effects of almost constant Allied heavy artillery and air bombardment had badly blunted these first weak and poorly organized Axis attacks.

On 25 October, Allied armour finally began to reach the front of their infantry penetration, and forward spearheads soon reported enemy armoured forces assembling for counter-attacks. At noon it appeared that a general Axis armoured counter-attack was imminent; but heavy air and artillery bombardment very effectively disrupted its development. Instead the Allies were faced with a series of piecemeal, unco-ordinated probes and small-scale counter-attacks during this day also. At 14:00hr, one of these approached 2 Armoured Brigade from the north-west, led by a company of Italian M14s from 51 Armoured Battalion of *Littorio*, supported by 5 German panzers and infantry. It came within range of 2 Armoured's Sherman tanks before turning aside into 20 Australian Brigade. They immediately came under heavy artillery fire, which quickly isolated the Axis armour from its infantry support. In spite of this, the M14s pressed home their attack with considerable dash, some even reaching the Australian

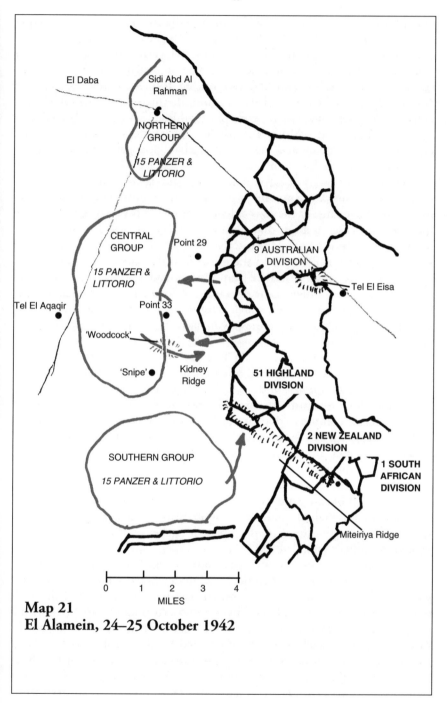

Map 21
El Alamein, 24–25 October 1942

outposts. They were halted and driven back by Australian anti-tank guns, supported by fire from 7 British Motor Brigade on their left and 2 Armoured to their south. The Germans later claimed that the Italians withdrew when their commander became a casualty. The Australians claimed twenty M14s knocked out during this encounter. In reply, 2 Armoured reported the loss of twenty-four Sherman tanks, mainly to Axis anti-tank guns and artillery. In terms of casualties, 20 Australian Brigade lost eighty-five men, and 7 Motor Brigade lost forty-nine, but claimed to have captured 173 German and sixty-seven Italian prisoners, the latter from *Trento* and *Littorio* Divisions. *Littorio* reported its overall tank strength down from 115 to sixty at the end of this second day of fighting.

At dusk on this day, Rommel arrived back from Europe by air at Hitler's request to take charge of the Axis defence. He would find himself faced with the most difficult situation that he had ever tackled, and it would swiftly deteriorate. At midnight, 24 Australian Brigade launched an attack on a small rise known as Point 29 in the north near the coast. The position was captured despite tough resistance from the German 164 Light Division, and created a dangerous bulge in the Axis front. It forced Rommel to allocate an important proportion of his scarce reserves to eliminate this threatening salient. This presented the Allies, who were not short of reserves, with opportunities elsewhere.

On 26 October, Rommel, who had rapidly familiarized himself with what was known about the Allied offensive, planned a major counter-attack involving most of *Littorio* and 15 Panzer. He also brought 90 Light and *Trieste* Divisions forward to assist. The first of a series of Axis armoured counter-attacks commenced at dawn, involving elements of 15 Panzer and *Littorio*, supported by the concentrated fire of all available Axis artillery. The attacks were met by intense Allied artillery barrages far heavier than anything available to the Axis. This severely disrupted the concentration and deployment, and delayed the timing of the early Axis attacks, which were consequently broken up quite easily. The M14 tanks and *Semoventi* of 4 and 51 Armoured Battalions of *Littorio* were turned back by intense Allied shelling that caught them in the open, long before they could get near enough to inflict much damage.

At 15:00hr, a more serious Axis counter-attack developed, involving tanks, guns and infantry, which deployed under Allied bombardment. This was a combined assault by 12 Armoured Battalion of *Littorio* and elements of 15 Panzer from the south, and by 4 and 51 Armoured Battalions with a group of *Semoventi* of *Littorio* and some German panzers from the north-west. The whole attack would be supported by all available Axis artillery. But the Axis assault forces were once again effectively disrupted by bombing and heavy artillery fire, and repulsed before reaching the Australian positions. 2 British Armoured Brigade now penetrated the main Axis front and was met by tanks from 15 Panzer and *Littorio*. Thirty-five M14s and a few *Semoventi* from *Littorio* counter-attacked and, in ferocious fighting, forced the British back through 7 Motor Brigade. The British finally drove the Italians back, claiming to have destroyed thirteen M14s.

This counter-attack was described by Davide Beretta, commander of the 1st Battery of the 554th *Gruppo Semoventi da 75/18*, attached to the *Littorio*:

> In front of our *Semoventi* there were some tens of M14 tanks of *Littorio* Division that were firing their 47/32 guns against some enemy anti-tank positions. Suddenly on the horizon there appeared overwhelming formations of heavy British tanks, Shermans and Grants, aiming their 75mm guns like hunters. Sometimes they stopped their advance, and then continued forward. Our tiny M14/41s moved towards them to shorten the range – the shorter the range, the better the chances of penetrating their armour with their small guns. The British were positioned about 1,500m from our tanks and began to put up a rapid fire. We observed this action with dismay, because the 47mm shells of the M14s were bouncing off the heavy armour of their tanks. We were confident, however, that our own 75mm guns would have a very different effect on the British. 'Watch out, they are advancing towards us!' 'Tally Ho!' We started to advance as well, and we reached our blazing M14s with guns ready! 'Range 700, 800, 900. . . Fire!' . . . We managed to destroy some Shermans and Grants, and the British halted their advance and tried to attack our flanks. We barely managed to stop their advance, and failed to force them to withdraw; but it was a miracle indeed that we stopped them. In the evening we counted twenty Shermans and Grants and some Valentines and Crusaders destroyed; but the price we paid in that uneven battle was far too high. We had no choice, we were so used to Death's presence that we did not fear it anymore; we understood that the most difficult courage lay not in dying, but in continuing to live and fight in that hell.

In the evening of 26 October, 23 *Bersaglieri* Battalion from *Littorio*, supported by 90 Light, finally succeeded in occupying the extreme western edge of Point 29 near the coast. They were, however, unable to take the summit, which remained a base for future Australian advances. At 21:00hr, Rommel finally decided to summon up 21 Panzer from the south to provide badly needed reinforcements. He had decided that the Allied main thrust was in the north, but wanted to keep *Ariete* in the south just in case of any attacks there. As a result of the disruption caused by Allied air attacks, 21 Panzer only managed to get under way at midnight. They also moved north very slowly since, although it was dark, the Allied bombing went on uninterrupted through the night by the light of parachute flares. As 21 Panzer made their way north, 20 Australian Brigade on Point 29 managed to destroy two Italian M14s sent to probe their positions. After midnight, 2 Rifle Brigade from 7 Motor Brigade advanced through Axis positions further south under cover of darkness, to a location known as 'Snipe'. On the way they had a short but sharp encounter with a leaguer of tanks from *Littorio*, and claimed one *Semovente* destroyed.

'Snipe'

At dawn on 27 October, 2 Rifle Brigade had just hastily completed some shallow foxholes for their 6pdr anti-tank guns, when they found a large leaguer of Axis tanks from *Littorio* and 15 Panzer to their north. The latter quickly came to life and prepared to deploy, not as the British initially feared for an attack, but to move westwards away from them. This Axis force was as yet completely unaware of the British presence, and proceeded to cross the field of fire of the concealed British anti-tank guns, exposing their vulnerable flanks. The British promptly opened fire and claimed six panzers, eight M14s and two *Semoventi* destroyed and two other panzers hit. The smoking remains of some of these casualties remained observable, while others were towed away later in the day for repair. In reply the Axis claimed three British anti-tank guns, and Axis artillery shelled their positions for almost an hour. They then came under fire from their own armour that had mistaken their positions for those held by the Axis.

At 10:00hr, some Italian *Bersaglieri* formed up for an attack on the western perimeter of the position, but were attacked by British Bren carriers and forced to scatter. A half hour later a more serious Axis attack developed, when a company of thirteen Italian M14s emerged from behind a low ridge to the west and advanced against 'Snipe'. They approached at high speed in a sector where only a few British anti-tank guns could engage them. The British nevertheless accounted for four M14s in the first salvo, and the remainder retreated behind the ridge. At the same time, 2 Armoured Brigade, supporting another part of 7 Motor Brigade near Kidney Ridge slightly to the north, claimed a further five panzers and two M14s before withdrawing temporarily. At around noon, both sides took the opportunity to snatch some welcome rest. Once again Davide Beretta describes these assaults:

> The next morning [27 October] we were ordered to counter-attack and recover the positions lost previously, whatever the cost. It was a foolish order indeed . . . we were already exhausted and decimated, and it would be a desperate task even to resist another British attack. However, we were beyond caring and prepared for another counter-

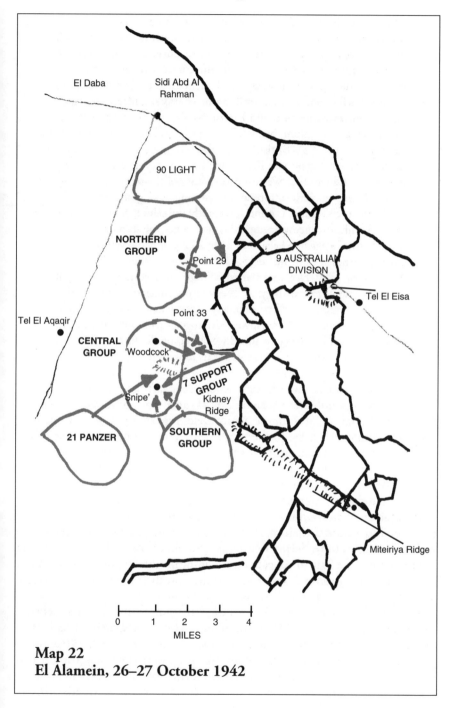

Map 22
El Alamein, 26–27 October 1942

El Daba

Sidi Abd Al Rahman

90 LIGHT

NORTHERN GROUP

Point 29

9 AUSTRALIAN DIVISION

Tel El Eisa

Point 33

Tel El Aqaqir

CENTRAL GROUP

'Woodcock'

7 SUPPORT GROUP

Kidney Ridge

'Snipe'

21 PANZER

SOUTHERN GROUP

Miteiriya Ridge

0   1   2   3   4
MILES

attack. Luckily, this time we would be supported by some German Panzer IIIs and IVs. As we advanced at least ten British tanks with infantry support appeared. We opened fire, but did not have time to congratulate ourselves for destroying three Crusaders before a tide of enemy tanks came up in support of them. The British 25pdr guns brought hell down on us as well. Some enemy infantry were wiped out by our machine guns and I must say that, in the heat of battle, when you killed without being killed, you were almost glad about the enemy's death. The British really did not expect our desperate counter-attack. Again the RAF came over to bomb us, destroying tanks and killing men. We counted seventy of them. Seventy deadly birds, flying in perfect formation, coming and going repeatedly. Suddenly everything was calm. It was only the calm before the storm, the next massive enemy armoured attack. Since the start of the battle the 554th *Gruppo* had been very lucky. We still had seven *Semoventi* with no losses at all. It was at 15.42 that we received the order: 'Open formation, Tally Ho!' So started a huge and confused dogfight involving tanks and artillery. ... We were encouraged by the fact that our 75mm gun was effective: many British tanks, even the most feared Shermans and Grants, were destroyed or immobilized by our guns. We could avenge our unlucky M14 comrades by these kills. ... Even though there was no chance for us to win.

The assaults resumed at 13:00hr when Axis artillery concentrated on 'Snipe', and a company of eight M14s and one *Semovente* from 12 Armoured Battalion of *Littorio*, which had moved up from El Wishka, appeared from over a ridge to the south-west. They probed the sector of the 'Snipe' defences that had suffered the heaviest losses, and were encouraged by the fact that all but one of the British anti-tank guns had fallen silent. This single 6pdr gun, however, managed to defeat the Italians, picking off five M14s and the *Semovente* from a range the M14s could not reach, before running short of ammunition. The three surviving M14s, gallantly manned, continued to advance, their machine guns firing on the British. They got to within 200yd (180m), deeply denting the shield of the 6pdr and wounding its crew before the British collected fresh ammunition and opened fire again. The three M14s promptly burst into flames and their brave crews perished. The entire Italian company had been wiped out.

At around the same time, 2 Armoured Brigade to the north attacked a small rise known as Point 33 but was repulsed by intense enemy fire. It then found itself facing a major counter-attack involving an estimated thirty panzers and ten Italian M14s, coming from the west. The Axis armour had been poorly briefed and advanced in open formation, apparently unaware of the British guns still at 'Snipe' to the south. In response to intense British anti-tank fire, about half the Axis tanks turned south. The combined fire of 2 Armoured and 2 Rifle Brigades caused significant losses to the Axis armour when they came within 200yd (180m). The British later claimed nine enemy tanks destroyed, several others hit, and one M14 captured. Three Axis tanks remained concealed in hull-down positions nearby and swept 'Snipe' with machine-gun fire for the rest of the afternoon. As dusk fell the Axis armour withdrew, 12 Armoured Battalion of *Littorio* having suffered severe losses, amounting to twenty-seven of the Division's remaining sixty runners.

The *War Diary* of 12 Armoured Battalion, commanded by Captain Preve, indicates graphically how these losses occurred:

04:25 hours. An order arrives from Colonel Amoroso [commander of 133 Armoured Regiment] to move . . . to attack the British forces in front in co-operation with the Barone Battery and in close collaboration with the Stiffelmaier Group – direction north-east.

05:30 hours. The battalion and the Barone Battery [Major Barone] are near 4 and 5 Companies, who are in the first wave: behind follow two *Semoventi* groups in line with 6 Company in the second wave.

06:30 hours. The battalion is ready to attack. Strength: 19 tanks, 9 *Semoventi*. In front of us, covering the British withdrawal, are at least ten 6pdr AT guns, dug in flush with the ground (as events proved later). Distance of the AT guns from our start line, 2,000m.

06:45 hours. Two tanks of 5 Company hit and immobilized. The *Semoventi* groups open fire on the forward AT gun.

07:00 hours. The battalion attacks. In spite of the violent enemy fire and the resultant initial losses of tanks and men, the battalion advances firmly but keeping a certain distance from the AT guns, which are extremely well dug in and camouflaged. Suddenly there is very violent fire from another eight or ten AT guns hidden on our left and in depth. A number of victims in the battalion, which halts very suddenly. Enemy fire becomes more and more violent. The survivors then show incredible proof of valour: Second-Lieutenant Camplani from outside his turret urges his own tanks on to the attack at the head of them, drives his own tank at full speed towards the foremost AT gun. He is stopped by a belt of mines in front of the AT positions and by a shell that breaks his tracks. Second-Lieutenant Stefanelli has his tank hit by an AP shell, which penetrates and explodes. At the head of his company Lieutenant Pomoni's tank is hit in the engine; the crew miraculously survived. Lieutenant Bucalossi's tank is hit and set on fire. Lieutenant Zilambo is wounded in the right leg and saved by Lieutenant Luciano (the adjutant). Second-Lieutenant Delfino continues the attack and is only stopped by the minefields.

> At 11:30 hours Colonel Teege gives the order to withdraw to the start line and disperse in the wadi behind. The tanks not burnt out were recovered.
>
> The following losses were reported: Tanks – 9 burnt, 3 hit and immobilized but recovered. Personnel – 4 dead, 11 wounded.

In spite of the heavy losses, these persistent Axis armoured attacks did have an impact, and during the night of 27/28 October, the shattered remnants of 2 Rifle Brigade withdrew from their exposed position at 'Snipe'.

The following day, 28 October, the Axis armour launched more counter-attacks on the now partially abandoned Allied salient. In the early morning they attacked 133 British Lorried Infantry Brigade: this company had been sent to relieve 'Snipe', but ended up to the north of it and was unable to dig its anti-tank guns into the rocky ground. The Axis assault virtually annihilated the British unit, knocking out their exposed anti-tank guns, killing sixty men, including their commander Colonel Murphy, and capturing 300 others. The British should have been supported by their armour, but once again the latter failed to appear. At this point *Littorio* had been reduced to a strength of between thirty and forty M14s, while *Ariete* in the south still had their original 129 tanks.

On the night of 28/29 October the Allies moved the battle of attrition to the coastal sector of the line, when 9 Australian Division struck north from Point 29 towards the coast. They almost succeeded in cutting off elements of 164 Light and *Trento* Divisions. The initial Axis response was to commit available elements of *Trieste*, 90 Light and 21 Panzer Divisions to block this dangerous advance. In the longer term, Rommel was keen to preserve the largely intact 21 Panzer by withdrawing their units from the front to form a new mobile reserve, and replacing them with the somewhat battered *Trieste*. Unfortunately, this dangerous Australian thrust was swiftly followed by alarming rumours of a powerful British force crossing the Qattara Depression in the far south. This aroused a fear that the entire Axis army might be outflanked, surrounded and annihilated. The response to these apparent dangers at opposite ends of the Alamein line was further confusion and indecision in the Axis command. They constantly feared committing all their armour at a single point in case the Allies exploited their numerical superiority to attack somewhere else. This was the nightmare scenario that now appeared to have arisen.

On the morning of 29 October, Rommel delayed the replacement of 21 Panzer on hearing reports of the Qattara advance. He was unable to concentrate fully on the real danger in the north, although he assumed personal command of the forces there. In the meantime, *Ariete* – his only other intact armoured formation – remained in the south to prevent a possible Allied breakthrough there. It and the infantry divisions in the southern sector were now placed under the command of General De Stefanis at XX Corps. These command changes were intended to provide more focus in the Axis response to Allied attacks. In the short term, however, the uncertainty and confusion caused by rumours and indecision effectively allowed the Allies time to prepare for any Axis reaction in the north. In late afternoon, therefore, when an Axis counter-attack finally sought to repair the breach on the coast, they were more than ready for it. The planned counter-attack against Point 29, by 15 Panzer and *Littorio*, was heavily disrupted and delayed by Allied bombing. Initially a few Italian M14 tanks reconnoitred positions occupied by 8 British Armoured Brigade, which returned fire and claimed several hits, but no tanks destroyed. The main Axis attack followed, but quickly disintegrated under the fire of 300 Allied guns. This furious barrage caused the surrender of large numbers of Germans, including more than 100 men from 15 Panzer Division.

The next morning, 30 October, Rommel finally learnt that the reports of an Allied advance across the Qattara Depression were no more than fantasy. This would be the only item of good news on this day, however. He realized that *Trieste* was now too weak to replace all of 21 Panzer, and that one infantry battalion would need to remain in the front line. In spite of this, he withdrew the rest of 21 Panzer and replaced it with *Trieste* during the following night. The newly released 21 Panzer and those elements of 90 Light not committed against the Australians were now Rommel's only mobile reserve in the north. He also discovered that 15 Panzer had only thirty-nine panzers left, and *Littorio* only twenty-three M14s, eight *Semoventi*, a single battery of captured 25pdr guns, and one anti-tank platoon, and most of these were emplaced forward in direct support of the infantry.

In the next two days, *Littorio* remained near the front line in support of the overstretched Axis infantry. They were now really too weak to play a significant role in Rommel's counter-attacks against the Australians, though they were still involved in local actions; but they could not escape the ever-present Allied bombing. On 1 November, the eve of their 'Supercharge' offensive, the Allies estimated Italian strength, fairly accurately, at 4,300 men and 140 tanks with *Ariete*, and 4,200 men and sixty tanks with *Littorio*, or 200 tanks in total. At this same point records indicate that *Ariete* had 124 tanks, *Littorio* only thirty-eight and *Trieste* twenty-seven, a total of 189 in all.

Tel el Aqaqir

On the night of 1/2 November, 50 British Infantry Division advanced through the badly overstretched Axis forward defences, including a number of disabled tanks dug in in hull-down positions. The preparatory artillery bombardment had been so intense that the Axis infantry were still suffering from shock when the British took them prisoner. Already by 04:00hr, the British had reached their objectives with relatively light casualties, many caused by fire from dug-in M14s from 12 and 51 Armoured Battalions of *Littorio*. The Italians also engaged in gun duels with eighty Valentine tanks, advancing in support of their infantry. The fighting lasted for an hour and a half before the Italian tanks were destroyed one by one and the British pushed forward in strength. The British captured 350 German and Italian prisoners during this advance, including many from *Littorio*.

On the morning of 2 November, 9 British Armoured Brigade, with a mixture of 130 Sherman, Grant and Crusader tanks, moved up behind 50 Division. They then engaged the main Axis anti-tank screen, claiming thirty-five anti-tank guns destroyed, mainly 47mm or 50mm calibre. However, they suffered heavy casualties in the process, being reduced from ninety-four to nineteen Sherman tanks. In spite of this they reached the area of the Rahman Track below a small height called Tel el Aqaqir. Rommel immediately directed the last mobile reserves from 15 Panzer and *Littorio* against this penetration, and ordered 21 Panzer down from the north. He had to organize counter-attacks against this dangerous Allied penetration. This took time, however – time that the British tanks used to dig themselves in beside their concealed anti-tank guns in preparation for Axis counter-attacks. This secured them the advantage in the forthcoming encounters, since the Axis tanks were forced, against their usual practice, to advance against enemy tanks and anti-tank guns in prepared positions. The result could only be further heavy losses for the Axis armour, losses that they, unlike the Allies, could not afford.

In spite of these disadvantages, the Axis forces mounted a number of hastily organized and unco-ordinated strikes against the Allied penetration, involving 21 Panzer from the north and 15 Panzer and *Littorio* from the west. They had no choice in the matter, since they had to prevent an Allied breakthrough at all costs. The western attacks involved 15 Panzer and the surviving M14s from 4 Armoured Battalion of *Littorio*. It is uncertain exactly how many tanks were involved in total, but the Axis tank crews found themselves at close quarters with large numbers of Shermans with their deadly 75mm guns. They were badly outnumbered and outgunned, and the Shermans were supported by concealed 6pdr anti-tank guns. The British tanks, for once, refused to be drawn out, and the Axis armour had to slug it out in the most disadvantageous circumstances. They had only a little support from their own anti-tank guns, artillery or infantry, and no air cover at all, while the British could call on assistance from all of these supporting arms. It was a shattering experience for the experienced Axis crews, but especially for the Italians in their flimsy M14s, which can often be seen in post-action photographs smashed to pieces.

In a two-hour period around noon, the most intense tank battle of the desert war raged as 21 Panzer and the sad remnants of 15 Panzer and *Littorio* Divisions tried to repulse the entire might of the reinforced 1 British Armoured Division. It involved around a hundred German and Italian tanks in attacks on more than 300 British tanks, including over a hundred Shermans, supported by anti-tank guns, artillery and aircraft. It was a battle of attrition that the heavily outnumbered Axis armour could not win. It is clear that before the day ended, most of the ninety German and fifty Italian runners were sucked into this attrition and ground up. The Axis infantry was entirely tied down holding the increasingly overstretched front. The Axis armoured attacks were eventually so weak that they amounted to little more than probes that were driven off by heavy Allied artillery and anti-tank fire. In these circumstances, the Axis armour was increasingly forced onto the defensive, retreating into hull-down positions and only engaging targets of opportunity. As dusk approached, only thirty-five German panzers and twenty Italian M14s remained in battle-worthy condition in the north; the rest were left smoking on the battlefield. The Allies had suffered fewer losses, and still had 7 Armoured Division in reserve to throw into the battle. They overestimated the surviving Axis tanks at eighty German and 160 Italian, including *Ariete.*

It was the tragic outcome of this desperate fighting that finally convinced Rommel, on the evening of 2 November, to order an Axis withdrawal. He called on General Arena to bring his almost unscathed *Ariete* up from its positions in the south, despite the poor condition of many of their M14 tanks. They would provide a strong reinforcement for the otherwise weakened Axis mobile forces that would have to cover the retreat. This would effectively expose the Axis southern flank, since there was insufficient fuel for them to return south, but it was now absolutely vital to prevent an Allied breakthrough in the north. On the following day Rommel intended to use the Axis armour, including *Ariete,* to cover the withdrawal of the non-motorized Axis infantry, most of it Italian. In the first phase of the withdrawal, the Italian infantry of X and XXI Corps would fall back to positions behind the Axis anti-tank screen along the Rahman Track; they would be covered by the Axis anti-tank screen, supported by the Axis armour and its artillery. In this plan *Ariete* would take up a position near Tel el Aqaqir on the right flank of the battered remnants of *Littorio* and *Trieste.* The reconstituted XX Corps would then be in the centre of the Axis line, with *DAK* and X Corps to their north and XXI Corps to their south. The Axis infantry would then withdraw towards Fuka, while the armour of *DAK* and XX Corps held back the Allies, before staging a fighting withdrawal late on 3 November so that they stood at dusk on a line running south from Ghazal on the coast. He requested permission for this withdrawal from Hitler, but initially heard nothing.

On 3 November, the Axis infantry formations started withdrawing to their fall-back positions according to plan. At 10:30hr, in the absence of a reply from Hitler, Rommel confirmed his withdrawal orders. The Axis infantry was to continue westwards, while *Ariete* was urged northwards with all speed. The tattered remnants of *DAK* and *Littorio* were told to hold their current positions, but were put on short notice to pull back to a line running south from Ghazal as soon as darkness fell. 90 Light and the Axis anti-tank screen would follow soon after as the final rearguard. This complex plan actually went reasonably smoothly considering the chaotic state of the battlefield. It was reported that a few formations, once on the move, continued towards the rear, leaving gaps in the new line. In the centre, 25 *Bologna* Infantry Division had reportedly abandoned their positions too hastily and *Ariete*, on its way north, had to halt temporarily north of Deir el Qatani to cover this gap. It was also said that *Trieste* had practically disintegrated, leaving a dangerous gap to the south of Tel el Aqaqir; however, this was filled by *Ariete* as it arrived from the south.

It was at this crucial point that Hitler finally responded to Rommel's request for permission to withdraw of the previous evening. He showed no understanding of the desperate Axis military situation, but instead issued an imperious order demanding no retreat. It was a devastating personal blow to Rommel, who had always been supported by Hitler while successful, but a savagely cruel blow for the Axis forces, now apparently doomed to defeat and destruction. The still faithful Rommel, although fully aware of the implications, tried nevertheless to implement this insane order. He vainly hoped to soften it by revealing in full the wretched state of his forces, and sent his ADC to report to Hitler personally. In the meantime, he reluctantly issued orders for the non-motorized Axis infantry to stand where they were, even if this was in open desert with no cover whatsoever. He allowed *DAK* and XX Corps, including the newly arrived *Ariete*, to fall back on Tel el Aqaqir, but only to bring them into line with the stranded Axis infantry along the Rahman Track. This new line in the sand, for it was little more than that, was to be held against several Allied armoured divisions now emerging through the old Axis front. This vain attempt to obey Hitler's incompetent halt order effectively doomed most of the Axis infantry and brought about the ruin of *Ariete*.

The result of this swift succession of order and counter order was complete chaos. The already weak Axis communications, that were constantly breaking down under the bombing and shelling, did not help matters. A number of Axis units never received the revised orders to stand and fight, and withdrew as originally planned, including 164 Light. Others received the halt orders, but many chose to ignore them and continue their withdrawal westwards. They viewed them with suspicion as at least garbled and unrealistic, if not insane, and possibly inspired by the enemy. A few ignored the halt orders deliberately, including some Italian infantry units that had already abandoned their best defensive positions and saw no sense in opposing Allied armour in the open desert.

The Rahman Track

It was along an unprepossessing desert track running south from Sidi abd el Rahman on the coast that the Axis armour would meet its fate at Hitler's order. 2 British Armoured Brigade tried to break out on the north of the Allied salient, but was held up in a series of desperate battles along this track by the surviving elements of *DAK* and the last few M14s from *Littorio*. In the afternoon, a little further south 8 British Armoured Brigade tried to break through the overstretched Axis lines; a few managed to reach the Rahman Track, though here they clashed with the newly arrived *Ariete* and were driven off by Italian artillery and tanks. The British reported the loss of sixteen Sherman and ten Crusader tanks.

At dawn on 4 November, the Axis forces had successfully organized a ragged new line along the Rahman Track to the west of the Allied breakthrough. In spite of the confused orders and incessant Allied pressure, the complex Axis withdrawals had gone much better than anyone could have expected, mainly because of the cautious nature of the Allied advance. In the north were 90 Light and X Corps, with *DAK* and XX Corps in the centre and XXI Corps slowly moving into line in the south. The Axis armoured strength now stood at a truly pitiful twenty-four German panzers and seventeen M14s of *Littorio*. The main Axis armoured strength now lay with *Ariete* and its 100 M14s, which, although in desperate need of repair and maintenance, would now bear the brunt of the fighting. It was this battered force that stood against the full strength of the Allies.

It was not until mid-morning that 22 British Armoured Brigade finally managed to escape the original and now undefended Axis minefields. They were leading the rest of 7 Armoured Division and made first contact with the new Axis line. They immediately came under fire from a thin screen of 88mm guns and probed southwards along the Rahman Track from Tel el Aqaqir, seeking a way around this. Instead of reaching open desert however, they ran into an extensive line of tanks and artillery. This was *Ariete*, under Arena, with its 100 M14s dug in and supported by the entire XX Corps artillery, including a number of 88mm guns. It also included the shattered remnants of *Littorio* and *Trieste*, with a few more tanks. The British quickly recognized that this powerful force was too strong to rush and too dangerous to leave on their flank. They therefore halted and brought up their own supporting infantry, artillery and anti-tank guns. The two sides meantime settled down to a long-range artillery duel that went on for many hours. In this, Arena made excellent use of the central direction of their

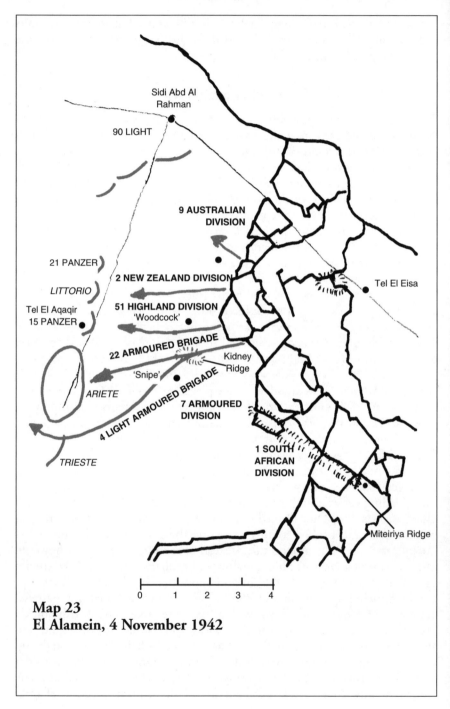

Map 23
El Alamein, 4 November 1942

corps artillery to achieve maximum firepower against any enemy movements or artillery batteries. In the meantime, 22 Armoured Brigade
prepared a set-piece assault against their old rivals, and *Ariete* soon reported
that it was heavily engaged.

The combination of artillery duel and armoured sparring between *Ariete*
and 22 Armoured raged all morning, through noon and well into the
afternoon, with neither side making any significant progress. The fighting
revolved around an intense artillery duel between the respective gunners,
and frequent bouts of heavy skirmishing between the tank crews. A tank
driver from *Ariete*, Antonio Tomba, described his impressions:

> . . . we spotted about sixty enemy tanks that, seeing us advancing
> furiously, had a moment of disorientation. Our poor M13s with
> their 47mm guns could never be effective against them – we could
> only hope to hit their tracks in order to immobilize them at least; our
> shells just bounced off when we hit their armour. In addition, while
> they numbered sixty, we had little over half of that. We did
> everything possible, giving our very best. ... We had no chance, but
> we proved a difficult opponent for the English: the secret lay in
> manoeuvring the tank properly. Our tactics were simple: always keep
> moving, never expose your flank to their guns, don't let them fire
> first, all the crew must act as a single unit: everyone must know what
> to do and when to do it, in complete harmony with each other. We
> managed to hold off the enemy that day, but they replaced their
> losses again while we could only count how many of us were left
> alive. We could never have resisted for another day. Everyone was
> good, really good, that day, everyone fought an unequal battle
> without complaint and without yielding, even when there was no
> water and no food. We were lucky when it started to rain as this
> slowed the English advance, and we, the last survivors of the *Ariete*
> Division, were able to escape their pursuit.

In addition to this frontal assault by 22 Armoured, 4 British Light
Armoured Brigade was already probing around *Ariete*'s largely open
southern flank. They attempted to encircle the Italians, but were delayed by
the fire of the entire XX Corps artillery. This intense Italian artillery fire only
finally ceased as British tanks appeared in their rear amongst the guns
themselves. In the late afternoon Arena reported: 'Enemy tanks penetrated
south of *Ariete*. *Ariete* now encircled. Location 5km north-west of Bir el
Abd. *Ariete* tanks now in action.' It was not long after this that Rommel
realized the game was up, and finally ordered a retreat, instructing 90 Light,
DAK and *Ariete* to withdraw under cover of darkness. The Italians were
instructed to retreat westwards through the desert to the south of the coast

road. The heavy pressure on *Ariete* had finally persuaded Rommel to ignore Hitler's order, and attempt to save what remained of his army.

It was not until nightfall, when Arena received this order, that the heavily outnumbered Italians finally fell back, and 22 Armoured occupied the field of battle. They counted the broken shells of twenty-nine Italian M14 tanks and a few ruined guns on the field, and captured about 450 prisoners against their own admitted losses of a single tank and a few casualties. In the south, 4 Light Armoured claimed an additional 300 prisoners and eleven guns. The German and Allied records leave us with the impression that *Ariete* was surrounded and destroyed in this battle, and a significant portion of the division was certainly lost. However, a remnant of *Ariete* nevertheless managed to escape the trap, and the events of the next day show that a large part of *Ariete* managed to disengage during the night and slip away. The dramatic day-long stand by *Ariete* at El Alamein, on 4 November, effectively stymied Allied plans to encircle and destroy the main Axis armoured forces. It allowed the surviving Axis mobile units, including *DAK* and 90 Light, to withdraw westwards largely unimpeded. They were unable, however, to save the Axis infantry that had no transport to carry them to the rear. These either forced to surrender where they stood, or were rounded up by British mobile forces as they marched through the desert. The end of *Ariete* was acknowledged by Rommel, who recorded that the Italian XX Corps 'had been completely destroyed after a very gallant action. In the *Ariete* we lost our oldest Italian comrades.'

On the night of 4/5 November, in response to Rommel's revised orders, those Axis formations that could do so, disengaged and fell back in the direction of Fuka. The Allies, immensely relieved that their long grinding battle of attrition was nearing its end and that organized resistance had melted away, retired into leaguers to await the dawn. They were anxious to reorganize and regroup before what they anticipated would be a resumption of battle the next day. There was no pursuit during the night. It was only overnight intelligence that persuaded them that the battle had actually been won, and that Axis forces were in full retreat.

In the early hours of 5 November, a confused gaggle of mixed-up Axis formations scrambled through the desert south of Fuka under constant air attack. They were relatively disciplined in the circumstances, but were in constant fear of being outflanked by pursuing Allied armour, which must have been on their heels. They were ordered to reorganize before moving to Mersa Matruh during the coming night. Rommel wanted to keep them moving, both to prevent them falling into Allied hands and to boost their flagging morale. The fighting power of all of his remaining units was at a very low ebb. The Italian XX Corps had been almost destroyed, and De Stefanis had no more than a few scattered units under his command which could no longer be brought into action as a cohesive whole.

At midday, 8 British Armoured Brigade, that had been sent to cut off the Axis armour, reached the coast road between El Daba and Fuka. They were just in time to net the only substantial group of Axis mobile troops successfully caught by British armour. The British waited in hull-down positions as a mixed column of tanks, trucks and marching infantry came unsuspectingly towards them. At almost point-blank range they opened fire, throwing the Axis column into such complete confusion that they offered little resistance. In a little over an hour, a total of fourteen panzers and twenty-nine M14s were claimed destroyed, and 1,000 prisoners taken, along with four guns and 100 vehicles. This ambush was interpreted by the British as the final destruction of the Italian XX Corps. This contradicts Axis reports indicating that the remnants of this corps were present at Mersa Matruh the next day. The records do not identify this captured Axis unit, and it may have been a mixed bag, perhaps including technicians and repaired tanks from the abandoned repair shops at El Daba.

On the morning of 6 November, the dejected and bedraggled Axis armour reached Mersa Matruh in pouring rain. They included the meagre remnants of the Italian XX Corps, with a grand total of only ten M14 tanks. The defeated Axis forces could not possibly hold this position, and halted only long enough to destroy supplies and repair facilities to prevent them falling into Allied hands. They replenished their own reserves before doing so, but could delay no longer. They had to keep in motion to avoid encirclement and destruction at the hands of Allied armour reportedly moving through the desert to the south. This was the beginning of an epic retreat that would eventually lead all the way back to Tunisia. It was carried out across difficult terrain, in frequently appalling weather, under intermittent bombing and the constant threat of encirclement. It was, however, assisted by the bad weather, as this slowed the Allied pursuit and grounded Allied aircraft. The pursuit was also delayed by Axis sabotage and booby traps, which made the Allied advance costly in lives and in time. In addition the long retreat reversed the previously prevailing balance of advantage in the supply war. The Allies found their supply lines lengthening as they advanced, and had to bring their supplies forward over an increasing distance. In contrast the Axis forces were able to fall back on existing stockpiles and dispense with the necessity to transport these to the front. This combination of factors limited the Allied pursuit to a relatively small force of two divisions.

On 7 November the Axis retreat continued to the Egyptian frontier without further losses. The pursuing Allies had been held back by heavy rain that had turned the desert into sticky mud, and by booby traps set by German and Italian engineers. They were further delayed by the disorganization that followed the breakout, and by increasingly tricky supply problems. This was fortunate, since the Axis forces were caught up in a massive 25-mile (40km) traffic jam through Halfaya Pass. It would take them two whole days to clear this bottleneck, in spite of ruthless traffic control measures, which dictated that broken-down vehicles were simply bulldozed off the road. It seemed all too likely that the Axis forces would be encircled by Allied armour moving around their open desert flank. This was a difficult time for an exhausted Rommel, who had to make some hard decisions to ensure that as many of his forces as possible escaped. He ordered the remnants of XX Corps to swing southwards through the desert to reach the top of Halfaya Pass by this route and ease congestion on the road. They were then instructed to protect the top of the pass from any Allied flanking moves. At the same time he directed Italian infantry reserves in the rear towards Mersa Brega to construct defences. This provided an early indication that he had no plans to stop before there, in spite of pleas from his superiors that the Egyptian frontier should be held.

It was at noon on 8 November that news arrived of the successful Allied landings in French North Africa. It was obvious that these new Allied forces would attempt to reach Tripoli before Rommel. This raised the spectre of the puny Axis forces being crushed between two superior Allied armies, and virtually ensured that Rommel would not defend Mersa Brega as he had done in the previous two years. It also finally compelled Hitler and Mussolini to send reinforcements to North Africa to prevent a complete Axis collapse. The very next day the first Axis units landed in Tunisia to prevent this vital area falling into Allied hands. They would soon be followed by others, including two panzer divisions that Rommel could have used at Alamein. It is important to note that these reinforcements landed at the ports of Tunis and Bizerta, which significantly expanded Axis port capacity. They could not have been landed or supplied through Tripoli without cutting supplies to Rommel's forces. They were also sent to shore up the endangered Axis position and prevent a military and political collapse; they would not have been sent to assist a successful Rommel in Egypt.

On 9 November, Rommel was still pushing his forces through the Halfaya Pass, while 90 Light acted as a rearguard. In reserve, above the pass, stood the XX Corps which had completed its swing through the desert with, remarkably, no further losses from amongst its worn-out vehicles. It was not until the following day that Axis forces finally cleared Halfaya Pass – and just in the nick of time, as the Allies stormed the pass and captured a small Axis rearguard. The main Axis forces were already heading for Tobruk, where they halted briefly to rest and replenish their supplies from their stores before destroying them.

At this point Rommel estimated his total strength as 2,000 Italian and 2,000 German infantry, fifteen German and a few Italian anti-tank guns, forty German and several Italian field guns, with an armoured force of 3,000 German and 500 Italian troops, eleven German and ten Italian tanks, twenty German anti-tank guns, twenty-four mixed AA guns and twenty-five mixed field guns. The only armoured reinforcement imminently available was the 131 *Centauro* Armoured Division, which landed at Tripoli in the middle of November. It consisted of 131 Armoured Regiment with 13, 14 and 15 Armoured Battalions, 5 *Bersaglieri* Regiment with 14, 22 and 24 *Bersaglieri* Battalions, and 131 Artillery Regiment, under General Giorgio Count Calvi de Bergolo, a fifty-five-year-old cavalry officer. It arrived without many of its artillery and engineer units, which had been lost in transit or left behind in Italy, and was due to undergo a process of acclimatization. This was, however, curtailed so that it could be sent to support the rapidly contracting Axis front. It almost immediately surrendered its 15 Armoured Battalion, which was sent to Tunisia to reinforce 50 Special Brigade.

On the night of 11/12 November, another serious traffic jam built up as the Axis forces pushed through the bottleneck presented by the minefields of the old Gazala line. The news that Allied armour had reached Acroma, next morning, caused momentary fear that they might be even further south and west. If so they might easily swing north to cut the coast road behind the exhausted Axis forces. As a result, Rommel immediately rushed his own forces into the Jebel Akhdar, where they would have some chance of defending themselves against Allied armour. However, they were also in danger of being cut off by a rapid Allied advance through the desert, like the advance that had brought about the disaster at Beda Fomm in 1941.

On 13 November the Italians, increasingly anxious to retain some small remnant of their African Empire, issued orders to hold Mersa Brega. They had already posted 80 *La Spezia* and 136 *Giovani Fascisti* Infantry Divisions and elements of Count Calvi's *Centauro* to the defences there. On 17 November, however, Rommel decided that Axis forces were not strong enough to hold this position and sent De Stefanis, commander of XX Corps, to Rome to persuade his superiors that Buerat offered a better prospect for the defence of Tripoli. De Stefanis was no longer needed, since XX Corps had been reduced to a regimental grouping, known as the *Ariete* Battle-Group.

On 18 November, Axis mobile forces were in the area of Benghasi, while Rommel was further back at Zuetina with the *Ariete* Battle-Group. He ordered the first M14s from *Centauro* to arrive at the front to Antelat to protect their exposed flank from any Allied forces approaching from across the desert. It was here that *Centauro* had their first encounter with the enemy when they clashed with forward units of 7 Armoured Division near Antelat on that day. An Italian column of fifteen lorries, five M14 tanks, five armoured cars and a single 75mm gun were moving along the foot of the escarpment from Schleidima when they were fired on from above by British armour and brought to a halt. The *Bersaglieri* quickly deployed from their lorries and sought cover, returning fire and deploying their armour. A force of three German armoured cars arrived to support them, and they were able to keep the British at bay while the main Axis forces slipped past to Mersa Brega.

On 19 November, the Soviets launched their huge counter offensive at Stalingrad, which would trap an entire German army and punch a massive hole in the Eastern Front in only five days. This disaster quickly made Russia the main priority for all reinforcements and supplies, and left Rommel to cope as best he could with what had already been transported to Tunisia. It strengthened his opinion that Mersa Brega could not be held, and that the Axis forces should fall back as far and as fast as possible. This clashed with the views of his superiors, who were anxious to hold on to part of Libya for political reasons. Precisely a month later, on 19 December, a second Soviet offensive further north destroyed a 200,000-strong Italian army defending the Don River. This second disaster eliminated the only other substantial Italian force engaged in front-line warfare. The loss of this huge army ended any prospect of significant Italian reinforcements reaching North Africa. It would, however, finally compel Italian leaders to reassess any hopes of saving their African Empire. In the meantime they believed that they should try to preserve what they could.

On the night of 23/24 November, the last Axis rearguards arrived in the refurbished Mersa Brega positions. The tattered remnants of the force that had entered battle at El Alamein only a month before were a sorry sight. The only mobile reinforcement that they had received was *Centauro*, the rest having been sent to Tunisia to defend the rear. The largely untried Italian infantry were positioned in static defences, and the few exhausted armoured forces available were posted on the open desert flank. Although strong, the Mersa Brega position was open to being outflanked by powerful British armoured forces using the desert to the south. This flank needed to be protected by strong Axis armoured forces, but those available were extremely weak after their long retreat. In spite of this, Rommel was under pressure from all sides to defend the position, largely for political reasons. Fortunately the Allies had no immediate plans to attack, fearing that if they did so without adequate preparation and overwhelming superiority, they might be repulsed, as in previous years. This extreme caution, and a long Allied supply line all the way back to Egypt, allowed the Axis troops time to recover from their recent experiences.

In early December, Rommel finally secured Italian agreement to construct a new fall-back position at Buerat, and to send the Axis infantry there to prepare defences. This breakthrough was vital since the Axis fuel situation remained desperate, and without fuel, the Axis forces might find themselves stranded and outflanked. The largely Italian infantry formations were sent back to Buerat in relays between 6 and 8 December, to minimize fuel consumption, to construct defences. By 9 December the last of them had withdrawn, leaving enough fuel to permit *DAK* and a combined battle group from *Ariete* and *Centauro*, stationed at El Agheila, to escape to Buerat at short notice. The intention was that the Axis armour would inflict maximum damage on the enemy before pulling out.

On 11 December, the combined *Ariete/Centauro* Battle-Group was stationed on the southern flank of the Axis front line. Its strength stood at fifty-seven worn-out M14 tanks and around 2,000 men, and it only had fuel for between 20 and 30 miles, like all of the Axis units, and therefore had to keep its activities to a minimum. It was now clear to the Axis forces that an Allied attack was imminent, and therefore orders were issued for the Axis armour to withdraw after dusk, leaving only a small rearguard to delay pursuit. This withdrawal went as planned, and by midnight the road was full of Axis tanks and guns all moving westwards. In response to intelligence about this, the Allies moved forward their planned assault on Mersa Brega, and on the night of 12/13 December, they attacked and broke through the Axis rearguard. The *Ariete/Centauro* Battle-Group, at the extreme southern end of the line, about ten miles from the coast, had further to retreat than most and across more difficult terrain.

On 13 December, *Ariete/Centauro* Battle-Group was at the tail end of the retreat when it was attacked by 8 Armoured Brigade near El Agheila. At 11:30hr, an Italian rearguard of four guns and three M14s was attacked and fired on by eighty British Shermans, and fell back under fire. An hour later the main Italian positions, spread out on either side of the coast road, were attacked. They responded with heavy artillery fire that destroyed a number of British vehicles. At 15:00hr, after a heavy artillery bombardment from British 25pdrs, a force of British tanks engaged *Ariete/Centauro*. An hour later, a company of twelve M14s attacked the British from the north-west until they were engaged by Shermans, which knocked out six M14s and two more half an hour later. The British then closed in on the Italian anti-tank screen, overrunning twelve 47mm guns and taking fifty prisoners. The Italians claimed twenty-two Shermans and two armoured cars destroyed in return. As usual the British subsequently leaguered for the night and allowed *Ariete/Centauro* to withdraw under cover of intermittent shelling by artillery. This tough fight by the weakened Italians brought warm praise from the Germans, including Rommel who enthused: 'The Italians put up a magnificent fight, for which they deserved the utmost credit.'

Minor successes like this, however, could not halt the Allied advance for any length of time. The Axis forces had retained their cohesion throughout the retreat and had held Cyrenaica longer than expected. This was largely due to the extremely cautious Allied pursuit, but it was also partly due to the determination and professionalism of the Axis forces. On 16 December they were back at Nofilia, and two days later at Sirte, which they hoped to hold until Christmas. Instead they were forced to abandon their festivities and fall back to Buerat, which they reached on the last day of the year, 31 December 1942. On 3 January 1943 the Italian infantry were withdrawn from Buerat to a final position before Tripoli at Homs-Tarhuna. They were replaced by the Axis armour, with *Ariete* Battle-Group at Beurat on the coast, 15 Panzer and 90 Light in the centre, and *Centauro* Battle-Group in the desert to the south.

On 9 January, Rommel had time to dine with the officers of *Centauro* and discovered that he had fought against Colonel Pizzolato during World War I. They exchanged views on that other war to escape the unwelcome shadow of this present one. On 13 January, 21 Panzer was sent back to Tunisia to protect the rear, but it surrendered its few remaining panzers to its sister division, 15 Panzer. On 15 January, the remnants of the *Ariete* Battle-Group were officially absorbed into the *Centauro* Battle-Group, and they moved into the centre of the Axis line, with 90 Light to the north and 15 Panzer to the south. The *Centauro* Battle-Group now had fifty-seven M14 tanks, ninety-eight field guns, sixty-six anti-tank guns and sixteen armoured cars. The Axis forces had fuel for 150 miles (240km), two-thirds of their normal ammunition issue, and rations for five days. On that same day the Allied armour attacked Buerat, while 2 New Zealand Division attempted to outflank it to the south; and at noon Rommel issued orders for a withdrawal that evening.

On 16 January, the New Zealanders managed to surprise and capture three M14 tanks from *Centauro* as they camped in the desert south of Buerat. As dusk fell, they fought a fierce two-hour action with fifteen panzers and fifteen Italian M14s, and knocked out two M14s and a number of vehicles and guns, while losing four Crusader tanks themselves. In the course of this encounter, a small gap opened up between *Centauro* and 15 Panzer in the south and 90 Light in the north. The Axis forces were running low on fuel and ammunition, and Rommel therefore ordered a further withdrawal back to Homs-Tarhuna under cover of darkness. A potentially dangerous situation was avoided by this rapid withdrawal and the Allied decision to leaguer for the night.

On 17 January, *Centauro* was briefly stationed in support of 90 Light at Beni Ulid, with the intention of delaying the Allied advance. In spite of this, 8 British Armoured Brigade penetrated their positions and forced them back to the Homs-Tarhuna positions. The following day these positions were held by Italian infantry on the coast with a mobile group, including *Centauro*, 15 Panzer, *Giovani Fascisti* and a reconstituted 164 Light on the desert flank, and 90 Light in reserve. In the evening of 19 January, Rommel became concerned that 4 Light Armoured Brigade might outflank his positions, and sent *Centauro*, *Giovani Fascisti* and 90 Light to the south-west of Tripoli to guard against this possibility. This apparent last stand outside Tripoli was, of course, only another holding action. On 23 January the Italian infantry forces were sent over the border into Tunisia in face of the threat of an Allied attack against Homs.

On 28 January, *Centauro* was redeployed to Tunisia to prevent the Axis forces from being cut off by an Allied thrust to the sea. The story of the exploits of the Italian armoured divisions in the desert came to an end. In this last phase of the campaign, they had fought against immense odds and emerged with some credit. *Littorio* and *Ariete* had fought against heavy odds in the biggest armoured battle of the campaign and been almost completely destroyed. The remnants of these shattered divisions had then withdrawn across 1,200 miles of desert in the face of vastly superior Allied forces and under constant attack by superior Allied airpower. They had done so in reasonably good order and had managed on occasion to strike back at their pursuers. *Centauro* had arrived too late for El Alamein, but participated in the latter stages of the Axis withdrawal, and clashed with superior Allied forces. It was, however, swept up in the chaos of the Axis retreat before it could make any real impact, and its destiny was increasingly shaped by events elsewhere. It would fight on in Tunisia for more than two months with variable results, but it could not on its own alter events or prevent an Axis defeat that was now inevitable.

8

Last Stand and Retrospective

On 8 November 1942 the Allies landed in French North Africa and in a few days secured Casablanca, Oran and Algiers and subsequently occupied Bougie and Bone on 11 and 12 November respectively. In an effort to forestall them, Axis forces were hastily landed by air and sea in Tunis and Bizerta in northern Tunisia from 11 November onwards. This led to a scramble between small *ad hoc* units to seize the key passes through the 300-mile (500km) mountainous spine of central Tunisia. It was the extreme southern end of this front that was particularly important for Rommel's retreating forces, which were hoping to reach the relative safety of the pre-war French defences at Mareth or the narrow Wadi Akarit position behind. The danger was that Allied forces would penetrate southern Tunisia and reach the sea at Gabes behind both of these positions. This had to be prevented at all costs, as it would leave Rommel trapped between two Allied armies.

The Allies were the first to venture into southern Tunisia, when US paratroops from Tebessa in Algeria occupied Thelepte and its airfields on 15 November. On 21 November, Axis forces responded by sending German paratroops to occupy Gafsa and a scratch force of Italians from Tripoli to occupy Gabes. The latter was designated 50 Special Brigade under General Giovanni Imperiali de Francavilla, and consisted of 6 Infantry Battalion, 557 *Semovente* Group and 15 Armoured Battalion from *Centauro* Armoured Division, and three artillery battalions. The result of these moves was that the opponents each controlled one of the central mountain spines: the Allies the Western Dorsale, and the Axis the Eastern Dorsale.

On 22 November, a small force of M14 tanks from 50 Brigade was heading inland from Gabes towards Gafsa, when it was ambushed by US paratroops, who knocked out five M14s. On 26 November the US paratroops raided Gafsa itself and destroyed some fuel dumps, but were driven back by Italian tanks from 50 Brigade. On 3 December, the reinforced US forces resumed their offensive and captured Faid Pass to the north. In reply, on 10 December, the reinforced Italians formally occupied El Guettar and Maknassy. The opposing sides clashed briefly at Maknassy on the night of 17/18 December when a column of Italian tanks was fired on before the front stabilized. The Italians held on to El Guettar with

German support, while the French held Gafsa with US support. There was regular patrol activity and occasional skirmishes, but no major offensives for the rest of that year.

In January 1943, US 2 Corps under General Fredendall recognized the weakness of the Axis position in southern Tunisia and planned to capture Sfax or Gabes and cut off Rommel's forces. He had 1 US Armoured Division and three supporting infantry divisions for this task against a single Italian brigade with some German support. On 24 January, he sent part of 1 US Armoured to raid Sened Station against weak forces from 50 Brigade. They captured ninety-six prisoners and inflicted 100 casualties with the loss of only two tanks themselves. This raid alerted the Axis forces to the vulnerability of this sector, and they quickly sought to reinforce it.

As a direct result, on 28 January 1943, 131 *Centauro* Armoured Division under General Giorgio Calvi di Bergolo, which had briefly entered the fray in Libya, found itself rushed to Tunisia to bolster the front at El Guettar. They were tasked to prevent US forces reaching the coast at Gabes, cutting off Rommel's retreat and dividing the Axis forces in two. It was a tall order, but they set to work blocking the mountain passes around El Guettar against any Allied penetration. The Tunisian terrain was very different from the deserts of Libya and Egypt, a land of high hills and narrow valleys covered in thick scrub and low trees, and often wet in winter. It provided a good living for farmers and was scattered with small villages and larger towns. It favoured defensive tactics, and required a different tactical approach, unfamiliar to desert veterans. It centred on the control of high ground, particularly at the passes, by infantry with artillery and armoured support, and it offered relatively few opportunities for mobile operations.

This style of fighting was familiar to those of *Centauro* who had experienced operations in Albania, Greece and Yugoslavia. In late January, *Centauro* entered the line south of 50 Special Brigade from Sened Station south to the salt marshes; they occupied the El Guettar defile north-west of Gabes and built a solid defensive position in the hills overlooking Gumtree Road. They were below their full establishment after the losses suffered during the Axis retreat from Libya, and the surrender of units to 50 Brigade.

Sened Station

On 31 January, the Allies planned an assault on Maknassy using elements of 1 US Armoured and 34 US Infantry Divisions. But the Axis forces pre-empted this by sending 21 Panzer Division to capture Faid Pass on 30 January. This attack forced the Allies to re-deploy part of 1 US Armoured Division to Faid and so weakened their own assault on Maknassy; the latter encountered stiff resistance from the recently arrived *Centauro*, which lasted for most of the day. The Americans finally captured Sened Station in the late afternoon of 1 February, but lost an infantry battalion that missed its objective and drove straight into Axis hands. Thereafter, US tanks advanced a few miles beyond the town, but were halted by Axis armour reinforcements and anti-tank guns well short of Maknassy. On 2 February, the appearance of Axis tanks caused some panic, and Allied forces were unable to advance any further. In the end, superior Allied airpower broke up the Axis counter-attack. The Americans cancelled this attack on receiving intelligence about Axis plans for offensives in mid-February.

In early February, Axis commanders realized that the southern sector of the Allied front in Tunisia, held by inexperienced US and French troops, offered them offensive opportunities. Unfortunately, the two leading Axis commanders developed rival plans, and there was no overall Axis authority to arbitrate between them. The result was chaos, with two contradictory plans being implemented one after another, but with neither allocated sufficient priority or resources to achieve their potential. Thus General Jurgen von Arnim of 5 Panzer Army planned to capture Sidi Bou Zid using 10 and 21 Panzer Divisions with their 200 tanks. At the same time Rommel, newly arrived from the desert, wanted to drive the 2 US Corps back from Gafsa to protect the rear of his new Mareth Line defences. He knew that his own much depleted armour, 15 Panzer and *Centauro*, was too small for this task and therefore requested 21 Panzer and its ninety tanks. The two Axis offensives could not both use 21 Panzer at the same time, and possession being nine-tenths of the law, Arnim's attack on Sidi bou Zid went ahead first.

Kasserine Pass

On 13 February, Rommel started to assemble his forces for the proposed attack on Gafsa. They consisted of a mixed Italo-German force, drawn from 15 Panzer and *Centauro* Divisions, initially under General Kurt von Liebenstein of the former. This *ad hoc* force would be known as *DAK* Assault Group. It currently had only fifty-three panzers from 15 Panzer and twenty-three M14s from *Centauro* based at El Guettar. At this point, *Centauro* under Calvi di Bergolo consisted of three *Bersaglieri* battalions from 5 *Bersaglieri* Regiment, two artillery battalions from 131 Artillery Regiment, one tank battalion with twenty-three M14s from 131 Armoured Regiment, and a single group of *Semoventi*. In the circumstances, Liebenstein viewed his mission as little more than a quick raid on Gafsa, followed by withdrawal to Gabes, and he was prepared to launch it any time after 15 February. In contrast, the opportunistic Rommel intended to push on to Tebessa in Algeria, if the Americans proved weak and Gafsa fell relatively easily.

In the afternoon of 15 February, Liebenstein learned that Gafsa had been

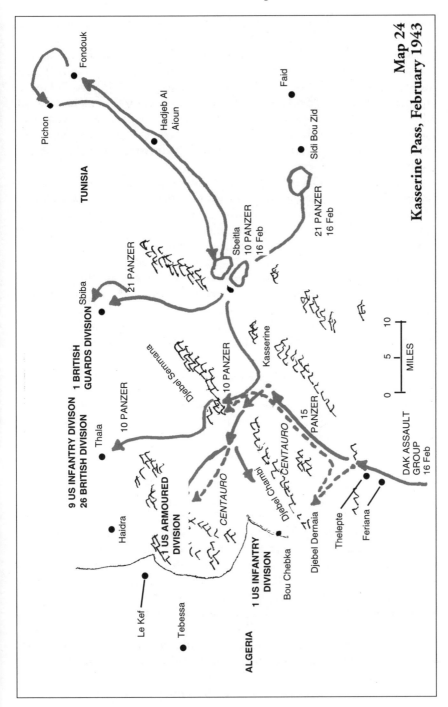

Map 24

Kasserine Pass, February 1943

evacuated by the Americans, and he therefore occupied the town unopposed that evening. He established 5 *Bersaglieri* Regiment from *Centauro* under Colonel Luigi Bonfatti in positions on the heights around the town, and sent out patrols towards Tozeur and Feriana, the latter from *Centauro*. In the late afternoon of 16 February, 10 Panzer requested that *DAK* Assault Group support its attack on Sbeitla the next day by threatening Feriana to draw off Allied reserves. This request was accepted since it fitted in with Rommel's plans to advance on Tebessa. He ordered *DAK* Assault Group to move against Feriana and Thelepte, but warned Liebenstein to avoid getting involved in any costly engagements in order not to spoil his own plans.

In the evening of 17 February, *DAK* Assault Group captured Feriana and Thelepte, including their airfields. It was now that Rommel confessed that he was too weak to reach Tebessa without the support of 10 and 21 Panzer Divisions, but Arnim refused to surrender them. There was no overall Axis authority to resolve this dispute, and Rommel had to postpone his attack. He therefore ordered *Centauro* and 15 Panzer back from Feriana and Thelepte to Gafsa in case they were counter-attacked in these exposed positions. On 18 February, Axis reconnaissance revealed no enemy concentrations opposite his forces, and an increasingly frustrated Rommel was forced to sit idly by while an apparent chance to advance on Tebessa went begging. He repeated his request for the two panzer divisions, and in the meantime sent *DAK* Assault Group to probe towards Tebessa and occupy Kasserine. He also urged them to attempt to link up with 21 Panzer at Sbeitla to the north.

It was not until the early hours of 19 February that Rommel was finally granted control of 21 Panzer, and at least part of 10 Panzer Divisions. He swiftly planned an early attack towards Sbiba and Kasserine Pass, with Le Kef and Tebessa as his ultimate objectives. He sent 21 Panzer north from Sbeitla to Sbiba, and directed *DAK* Assault Group forward from Gafsa to capture Kasserine Pass. He would use 10 Panzer, when it arrived from Sidi bou Zid, to reinforce whichever advance seemed most promising. He sent *Centauro* north from Gafsa through difficult terrain at Dernaia and Bou Chebka towards Tebessa. The Italians would find it very difficult to advance through this mountainous area. He hoped that this would broaden his attack and divert enemy forces from the main thrust at Kasserine. A series of unwelcome developments soon forced Rommel to alter these ambitious plans. 21 Panzer was halted before Sbiba by British reinforcements; 15 Panzer started late and failed to capture Kasserine Pass; and when 10 Panzer finally turned up, it was not at full strength. He therefore recalled *Centauro* from its now useless diversion to Dernaia, and brought it up to reinforce 15 Panzer at Kasserine Pass. They arrived during the night with their M14 tank battalion and part of 5 *Bersaglieri* Regiment.

At 08:30hr on 20 February, *DAK* Assault Group resumed their attack on

Kasserine Pass with help from a battalion of Bonfatti's 5 *Bersaglieri* on the right flank. They were supported by all the available Axis artillery, including the familiar 88mm guns and a battery of new *Nebelwerfer* rocket launchers, the first time the latter had been used in action. In reserve ready to exploit any breakthrough towards Tebessa were 15 Panzer and the armoured battalion from *Centauro*. The Axis infantry were slowed down by difficult terrain and accurate Allied artillery and mortar fire. The élite 5 *Bersaglieri* finally took Djebel Semmana after a bitter struggle in which their commander was killed. The new commander of *DAK* Assault Group, General Bulowius, complimented them on their élan, which contributed significantly to Axis success. The Italian action was instrumental in breaking through the US positions and in opening up the road to Thala and Tebessa. In mid-morning, the Axis forces poured through the pass and routed the Americans, who abandoned much of their equipment including twenty tanks, thirty half-tracks and many guns. 15 Panzer was sent towards Thala and reported that organized resistance had melted away, while the armoured battalion from *Centauro* made a heady five-mile dash along the road to Tebessa and encountered no enemy forces, apart from burning and abandoned vehicles. It seemed as if a clear breakthrough had been achieved – although Rommel suddenly became more cautious and ordered both advances halted. He feared that the Americans would launch heavy counter-attacks the next day, and therefore wanted to keep his forces concentrated near defensive positions at Kasserine Pass.

Early on 21 February, Rommel sent reconnaissance forces, including a small number of M14s from *Centauro*, to the north-west of Kasserine Pass. They pushed forward until they ran into part of 1 US Armoured Division, which briefly blocked their progress, before withdrawing east out of range at dawn. This seems to have reassured Rommel that no Allied counter-attack was imminent. At 14:00hr, 15 Panzer and *Centauro* therefore moved forward from Kasserine Pass to seize Djebel el Hamra. They set out boldly north-west, only to come under increasingly heavy Allied artillery fire; they then ran into tanks of 1 US Armoured in hull-down positions. This time the US Sherman tanks refused to be drawn onto the Axis anti-tank screens, and only one was lost. This determined opposition forced the Axis forces to withdraw at dusk. They were still a few miles short of Djebel el Hamra on the open plain. The other Axis advances on Thala and Sbiba had also been halted by fierce Allied resistance. After nightfall Bulowius sent a mixed force of 300 infantry from *Centauro* and 15 Panzer on a wide outflanking move through difficult terrain to attempt to sweep around Djebel el Hamra towards Tebessa.

On 22 February, 5 *Bersaglieri* from *Centauro* was holding a line below the American positions on Djebel el Hamra against strong counter-attacks. In the morning, 15 Panzer, supported by a *Semovente* group from *Centauro*, launched an attack on the US positions. This briefly relieved the pressure on the *Bersaglieri* before running into powerful anti-tank defences and devastating artillery fire. An American counter-attack in the late afternoon finally drove the weak and exhausted Axis forces back, causing them to abandon some US field guns and vehicles, captured earlier in the day. The final straw was the intervention of a number of US Sherman tanks that scattered the strung-out 5 *Bersaglieri*. The latter, after suffering heavy casualties, withdrew in some disorder all the way back to Kasserine Pass. Rommel was now anxious about the Mareth Line, where he expected a major Allied offensive any day now. He therefore cancelled the offensive and ordered a phased withdrawal all the way back to Gafsa.

In the meantime, the Axis infantry sent by Bulowius the previous night to circle behind the US positions had run into a violent rainstorm in the dark, which delayed them severely. They managed to make slow progress, through difficult terrain and recurrent downpours; but instead of heading towards Tebessa, they strayed onto a camel trail that turned south. At dawn on 22 February, they found themselves lost in the midst of US positions near Bou Chebka Pass. Initially they were concealed by the early morning mist, which enabled them to infiltrate the enemy artillery positions and, briefly, capture five howitzers, thirty vehicles and several anti-aircraft guns. The sudden appearance of Axis troops in their midst caused considerable panic in the Allied lines. It took the Allies a whole day to restore the situation and eliminate this Axis force, which was eventually forced to surrender when, confused and exhausted, they stumbled into a hollow for shelter – only to find it was overlooked by a company of Sherman tanks. This brief action caused the Americans to cancel a proposed assault on Italian troops holding Bou Chebka Pass to the south.

On 23 February Axis forces withdrew from Djebel el Hamra and Kasserine, unhindered by Allied pursuit, and mined the roads behind them. The surviving units of *Centauro* were relieved at Feriana and Thelepte by 15 Panzer and returned to Gafsa, where they once again adopted a defensive posture. Rommel had by this time already returned to Mareth, where a major Allied attack was expected in the very near future.

Rommel would never command *Centauro* or any other Italian armoured formation in action again. He had led these formations during the period when they had registered their best achievements, but always compared them unfavourably to their German equivalents. He understood the technological reasons for their weakness, but still had a tendency to ignore these and blame them for Axis failures that were usually the result of Allied superiority or his own errors.

Gafsa

In mid-March 1943 there were proposals for *Centauro* to be transferred to the Mareth Line in southern Tunisia as part of a wider reshuffling of forces. In the event, however, the transfer never happened, since reshuffles seemed inappropriate in the face of potential Allied threats towards both Mareth and El Guettar. Instead, *Centauro* and 10 Panzer Divisions were retained at Gafsa, where they had been posted after the end of the Kasserine offensive, and 21 Panzer was sent to support them against an anticipated attack by US 2 Corps. On 15 March Axis forces were planning a spoiling attack from Gafsa involving 21 Panzer and *Centauro*, but a major US attack effectively pre-empted these plans.

At 11:00hr on 17 March, the US 2 Corps, with 90,000 men under General George S. Patton, sought to capture Gafsa in what they termed, in insulting reference to their Italian opponents, Operation *Wop*. The assault was intended to occupy the attention of *Centauro* and 10 Panzer – fifty panzers and thirty M14 tanks, and 7,100 men – while the Allies attacked the Mareth Line to the south. The US forces had a numerical superiority of more than ten to one, not to mention their enormous material advantage. It should have been an easy victory, but Patton nevertheless took a fairly cautious approach in the light of recent experiences. He wanted a certain victory to restore shaken American morale and confidence. A heavy preliminary air and artillery bombardment preceded the attack, but this fell largely on empty and abandoned Italian positions. Before dawn, 5 *Bersaglieri* had withdrawn behind a screen provided by the Axis armour, leaving a range of elaborate booby traps behind. The 1 US Armoured and 1 US Infantry Divisions, which moved forward behind the Allied bombardment, occupied Gafsa before advancing eastwards to occupy an abandoned El Guettar. They were delayed by booby traps and heavy rain, and failed to catch the retreating Axis forces.

El Guettar

The remnants of *Centauro* fell back to positions east of El Guettar along Keddab Ridge, which dominated Gumtree Road to Sfax and also overlooked the road to Gabes further south. There the Italians constructed some very strong defensive positions that extended southwards on to the lower ridges dominating the Gabes road itself. The Italians garrisoned the hills on either side of these roads, and in the north exploited a deep wadi running across Gumtree Road as a natural anti-tank ditch. They were supported by a remnant of their own armour, and the infantry, artillery and panzers of 10 Panzer Division. The US forces recognized the strength of this Axis position, and knew that a frontal attack would be costly – but their

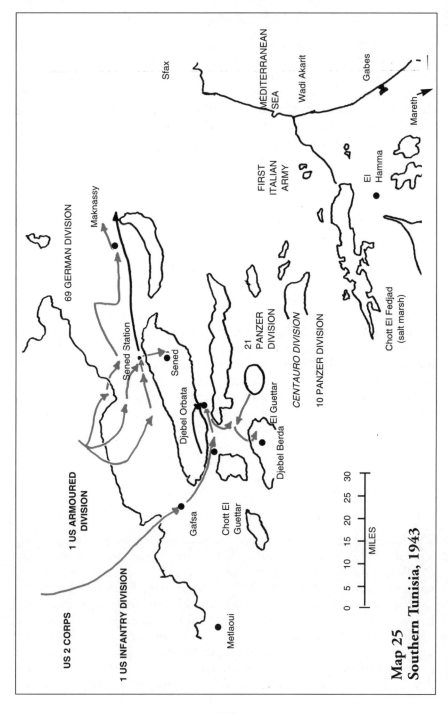

Map 25
Southern Tunisia, 1943

options were limited by the difficult terrain in the hills.

On the evening of 20 March, 500 US Rangers with seventy mortars were sent into the 3,700ft (1,100m) high hills to the north of Gumtree Road with orders to outflank this position. They climbed through rugged terrain for more than 10 miles before they emerged on the slopes of Djebel el Ank, which overlooked *Centauro*'s positions on Djebel Orbala, north of Gumtree Road. They remained undetected by the Italians, who had not anticipated such an advance, and were able to observe the Italian positions closely for a time. At dawn the next morning the US Rangers charged and the *Bersaglieri*, below them, were taken completely by surprise. Many of them were killed in the first assault, and the shocked survivors either surrendered or fled eastwards along Gumtree Road. The Rangers were now able to fire on the Italians to the south of the road, and under cover of this fire 1 US Infantry Division advanced along the valley against the Italian front line. They succeeded in breaking through the main Italian positions, and captured about a thousand prisoners from 5 *Bersaglieri* before advancing about fifteen miles along Gumtree Road. The Italians hastily withdrawing to the east were not pursued, however, since this rough track did not offer a useful route to the sea; this lay along the Gabes road to the south, where other Allied forces were attacking.

On the same night, 18 US Infantry Division attacked south-eastwards from El Guettar into the hills adjacent to the Gabes road under a hazy moon. They struck hard at the positions held by *Centauro*, and took 415 prisoners. As dawn broke, however, the Axis forces brought them under artillery fire and air attack, and it was only after some tough fighting that the Americans reached their initial objectives at noon on 21 March. On the following day, *Centauro* and 10 Panzer made several attempts to counter-attack the Americans, but whenever they assembled their tanks or mounted an artillery barrage the enemy responded with heavy artillery fire or air strikes. This prevented any effective counter-attacks from being launched. On 23 March, 10 Panzer mounted a small counter-attack that failed utterly, with the loss of thirty-seven of their fifty-seven panzers. They were quick to blame this failure on the Italians protecting their flanks at Djebel Berda to the south. The Allies halted this offensive to reorganize their forces for another attempt, timed to support the Allied attack on Mareth to the south. It was intended to prevent Axis forces at El Guettar from reinforcing the Mareth Line.

In the event the Allies broke through the Mareth Line on 27 March, earlier than anticipated, and this caused 2 US Corps to launch 1 and 9 US Infantry Divisions towards Gabes, prematurely, in an attempt to cut off Axis forces withdrawing from the Mareth Line. They faced strong defensive positions in the hills manned by *Centauro* and 10 Panzer Divisions, concentrated in a number of strongpoints supported by artillery and mortars. The northern flank at Djebel el Mcheilat was held by 10 Panzer, while *Centauro* held the southern flank at Djebel Berda. The tough Axis defence was described by Count Calvi di Bergolo's chief of staff:

> Our artillery and minefields several times stopped the repeated attacks of hundreds of tanks three times as heavy as ours; on the second day with two *Semoventi* and fourteen tanks, we even carried out a surprise counter attack on the flank of a large armoured formation ... The American infantry that followed the tanks, even when the latter were forced to retire, continued without respite to attack our lines with an impressive superiority of fire . . .
>
> For four consecutive days we succeeded first in holding, and then in recapturing the strongpoints that fell one by one, successively using all the reserves that we had saved at Gafsa. It was useless to call for the support of our own aircraft; the sky above the battle was permanently dominated by the enemy aircraft, and our anti-aircraft defences, equipped only with small-calibre weapons, succeeded only in putting off low-level machine-gunning.

Thus the Axis defenders successfully drove back the badly co-ordinated US forces with heavy losses. On 30 March, a reinforced 2 US Corps offensive fell on the depleted Axis forces – 10 Panzer with fifty panzers, and *Centauro* with ten M14s, reinforced by 21 Panzer with forty panzers. In spite of these odds, the Axis forces drove back the US forces after some fierce fighting.

On 3 April the Axis armoured forces at El Guettar, including 10 and 21 Panzer and *Centauro* Divisions, counter-attacked the US forces, but failed to drive them back. The Axis forces were just about holding on against superior forces, but they could not keep this up for long. On 6 April the Allies to the south broke through the new Axis defences at Wadi Akarit and forced them northwards into the rear of *Centauro* and the Axis forces opposing the 2 US Corps at El Guettar. This spelled the end of their long and determined resistance, and that night they withdrew under cover of a heavy artillery bombardment. The next US attack, on 7 April, fell on their abandoned positions, while 10 and 21 Panzer and *Centauro* Divisions withdrew safely to the north-east.

In the Axis last stand in Tunisia, *Centauro* had been posted at Gafsa and El Guettar to prevent an American breakthrough to the sea, which would have cut off the Axis forces retreating from the desert to Mareth and Wadi Akarit. They had been completely successful in this task, with German support against superior Allied forces, and had managed this in the face of often superior numbers and always superior weaponry. They had made skilful use of high ground and complex defensive positions with artillery support and armoured counter-attacks. They had even participated in

Rommel's major counter-attack at Kasserine, which had briefly caused the Allies some anxiety about their position in North Africa. This was a considerable achievement for an under-strength Italian armoured division with no possibility of reinforcement. Furthermore, it had held on to its positions in spite of the drain of constant losses.

Its chief purpose now ended, on 8 April *Centauro* with 10 and 21 Panzer formed a rearguard for the Axis forces withdrawing from Wadi Akarit some 300 miles (500km) north to Enfidaville. On 12 April *Centauro* was attached to 15 Panzer on the extreme left of the new Axis positions near Takrouna, where its *Bersaglieri* supported the defence. On 26 April its last ten M14 tanks were sent to reinforce 10 Panzer and *Centauro* was officially dissolved. This was the end of the road for the Italian armoured divisions in North Africa, although a few individuals from these units fought on until the end. The last forces to surrender in North Africa were the 1st Italian Army, which included survivors from the various Italian armoured divisions. It finally surrendered to the Allies on 12 May 1943, and the war in North Africa came to an end. It had been a desperate last stand against the odds as Allied power waxed inexorably and Axis power waned.

A Retrospective on the Performance of the Italian Armoured Divisions

In the summer of 1940, when Italy entered World War II, the future had seemed very different, with France already beaten and Britain apparently soon to follow. At that point, numerically superior Italian forces stood on the borders of Egypt, which appeared to be theirs for the taking. The Italians, who were not fighting for a clear cause or defined aims, completely failed to exploit this early advantage. They hesitated, while the Battle of Britain was fought and won, and Britain was freed from the immediate threat of invasion at home. They failed to concentrate their efforts against the British, but rather dispersed them, launching an ill-conceived and poorly prepared invasion of Greece. The abject failure of this invasion undermined Italian morale while increasing the confidence of their opponents. It encouraged the British to try their hand against the Italians in the Mediterranean and in North Africa. And finally, perhaps most importantly for Italian prospects in North Africa, they failed to deploy any of their available élite armoured and motorized divisions to this theatre. The result was disaster, when a British offensive, employing armoured and motorized forces, destroyed the few small Italian armoured units, and isolated, surrounded and captured the largely immobile Italian infantry.

This disaster might have ended the fighting in North Africa had it not been for two important new factors. The first was the arrival of a small German armoured force under Rommel, which would quickly rise to legendary status. This force is almost universally acknowledged to have transformed the North African campaign from an easy British victory over the Italians into a tough see-saw conflict. The second factor, which has been almost universally ignored, was the arrival of a first Italian armoured division, *Ariete*. A natural British and German tendency to focus attention on the actions of their own forces and a reluctance to dismiss deeply ingrained racial stereotypes have meant little attention has been paid to the impact of *Ariete* on the campaign. If an effort is made to examine their activities this deficit can be redressed.

In the first half of 1941, *Ariete* was clearly not as powerful as a British or German armoured division, being much smaller than either. They also lacked their full planned establishment of M13 tanks, and still had a significant number of useless L3/35 light tanks. This meant that they lacked the ability to face British armoured forces in most circumstances. They could not therefore be deployed as a single entity against a British armoured division in open warfare with confidence. This did not prove to be an issue, however, since the *ad hoc* nature of the first Axis offensive of spring 1941 meant that Axis forces were deployed in *ad hoc* mixed units, rather than complete formations. In the course of this short offensive the Italians had already demonstrated their mobility and power by advancing rapidly across difficult desert terrain to Mechili, and playing an important part in defeating 3 Indian Motor Brigade there. They went on to meet defeat in attacks on the well-prepared defences at Tobruk, which has counted against them. In fact, they took part in these attacks against the advice of their commander, Baldassare, who knew that they were not prepared for attacks on such fixed defences. They were unable to attack as a complete formation, since several infantry and artillery units were deployed elsewhere, and they had only a few artillery pieces and anti-tank weapons, and just a handful of medium tanks to support the attacks. In these circumstances, defeat was not unexpected, and the same fate had already befallen the superior forces of their German allies. The latter were only too happy to shift the blame onto the Italians when the defeats at Tobruk were due to Rommel's inadequate preparations and to the weakness of the thinly spread Axis forces, rather than anything else. *Ariete* was still developing at this point, and would grow into a more credible threat in the next phase of fighting.

In November 1941 *Ariete* had been restored to its full establishment, including a full complement of M13 tanks. They would also, for the first time, operate together as a single entity for most of the forthcoming fighting. Their opponents still had a slight advantage in armour, but the Italians could now hope to stand up to an equivalent British formation. This was proved in the opening phase of the British offensive when *Ariete* inflicted a bloody nose on the overconfident 22 Armoured Brigade at Bir el Gubi. This action inflicted a delay on the British, which disrupted the entire subsequent course of their offensive. *Ariete* went on to assist the German armour in crushing 5 South African Brigade, although their role was a supporting one: they kept 1 South African Brigade and the British armour occupied for long periods, and prevented them supporting the New Zealanders in lifting the siege of Tobruk. In the same period, their German allies staged a dramatic but ultimately futile advance to the Egyptian frontier, which almost allowed the British to lift the siege of Tobruk. In the crisis that followed, *Ariete* captured a vital piece of high ground from 2 New Zealand Division and held off the British armour while the Germans destroyed the New Zealanders. This phase of fighting ended in defeat for the Axis because of overall Allied numerical superiority, rather than any specific Italian weakness. The effects of attrition meant that Axis losses could not be replaced, and they eventually had too few men and tanks left to hold out. *Ariete*, although still playing a supporting role, was now making a significant contribution to Axis successes.

In the spring of 1942, *Ariete* was rebuilt and re-equipped for the next phase of the campaign. They would be faced with increased numbers of British forces with superior equipment, including 75mm-equipped Grant tanks. In response, *Ariete* itself was reinforced with additional field and anti-tank guns and *Semoventi da 75/18*, which increased its fighting power. In addition, the Italians now sent a second armoured division, *Littorio*, to North Africa.

In the summer of 1942, *Ariete* took part in the major Axis offensive against the Gazala line and the fortress of Tobruk. They almost completely destroyed 3 Indian Motor Brigade on the opening day of the offensive, but also endured a bloody repulse at the hands of the French at Bir Hacheim. They have been criticized for this failure, and were certainly misled by their earlier easy victory over the Indians. The criticism is unjustified, however, since Bir Hacheim held out against everything the Axis threw at it until it was evacuated on 11 June. In spite of their losses on this first day, *Ariete* went on to protect the rear of their German allies while they crushed the 150 British Infantry Brigade in the Gazala line. In the process, with the help of German artillery *Ariete* held out against a major counter-attack involving one armoured and two infantry brigades, with the help of German artillery. They then took part in a counter-attack that destroyed two enemy infantry brigades. They also took part in the capture of Tobruk, where they faced tough resistance without the benefit of the sort of artillery or air support provided for their German allies.

In June 1942 the fall of Tobruk opened the Axis road into Egypt, and both Italian armoured divisions, *Ariete* and *Littorio*, took part in the hectic pursuit to El Alamein. They were, however, now mere shadows of their former selves, *Ariete* severely reduced by breakdowns and losses suffered during the recent fighting, and *Littorio* plundered to compensate *Ariete*.

Indeed, the whole Axis army was not only running on borrowed fuel, but living on borrowed time. They needed some sort of British collapse in order to break through, but none was forthcoming, and they encountered a barrier at Alamein that they could not breach. In particular, *Ariete* suffered a serious reverse at Alam Nayil at the hands of the New Zealanders, and was roundly condemned by Rommel for this failure. It should be noted, however, that this reverse only occurred after stronger German forces had already failed to break the British line. The tough German 90 Light Division had refused to advance and was on the verge of mutiny, and it is not surprising that the weaker Italians failed in similar circumstances. In spite of this reverse, *Ariete* soon joined *Littorio* and the German mobile forces in holding out against British counter-attacks until the main Axis infantry forces arrived to occupy the Alamein line. In August, both of the Italian armoured divisions participated in Rommel's futile Alam Halfa offensive, and *Littorio* actually managed to breach the British minefields alongside the Germans.

In the autumn of 1942, the Axis forces were facing inevitable defeat with the numerical odds stacked against them in every respect. The arrival of new Allied equipment removed any previous German superiority in weaponry. It was only a question of time, and that time came on 23 October with the start of the El Alamein offensive. The Axis forces were forced to fight a battle of attrition that they could not win and the weaker Italians were particularly vulnerable in these circumstances. But in spite of the odds against them, *Littorio* played its part in the Axis defence, with German support, right to the end. It was ground to pieces in a series of desperate counter-attacks against superior Allied Sherman tanks and 6pdr anti-tank guns. It was now that their puny M14 tanks truly earned their reputation as 'iron coffins' or 'self-propelled coffins', as they fell to the superior weapons of the enemy. As the inevitability of Allied victory became clear, Rommel made plans for a staged withdrawal and *Ariete*, which had not been involved in the slaughter until now, was intended to play a crucial role in this. Unfortunately Hitler's intervention, in a campaign where he had previously allowed Rommel complete freedom, transformed a planned retreat into a dreadful last stand. It doomed *Ariete* to destruction by forcing them to stand in the open desert against 7 Armoured Division; although in spite of the odds against them, *Ariete* stood firm for more than twenty-four hours by making skilful use of their artillery and armour. They granted the Germans some crucial extra time to extract their surviving armour from the battle, and in the end, *Ariete* only withdrew when 4 Light Armoured Brigade outflanked them and attacked their artillery from the rear.

In the long retreat from El Alamein to Tunisia the shattered remnants of *Ariete*, which was not entirely destroyed at Alamein, were still able to turn on their pursuers. It was only now that the third and last of the Italian armoured divisions, *Centauro*, arrived in North Africa, and they were already too late to change anything. They were a vital reinforcement for Rommel, who otherwise had none at a time when Axis reinforcements were being sent direct to Tunisia. This new force joined forces with the veterans of *Ariete* to inflict a sharp lesson on 8 Armoured Brigade at El Agheila in December. At the end of January 1943, *Centauro* was sent to Tunisia to prevent the Americans from advancing to the sea at Gabes and cutting off Rommel's forces. With German support they were successful in this task against the better equipped Americans until 6 April, and it was only then, when an Allied breakthrough against other Axis forces at Wadi Akarit threatened their rear, that they were finally forced to withdraw. In February they had even experienced a brief taste of success when they took part in Rommel's short offensive at Kasserine Pass.

How do we rate the performance of the Italian armoured divisions in this campaign? The *Ariete, Littorio* and *Centauro* were clearly very different formations from those Italian divisions beaten and written off by the British back in 1940–41. They were better trained and equipped than Italian infantry formations, and most importantly, more suited to the needs of mobile warfare. They were never a match for British armoured divisions either in size or equipment, but they could, and did, meet British armoured brigades on almost equal terms. They did not compare with the panzer divisions of their allies for similar reasons, and did not have the same impact on the battlefield. The Italians, however, shared one advantage with the Germans that the British failed to achieve during this campaign. They constructed and operated their armoured divisions as all arms formations, and functioned best when operating these arms in combination, as at Bir el Gubi in November 1941, 'The Cauldron' in June 1942, or at El Alamein in November 1942. They always had to be more cautious than the Germans because of their relative weakness in heavy armour and heavy artillery, but within these limits they operated well. In the course of the long campaign, they admittedly gradually fell behind their allies and opponents in equipment quality, but they did manage to introduce a few improvements, including the 90mm anti-tank gun and the *Semovente*.

It would be wrong to suggest that the Italian armoured divisions ever played a decisive role in this campaign, but within their limitations they performed with considerable credit throughout. They participated in every major action, and were usually not far behind their German allies. They had their share of successes – Mechili, Bir el Gubi, Taieb el Esem, Point 175, Point 171, 'The Cauldron' – and their share of failures – Tobruk, Bir Hacheim, First Alamein, Alam Halfa and Second Alamein. It should be noted that both these successes and these failures usually chime with those of their German allies. It was a joint Axis effort after all, and it was this that triumphed or fell short. The Italians have often served as the scapegoats for

Axis failures, but these were more often attributable to superior Allied forces. The Germans relied on their Italian allies, a fact that becomes obvious if we consider what might have occurred if the Italians had not been present. In this scenario, it seems unlikely that Rommel would have been able to launch his initial offensive of March 1941, or if he had, that he would ever have reached Tobruk. He would almost certainly never have invaded Egypt. The narrow German focus on the Eastern Front in Russia meant that their minimal effort in North Africa needed Italian support just as much as the Italians needed them. This is something that is often overlooked by those content to minimize or ignore the Italian contribution. It is probably true to say that the Italian armoured divisions usually worked best in co-operation with their German allies. This was the case because the Germans could offer support from the kind of heavy weapons that the Italians themselves lacked. The Italians also learned from the tactical skills of their allies. In turn the Italians provided their German allies with the numbers that they lacked. They provided the additional infantry and artillery to hold ground while on the defensive, and to protect their flanks and rear, and to offer extra flexibility while on the offensive. One motorized and two panzer divisions could not have achieved what they did without Italian support, and, in particular, support from élite Italian armoured divisions. The Axis forces in North Africa were not independent, but integral parts of a whole. They fought together, they advanced together, they retreated together, they died together, and in May 1943 they surrendered together. More than sixty years after the event, it is high time that this was recognized by more of those writing about the North African campaign.

This is what actually happened. In the absence of any fundamental political or economic changes, could the Italians have done any better? The answer to this is almost certainly affirmative. They could have substantially reduced the overall number of army divisions, from an inflated seventy or so, to provide a much smaller number of fully equipped divisions. They could have afforded greater priority to tank design and production, and equipped all of their armoured divisions with the M13/40 before the war. They could have concentrated their limited military resources in the Mediterranean and North Africa. They could have sent three armoured and two motorized divisions to North Africa in summer 1940 instead of useless infantry formations. Any one of these actions, or all of them together, might have made a difference and maybe even a significant difference to the course of the campaign. It is unlikely, however, that they would have changed the overall outcome of the war, which was decided elsewhere by the economic superiority of the United States and the Soviet Union.

What about the 'myth' of Italian military failure mentioned in the introduction? The wartime performance of the Italian armoured divisions in North Africa would suggest that this was indeed a myth. The myth originated in the opening phase of the war when Italian forces collapsed under Greek and British attack. The Italians, however, were not alone in suffering a sequence of disasters in their first encounters with the enemy. The early British experiences in Norway, Belgium, France, North Africa, Greece and Malaya spring to mind. The Soviets also suffered early disasters at Smolensk and Kiev before their recovery at Moscow. The Americans also suffered some embarrassing reverses in Tunisia and the Philippines before the tide turned. This situation was commonplace, and each of these nations learned from its mistakes and put things right. The Italians also learned from their early failures and managed to stem the routs in Albania and North Africa, a fact ignored by those who prefer to attribute this to German intervention. The effective operations of Italian armoured divisions in North Africa themselves indicate how much Italian performance improved since 1940–41.

The courage of Italian soldiers should also not be in doubt. The myth of their cowardice also originated in the opening phase of the war, when 130,000 Italians surrendered to the British. They were not alone, however, in making large-scale capitulations. The British surrendered 30,000 men at Tobruk and 85,000 at Singapore, both in 1942, and would also have lost men in France and Greece had it not been for their navy. The Soviets surrendered 310,000 men at Smolensk and 600,000 at Kiev. The Germans surrendered 90,000 at Stalingrad, and 250,000 Axis soldiers surrendered in Tunisia. Numbers alone have little to tell about courage, since men may suffer terribly before they opt to surrender, and many have no choice in the matter. The Germans, who were not at all enthusiastic about their allies and were apt to blame them for any Axis failures, nevertheless widely acknowledged their courage. In this difficult matter, it is perhaps simplest to ask who is the most courageous in the following situations: the Italian *carristi*, who goes into battle in an obsolete M14 tank against superior enemy armour and anti-tank guns, knowing that they can easily penetrate his flimsy protection at a range where his own small gun will have little effect; the German panzer soldier or British tanker who goes into battle in a Panzer IV Special or Sherman respectively against equivalent enemy opposition in the knowledge that he can at least trade blows with them on equal terms; the British tanker who goes into battle in a Sherman against inferior Italian armour and anti-tank guns, knowing confidently that he can destroy them at ranges where they cannot touch him. It would seem to be clear that, in terms of their motto *Ferrea Mole, Ferreo Cuore* and the title of this book, the Italian *carristi* really had 'iron hearts', even though as the war went on their 'iron hulls' increasingly let them down.

Appendix I
Italian Armoured Divisions: Orders of Battle 1941–42

April 1941

132 *Ariete* Armoured Division
General Ettore Baldassare

132 Armoured Regiment
1, 2 and 3 Light Armoured Battalions
7 Medium Armoured Battalion

8 *Bersaglieri* Regiment
5 and 12 Motorized *Bersaglieri* Battalions
3 Motorcycle *Bersaglieri* Battalion

132 Artillery Regiment
1 and 2 Artillery Groups (75/27mm)

November 1941

Corpo d'Armata di Manovra (*CAM*) or
Mobile Army Corps
General Gastone Gambara

132 *Ariete* Armoured Division
General Ettore Baldassare

132 Armoured Regiment
7, 8 and 9 Armoured Battalions

8 *Bersaglieri* Regiment
5 and 12 Motorized *Bersaglieri* Battalions
3 Motorcycle *Bersaglieri* Battalion

132 Artillery Regiment
1 Artillery Group (75/27mm)
2 Artillery Group (105/28mm)
501 AA Group (90/53mm)

101 *Trieste* Motorized Division
General Alessandro Piazzoni

May 1942

XX Motorized Corps
General Ettore Baldassare

132 *Ariete* Armoured Division
General Giuseppe de Stefanis

132 Armoured Regiment
8, 9 and 10 Light Armoured Battalions

8 *Bersaglieri* Regiment
2, 5 and 12 Motorized *Bersaglieri* Battalions

132 Artillery Regiment
1 and 2 Artillery Groups (75/27mm)
5 and 6 *Semovente* Groups (*Semovente da
75/18*)
501 AA Group (90/53mm)
31 AT Group (88/55mm)

101 *Trieste* Motorized Division
General Arnaldo Azzi

July 1942

XX Motorized Corps
General Giuseppe de Stefanis

132 *Ariete* Armoured Division
General Francesco Arena

132 Armoured Regiment
8, 9 and 10 Light Armoured Battalions

8 *Bersaglieri* Regiment
2, 5 and 12 Motorized *Bersaglieri* Battalions
132 Artillery Regiment
1 and 2 Artillery Groups (75/27mm)

Appendix I

5 and 6 *Semovente* Groups (*Semovente da 75/18*)
501 AA Group (90/53mm)
31 AT Group (88/55mm)

133 *Littorio* Armoured Division
General Gervasio Bitossi/General Carlo Ceriana-Mayneri

133 Armoured Regiment
4, 12 and 51 Armoured Battalions

12 *Bersaglieri* Regiment
23 and 36 Motorized *Bersaglieri* Battalions
5 Motorcycle *Bersaglieri* Battalion

133 Artillery Regiment
1 and 2 Artillery Groups (75/27mm)

101 *Trieste* Motorized Division
General Arnaldo Azzi

October 1942

XX Motorized Corps
General Giuseppe De Stefanis

132 *Ariete* Armoured Division
General Francesco Arena

132 Armoured Regiment
8, 9 and 10 Light Armoured Battalions

8 *Bersaglieri* Regiment
2, 5 and 12 Motorized *Bersaglieri* Battalions

132 Artillery Regiment
1 and 2 Artillery Groups (75/27mm)

5 and 6 *Semovente* Groups (*Semovente da 75/18*)
501 AA Group (90/53mm)
31 AT Group (88/55mm)

133 *Littorio* Armoured Division
General Gervasio Bitossi

133 Armoured Regiment
4, 12 and 51 Armoured Battalions

12 *Bersaglieri* Regiment
23 and 36 Motorized *Bersaglieri* Battalions
21 Motorcycle *Bersaglieri* Battalion

3 Mobile Artillery Regiment, *Duca d'Aosta*
2 Artillery Group (75/27mm)
332 Artillery Group (100/17mm)
554 and 556 *Semovente* Groups (*Semovente da 75/18*)

101 *Trieste* Motorized Division
General Francesco La Ferla

November 1942

131 *Centauro* Armoured Division
General Giorgio Count Calvi di Bergolo

131 Armoured Regiment
14, 15 and 17 Armoured Battalions

5 *Bersaglieri* Regiment
14 and 24 Motorized *Bersaglieri* Battalions
5 Motorcycle *Bersaglieri* Battalion

131 Artillery Regiment

Appendix II

Comparative Performance of Tank Weaponry 1941–42

Vehicle	Armament	Penetration @ 1,000yd	Armour
Italy			
M13/40	47mm	32mm	40mm
M14/41	47mm	32mm	40mm
Semovente da 75/18	75mm	50mm	42mm
Great Britain			
Crusader II	2pdr (40mm)	40mm	40mm
Stuart	37mm	46mm	51mm
Valentine II	2pdr (40mm)	40mm	65mm
Grant/Lee	75mm	38mm	50mm
Crusader III	6pdr (57mm)	52mm	51mm
Sherman	75mm	38mm	42mm
Churchill II	6pdr (57mm)	52mm	102mm

Bibliography

General

Abse, T. 'Italy' in J. Noakes *The Civilian in War* (Exeter 1992)

Bosworth, R. J. B. *Mussolini* (London 2002)

Burgwyn, H. J. *Italian Foreign Policy in the Inter-War Period 1918–1940* (Westport 1997)

Cannistraro, P. V. *A Historical Dictionary of Fascist Italy* (Westport 1982)

Ciano, G. *Diary 1937–1943* (New York 2002)

Corvaja, S. *Hitler and Mussolini* (New York 2001)

Coverdale, J. *Italian Intervention in the Spanish Civil War* (Princeton 1975)

Deakin, F. W. *The Brutal Friendship* (Harmondsworth 1966)

Hibbert, C. *Mussolini* (London 1972)

Knox, M. *Mussolini Unleashed 1939–1941* (Cambridge 1982)

Lamb, R. *Mussolini and the British* (London 1997)

Mack Smith, D. *Italy and its Monarchy* (London 1989)

Mack Smith, D. *Mussolini* (London 1981)

Mack Smith, D. *Mussolini as a Military Leader* (Reading 1974)

Mack Smith, D. *Mussolini's Roman Empire* (Harmondsworth 1976)

Mockler, A. *Haile Selassie's War* (Oxford 1984)

Morgan, P. *Fascist Italy 1919–1945* (London 1995)

Robertson, E. M. *Mussolini as Empire Builder* (London 1977)

Sbacchi, A. *Ethiopia under Mussolini* (London 1985)

Segre, C. *Italo Balbo: a Fascist Life* (Berkeley 1987)

Whittam, J. *Fascist Italy* (Manchester 1995)

Wiskemann, E. *The Rome-Berlin Axis* (London 1949)

Zamagni, V. 'Italy: How to Lose the War and Win the Peace' in M. Harrison *The Economics of World War II* (Cambridge 1998)

Military Background

Alvarez, D. 'Axis Sigint Collaboration: A Limited Partnership' in D. Alvarez *Allied and Axis Signals Intelligence in World War II* (London 1999)

Barker, A. J. *The Rape of Ethiopia 1936* (New York 1971)

Belchem, D. *All in the Day's March* (London 1978)

Cervi, M. *The Hollow Legions* (London 1965)

Ceva, L. 'Italy' in I. C. B. Dear and M. R. D. Foot *The Oxford Companion to World War II* (Oxford 2001)

Creveld, M. V. *Supplying War* (Cambridge 1977)

Dunning, C. *Courage Alone* (Aldershot 1998)

Ellis, J. *The World War II Data Book* (London 1993)

Gooch, J. 'Clausewitz Disregarded: Italian Military Thought and Doctrine' in M. I. Handel *Clausewitz and Modern Strategy* (London 1986)

Greene, J. *Mare Nostrum* (Watsonville 1990)

Hinsley, F. H. *British Intelligence in the Second World War* Volume II (London 1981)

Knox, M. *Common Destiny* (Cambridge 2000)

Knox, M. 'Fascist Italy Assesses Its Enemies 1935–1940' in E. R. May *Knowing One's Enemies* (Princeton 1986)

Knox, M. *Hitler's Italian Allies* (Cambridge 2000)

Knox, M. 'The Italian Armed Forces 1940–43' in A. R. Millett and W. Murray *Military Effectiveness* Volume III: *The Second World War* (London 1988)

Bibliography

Madej, W. V. *Italian Army Handbook* (Allentown 1984)

Madej, W. V. *Italian Army Order of Battle 1940–1943* (1982)

Mallett, R. *The Italian Navy and Fascist Expansionism* (London 1998)

Mueller-Hillebrand, B. *Germany and its Allies in World War II* (Maryland 1980)

Ogorkiewicz, R. *Armoured Forces* (London 1970)

Sadkovich, J. *The Italian Navy in World War II* (Westport 1994)

Smyth, H. M. 'The Command of the Italian Armed Forces in World War II' in *Military Affairs Volume 15/1* (1951)

Sullivan, B. R. 'The Impatient Cat: Assessments of Military Power in Fascist Italy, 1936–1940' in W. Murray and A. R. Millett *Calculations: Net Assessment and the Coming of World War II* (London 1992)

Sullivan, B. R. 'The Italian Armed Forces 1918–40' in A. R. Millett and W. Murray *Military Effectiveness Volume II: The Interwar Period* (London 1988)

Sullivan, B. R. 'The Italian Soldier in Combat, June 1940–September 1943: Myths, Realities and Explanations' in P. Addison and A. Calder *Time to Kill: The Soldier's Experience of War in the West 1939–1945* (London 1997)

Sweet, J. J. T. *Iron Arm: The Mechanization of Mussolini's Army 1920–1940* (Westport 1980)

Trye, R. *Mussolini's Soldiers* (Shrewsbury 1995)

Whittam, J. 'The Italian General Staff and the Coming of the Second World War' in A. Preston *General Staffs and Diplomacy before the Second World War* (London 1978)

Wise, T. *World War Two Military Vehicle Markings* (Cambridge 1981)

The North African Campaign

Agar-Hamilton, J. A. I. and Turner, L. F. C. *The Sidi Rezeg Battles: 1941* (Oxford 1951)

Agar-Hamilton, J. A. I. and Turner, L. F. C. *Crisis in the Desert: May–July 1942* (Oxford 1951)

Atkinson, R. *An Army at Dawn* (London 2003)

Bates, P. *The Dance of War: The Story of the Battle of Egypt* (London 1992)

Baxter, C. F. *The War in North Africa 1940–1943* (Westport 1996)

Behrendt, H. O. *Rommel's Intelligence in the Desert Campaign 1941–1943* (London 1985)

Bharucha, P. C. *The North African Campaign 1940–1943* (New Delhi 1956)

Beirman, J. and Smith, C. *Alamein: War without Hate* (London 2002)

Blumenson, M. *Rommel's Last Victory: The Battle of Kasserine Pass* (London 1968)

Bungay, S. *Alamein* (London 2002)

Burdon, R. M. *24 Battalion* (Wellington 1953)

Caccia-Dominioni, P. *Alamein 1933–1962: An Italian Story* (London 1966)

Carver, M. *Alamein* (London 1962)

Carver, M. *Dilemmas of the Desert War* (London 1986)

Ceva, L. 'The North African Campaign 1940–43: A Reconsideration' in J. Gooch *Decisive Campaigns of the Second World War* (London 1990)

Clifford, A. G. *Three Against Rommel: the Campaigns of Wavell, Auchinleck and Alexander* (London 1943)

Cody, J. F. *21 Battalion* (Wellington 1953)

Cody, J. F. *Maori Battalion* (Wellington 1956)

Dawson, W. D. *18 Battalion* (Wellington 1955)

Doherty, R. *The Sound of History: El Alamein 1942* (Staplehurst 2002)

Ferris, J. 'The "Usual Source": Signals Intelligence and Planning for the Eighth Army "Crusader" Offensive 1941' in D. Alvarez *Allied and Axis Signals Intelligence in World War II* (London 1999)

Forty, G. *The First Victory: O'Connor's Desert Triumph* (London 1990)

Forty, G. *The Armies of Rommel* (London 1997)

Greene, J. and Massignani, A. *Rommel's North African Campaign* (Conshohoken 1994)

Greene, J and Massignani, A. *The Naval War in the Mediterranean* (London 1998)

Harrison, F. *Tobruk: The Great Siege Reassessed* (London 1996)

Hastings, R. H. W. S. *The Rifle Brigade in the*

Second World War 1939–1945 (Aldershot 1950)

Holmes, R. *Bir Hacheim: Desert Citadel* (London 1971)

Howe, G. F. *Northwest Africa: Seizing the Initiative in the West* (Washington 1957)

Humble, R. *Crusader* (London 1987)

Jackson, W. G. F. *The North African Campaign 1940–1943* (London 1975)

Kelly, O. *Meeting the Fox* (New York 2002)

Kippenburger, H. K. *Infantry Brigadier* (London 1949)

Latimer, J. *Alamein* (London 2002)

Lewin, R. *The Life and Death of the Afrika Korps* (London 1977)

Liddell-Hart, B. H. *The Rommel Papers* (London 1953)

Lucas, J. *The War in the Desert: The Eighth Army at Alamein* (London 1982)

Luraghi, R. 'The Italian Forces at the Battle of al-Alamein: "Ferrea Mole Ferreo Cuore"' in J. Edwards *Al-Alamein Revisited* (Cairo 2000)

Mackenzie, C. *Eastern Epic* (London 1951)

Macksey, K. *Beda Fomm: the Classic Victory* (London 1971)

Macksey, K. *Crucible of Power: The Fight for Tunisia 1942–43* (London 1969)

Maughan, B. *Tobruk and El Alamein* (Canberra 1966)

Messenger, C. *The Tunisian Campaign* (Shepperton 1982)

Messenger, C. *The Unknown Alamein* (Shepperton 1982)

Mitcham, S. *Rommel's Desert War* (New York 1982)

Mitcham, S. *Triumphant Fox* (New York 1982)

Murphy, W. E. *The Relief of Tobruk* (Wellington 1962)

Pitman, S. *Second Royal Gloucestershire Hussars: Libya–Egypt 1941–1942* (London 1950)

Pitt, B. *The Crucible of War* (Volumes 1 & 2) (London 1980/1982)

Rolf, D. *The Bloody Road to Tunis* (London 2001)

Sadkovich, J. J. 'Of Myths and Men: Rommel and the Italians in North Africa' in *The International History Review* Volume 13, 2 (1991)

Schmidt, H. W. *With Rommel in the Desert* (London 1951)

Scoullar, J. L. *Battle for Egypt: the Summer of 1942* (Wellington 1955)

Sinclair, D. W. *19 Battalion* (Wellington 1954)

Stevens, W. G. *Bardia to Enfidaville* (Wellington 1962)

Trye, R. *Mussolini's Afrika Korps* (Bayside 1999)

Verney, G. L. *The Desert Rats: the History of the 7th Armoured Division 1938 to 1945* (London 1954)

Von Mellenthin, F. W. *Panzer Battles* (New York 1956)

Walker, R. *Alam Halfa and Alamein* (Wellington 1962)

Westphal, S. *The German Army in the West* (London 1951)

Italian Armour

Anon. *Preliminary Report No. 14: Semovente* (Chertsey 1943)

Anon. *Preliminary Report No. 18: Italian Tank M13/40* (Chertsey 1943)

Geibel, A. *Iron Coffins: Italian Medium Tanks M13 and M14* (Darlington 1994)

Pignato, N. *Italian Medium Tanks in Action* (Carrollton 2001)

Pignato, N. and Simula, C. *M13/40* (Great Brookham 1967)

Riccio, R. *Italian Tanks and Fighting Vehicles of World War Two* (Watford 1975)

Italian Language Sources

Anon. *La Prima Controffensiva Italo-Tedesca in Africa Settentrionale* (Roma 1974)

Anon. *Seconda Controffensiva Italo-Tedesca in Africa Settentrionale da El Agheila a El Alamein* (Roma 1971)

Ceva, L. *Africa Settentrionale 1940–1943* (Roma 1982)

Ceva, L. *La Condotta Italiana della Guerra* (Milano 1975)

Luciano, A. *Guerra dei Corazzati in Africa Settentrionale* (Milano 1980)

Montanari, M. *Le Operazione in Africa Settentrionale* (3 vols) (Roma 1989–1993)

Pafi, B., Falessi, C. and Fiore, G. *Corazzati Italiani 1939–45* (Roma 1968)

Serra, E. *Tempi Duri* (Bologna 1996)

Vincenti, L. *Bersaglieri* Volume 3 (Milano 1980)

Index

206

Index